To Hell on
a Bike

www.transworldbooks.co.uk

To Hell on a Bike

Riding Paris–Roubaix: The Toughest Race in Cycling

Iain MacGregor

BANTAM PRESS

LONDON · TORONTO · SYDNEY · AUCKLAND · JOHANNESBURG

TRANSWORLD PUBLISHERS
61–63 Uxbridge Road, London W5 5SA
www.transworldbooks.co.uk

Transworld is part of the Penguin Random House group of companies
whose addresses can be found at global.penguinrandomhouse.com

Penguin
Random House
UK

First published in Great Britain in 2015 by Bantam Press
an imprint of Transworld Publishers

A CIP catalogue record for this book
is available from the British Library.

ISBN 9780593074473

Typeset in Times New Roman 11/15pt by Falcon Oast Graphic Art Ltd.
Printed and bound by Clays Ltd, Bungay, Suffolk.

Penguin Random House is committed to a sustainable
future for our business, our readers and our planet. This book
is made from Forest Stewardship Council® certified paper.

MIX
Paper from
responsible sources
FSC
www.fsc.org   FSC® C018179

1 3 5 7 9 10 8 6 4 2

In tribute to my past: Elizabeth and Gordon MacGregor,
and, to my present and future: Joanna, Cameron
and Isla. With much love.

Great sports are about much more than the rarefied activities of their elites. Their souls come from the mediocre majorities who know how difficult the achievements of the superstars really are . . . The knowledge and passion of the also-rans are what give meaning to the activities of the elite. If the elite aren't interested in our perspective, they should be.

(Richard Askwith, *Feet in the Clouds – A Tale of Fell-Running and Obsession*)

Contents

Prologue – the Package   1

Two Men and a Velodrome   11
The Hell of the Minute   26
A Promise Made   38
The Hell of the North   41
Fit for Purpose   53
Here Come the Belgians!   64
Chasing Sky   76
The Hell of the Black Country   83
Even Hitler Couldn't Stop It   98
Stranger in a Strange Land   103
The Man from the *Pavé*   120
The Wrong Coppi   136
Eurovision   145
The Best of British   155
Day of Days   178
Into the Unknown   187
Descent into Hell – the Arenberg Forest   196
Punctures and Death by Tractor   204
Drunken Aussies and Eating the Velodrome   217

Epilogue   235
Paris–Roubaix Winners   241
Bibliography   247
Acknowledgements   249
Index   251

NORTHERN FRANCE

North Sea

NETHERLANDS

Dover

Strait of Dover

Ostend

Bruges

Antwerp

Ghent

Dunkirk

Calais

Passchendaele

Ypres

BRUSSELS

BELGIUM

Boulogne

Lille

Roubaix

Mons

Charleroi

Arras

Valenciennes

Cambrai

Busigny

Abbeville

Somme

Amiens

Saint-Quentin

Reims

Seine

Chantilly

PARIS

FRANCE

Chartres

N

0   km   50

0   miles   50

Orleans

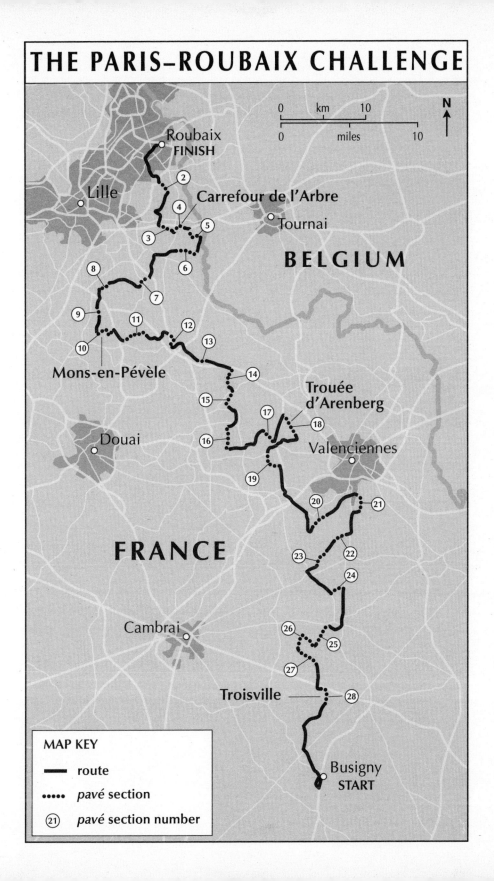

THE PARIS–ROUBAIX CHALLENGE

N

Roubaix
FINISH

Lille

② Carrefour de l'Arbre

④

③ ⑤ Tournai

⑥ **BELGIUM**

⑧

⑦

⑨

⑪ ⑫

⑩ ⑬

Mons-en-Pévèle ⑭

⑮ Trouée
d'Arenberg

⑰ ⑱

Douai ⑯ Valenciennes

⑲

⑳ ㉑

FRANCE ㉓ ㉒

㉔

Cambrai ㉖ ㉕

㉗

Troisville ㉘

Busigny
START

MAP KEY

— route

•••• *pavé* section

㉑ *pavé* section number

Prologue – the Package

Gleeful little voices squeal at me. 'Daddy, what have you bought? What is it? Daddy, tell us!' I haul the giant cardboard box through the front door and into the living room, the task made harder by my six-year-old twins dancing around me.

'Is it presents? For us?' They seem on the verge of self-combustion as the box is finally docked by the sofa, pushing each other out of the way in their eagerness to get to it.

'No, guys,' I say, 'it's for me.' Their smiles shrink and their excitement drops a few notches. I feel a pang of shame. And then I have another thought: my wife, Jo. It is 8.30 a.m. on a Saturday morning – slap bang in the middle of her lie-in, the few hours of well-deserved peace she gets at the end of a long week of looking after two noisy little ones. If the deliveryman didn't wake her up when he rang the doorbell, then it's as good as certain the children did when they saw the huge box.

I try to be a good husband and father. I really do. Right now, though, my performance is somewhat below par. Because of me, my children are disappointed and my wife might no longer be enjoying her sleep. And then I look at my box and my guilt vanishes. Why? Any cyclist familiar with buying kit online will know the excitement I feel right now. No Christmas compares to this. I can't wait any longer. I tear open the side of the cardboard box, and pull out the package. Silence reigns for what feels like minutes, but in fact is probably seconds. 'It's a big bike,' my son says.

'Yes,' I say, dreamily. We are looking at a gleaming, brand new road bike. A Raleigh SP Comp, carbon-fibre frame, with Shimano 105 gearing, Mavic Open Pro wheels, and RS10 rims. Beautifully painted in silver, black and red – and all mine. For a moment I am lost in a world of engineering perfection. Then my son snaps me out of it.

There were so many reasons for having this bike, dear reader, and why buying it was such a great idea – if, like me, you're middle-aged and into cycling, then I don't think I have to explain any further. We all have New Year resolutions – of wanting to get fit again, of carving out a new challenge to keep motivated; and, of course, there's losing the love handles too. I tick all those boxes – maybe you do, too?

I love cycling, and I used to be serious about it – I cycled from John O'Groats to Land's End in the mid-1990s. But recent years of raising twins and working (including a move back from Edinburgh to London for a new job) weakened my enthusiasm for real athletic challenges. For a while I rode my trusty racing-green Brompton through the various parks of west London to work each day, which was enjoyable enough but not entirely life-enhancing. Now, as I'm hitting 45 years of age, an unexpected fire has awoken in me, one which involves taking on a challenge, preferably using pedals.

This need to target, train for and accomplish a big challenge on a bike now brought me to this moment at the beginning of 2013, with our children staring at a beautiful racing machine propped up against our living-room sofa. I simply wanted to get back on my bike. I needed a big challenge and I needed to get myself fit. My goal for the summer of 2013, therefore, was to train as regularly as I could, with the intention of riding *L'Étape du Tour*.

The *Étape* is a stage of the official Tour de France, and every year the organizers of the race pinpoint one of the stages, usually a mountain stage in the Pyrenees or the Alps, and offer thousands of amateur enthusiasts a chance to live the dream by completing exactly the same stage which, in this case, the professionals will race two weeks later. I had registered for this event the previous November – stage 20, Annecy to Semnoz, 128 kilometres, taking on six categorized climbs, and finishing on top of the ski resort of Semnoz, overlooking the beautiful lakeside resort of Annecy. The purchase of a thoroughbred capable of getting me up that climb meant I was all set to go.

Over the next few months I mapped out a training plan, decided to go on a diet (I was at that time 14 stone – quite heavy for my height of 6 feet) and began turbo training (more of that later). Losing my job was an unexpected bump in the road, but it happened at the start of spring so I then spent four months (while looking for a new job) training like a pro and thus, come July, I weighed in at a trim 12 stone, was a lot fitter, more mentally focused, and tough enough to complete the mission. Yes, I did indeed reach my El Dorado.

The end of the Étape: the final climb up to summit of Semnoz: 3 p.m., 7 July 2013

Twisting little roads for most of the way to the final steep kick up to the ski station above Annecy, with its spectacular views; the brevity of this stage is intended to ensure action from the off with the contenders having enough in the tank to ensure it's more than a grind to the finish. Anyone who can climb can win here, and the stage isn't long enough to guarantee that the early break will stay clear at the finish.

William Fotheringham (the *Guardian* Tour de France preview, 21 June, 2013)

'*Bon courage! Bon courage!*'
  '*Allez!*'

It's mid-afternoon and I'm surrounded by voices shouting encouragement to me and my fellow riders. But I need more than just words – I am really struggling now. My Garmin computer is bleeping frantically, telling me that it's 95 degrees out here on this winding road, which leads up to the summit of Semnoz. I am, though, past caring what my computer says.

All I can see is a blurred vision of the long, long line of my fellow riders trundling up the ascent ahead of me. My brain cannot comprehend how far this procession continues, it just seems endless, disappearing into the distance and ending who knows where. There's hardly any shade and zero breeze to cool me down or calm the growing anxiety I'm feeling. I look down between my legs at my rear sprocket to see what gear I'm in. I hope I have some left in the bank, because the gears are the only thing which could ease this torture.

No, I don't. I'm in gear 27 out of 27 already and I still have more than 7 kilometres to go. There is nothing I can do except keep on pedalling. This gradient just doesn't want to ease up; in fact, it feels like it's getting steeper, which is probably my imagination at work. The previous climb up Mont Revard, which I completed a few hours ago, was much longer at 16 kilometres, but the winding hairpins and a few heaven-sent sections of level tarmac at least gave you a bit of rest. I actually enjoyed it. But this is payback. This climb is an unforgiving, unrelenting, exhausting bastard. It's lovely that hundreds of spectators are here, cheering us all on, and I appreciate the effort they've put in, but none of them have any water so part of me hates them at the same time.

I knew I shouldn't have ignored the last feed station. It's my own fault, because I was enjoying myself too much. At that moment I really was living the dream: riding at a brisk 40 k.p.h. in a string of a dozen or so riders through the hamlet of Quintal, with the crowds out and making noise and making me feel like Sir Bradley Wiggins himself. But that was a long time ago. I'm in a different place now. I need help, desperately. With both *bidons* empty, I reach back in my jersey pocket for an energy gel, but I just can't get another one down. I need the calories but its gluey consistency is sticking in my throat and making a tough situation intolerable. My legs are beginning to crack, the cadence is decreasing rapidly down from a healthy 80 r.p.m., to a standing still 45. I start weaving across the road, ignoring the beginnings of a painful throbbing in my right knee.

My predicament is not exceptional, rather it's the norm because the sides of the steaming hot road are literally blanketed with dozens of cyclists, lying by their gleaming road bikes of all designs and colours, and who cannot, will not, continue up this road. Some have their heads in their hands, a few are actually in tears, and one guy is being wrapped in a foil blanket by paramedics and looks like he's had heart failure of some description. We resemble an army in retreat, blindly trying to move forward to escape the dreaded 'broom wagon', the official vehicle bringing up the rear of the race, which tells the stragglers their time is up. Like being kicked out of the Foreign Legion, the fear of having one's race number torn off you and being disqualified for being out of time is an incredible stimulant. And right now it's all I have.

But, for every site of tragedy, there is one of victory, too. The organizers have, in their wisdom, split the route down the middle of the road. So, while we struggle like the cycling dead to try to reach the summit, on the other side of the barrier, laughing and chatting happily, are those hundreds of riders (out of a field of 13,000) who have reached nirvana and, with gravity at their backs, are now flying back down the mountain to Annecy, where at the tented village they will be awarded their medals and supplied with copious amounts of pasta and ice-cool bottles of Coke. I hate them all. *Don't give up, keep the rhythm. Whatever you do, don't stop!* I say to myself.

But there is another voice in my head, one from the Dark Side, and it is winning the argument. It says, 'Just take a few minutes' rest by that shade across the road under the foliage of that tree, where those riders are chatting. Look, they seem happy to have stopped. No one will know.'

Then the other side strikes back powerfully: 'You've trained too long,' the voice yells. 'You can't come all this way, posting your boasts and pictures on Facebook, and NOT finish this fucking race! Just aim for the next hairpin, that one about 600 yards up there. Carry on until you get there.' Six hundred yards? I'm close to tears.

My jersey now resembles a baby's nappy after one too many juice drinks. I am soaked in sweat. And I'm heating up to the point of blurred vision, which must be dangerous. I want to stop. I *need* to stop. 'Keep going!' someone shouts.

'*Allez, allez,* Mapei!' someone else yells. Mapei? That's a professional team, one of the biggest names of all time, but which was shut down after a doping scandal a few years ago. What's going on? My answer arrives as a rider dressed in the distinctive kit of the famous Mapei cycling team – the colours of the rainbow arranged in random blocks – storms past me as if I were standing still. With thighs and calves bulging he is motoring up the mountain, much to the crowd's delight. After that blow to my self-esteem, I take a big step closer to cracking and start looking for a secluded place with no spectators where I can stop for a breather. I'm convinced I'm at the point where I'll fall off the bike if I don't have a rest.

Then, on the shaded curve of the next bend, the spot where I was planning to hide for a few minutes, a beautiful sight appears. An old woman stands there alone, with what looks like a hose in her hands, and it is gushing with water. Cool, clear and, judging by the manic gulps the rider alongside her is taking, drinkable water. I manage to unclip my right foot and finally come to a depressing halt beside them both, to be the next in line for absolution.

'*L'eau est gratuite pour vous*,' she says. I know enough French to understand that the water is free. Before I drink I ask her if I may have it on my head instead which, under my helmet, feels at this moment like it is about to explode. Like an angel dispensing kindness, she quickly lifts her arm, stands on tiptoes and just manages to reach the vents so she can pour the liquid of life on to me. Within minutes I am a man reborn – it's like a scene from the *Road Runner* cartoons. I really do mean that, it was like a switch had been turned back on. I'm able to focus sharply and start thinking about what I have to do to finish this bloody race. The delirium and confusion in my mind have been blasted away. My legs are still shot, though. Let's not get carried away – this isn't Hollywood.

The next 7 kilometres took me an agonizing hour, feeling like I was fighting my bike every inch of the way to the top. The greenery decorating the sides of the road made way for moss, bracken, granite boulders and ski lifts as the route reached the top of Semnoz. The final 300 metres were joyous, except for the moment some smartarse pulled a wheelie as he breezed past me to the finish line. And then it was over. Done. No more pain, no more turbo training down the gym. A woman congratulated me in French and placed an official finisher's sticker on my handlebars. I burst into tears.

But that isn't the story I want to tell you. No, my truly epic cycling adventure starts with another conversation with my wife, almost a year to the day after that beautiful new bike arrived, on a winter's morning in Paris. I'm sitting in a restaurant opposite the Louvre with Jo. We're on a day trip to celebrate our wedding anniversary. The kids are under the watchful and expert eyes of their grandparents back home. We are relaxed and blissfully happy. It is time, I think, to talk about cycling.

'Why do I love going out on my bike?' I muse. 'I mean, I'm forty-six. What is it about dressing up in layers of lycra before the

sun is up so I can ride through the streets of south-east London
into the Kent countryside on a cold December morning?'

Jo stares into her coffee, stirring the spoon slowly and methodically. After a few minutes she stops, puts the cup to her lips, takes
a lingering drink and smiles at me while placing it down on to the
table. 'Because you get time off to yourself and love the exercise,'
she says. 'Or maybe it's because you have an excuse to buy more
stuff and talk endlessly about what you did last summer, and get
to pose in lycra?' She isn't being dismissive – those words were said
with a smile, after all. We're doing a lot of that today, as we bask
in our day of freedom, enjoying ourselves without the kids and
with the sun shining. What Jo doesn't know is that I have another
plan, and this time it's not going to be hamstrung by an over-eager
delivery man or the kids.

'Maybe,' I say, 'I don't want to lose any of the good things I got
from the *Étape*, my fitness and so on. I'm not getting any younger
and I was hoping doing that race would spur me on . . .' I pause
so I can give the impression I haven't really been rehearsing this
speech for the past fortnight '. . . and actually, now I come to think
of it, it really has, and I think I'd maybe like to do another big race
one day. Maybe. I mean, if I do another one, it would have to be
different this time. You know, closer to home and . . .' I run out
of waffle.

'All right,' Jo says, seeing right through me. 'What do you want
to do now?'

I pull out a book, and place it on the table in front of her. On the
cover is a figure, a cyclist, though he is so covered in mud, grit and
oil you can barely see his facial features, just the whiteness of his
clenched teeth and bulging eyes, such is the effort he is putting into
pushing his bike through what looks like a scene from the Great
War. Around him is a colourful spectacle of grinning, cheering
and happy spectators, who are waving flags and urging him on.

'Paris–Roubaix,' I say. 'It's known as "the Hell of the North".

Every cyclist who is familiar with professional racing knows about it. The competitors are the superhuman athletes of cycling. They ride through two hundred and sixty kilometres of muck and filth, but the worst part, the part which destroys countless bikes and riders, is the cobbles. There are twenty-eight stretches of cobbles covering fifty-two kilometres in total and they are hellish. It's an endurance test like no other, and it's the one I always fancied a crack at.'

I get all this out before Jo can speak. She is still staring at the book's cover and starts to flick through it – images jump from each page, some in monochrome from decades ago, and others dazzlingly colourful from more modern times. All show cyclists fighting their bikes to stay up straight and keep racing.

Silence.

I carry on.

'Completing the *Étape* gave me confidence and I would love to try this race before I reach fifty. That's my new challenge for 2014, and with my base fitness and three-and-a-bit months to train and prepare myself, I'm in a good place to start from.' It sounds so simple put like that. A smile starts to grow across Jo's face as she starts reading one section. Jo knows her sport better than I do and, indeed, before becoming parents we had travelled to Paris to watch Armstrong win the Tour de France. She had also cycled coast to coast across England with me in the 1990s. If anyone appreciates what I want to do, it's her, and her opinion matters. Her smile spreads and she passes over the book (*Paris–Roubaix: A Journey Through Hell*) and points to the relevant paragraph for me to see what is so funny: 'The American television channel CBS covered Paris–Roubaix in the 1980s. Theo de Rooij, a Dutchman, had been in a promising position to win the 1985 race but had then crashed, losing his chance of winning. Covered in mud, he offered his thoughts to CBS's John Tesh after the race: "It's a bollocks, this race!" said de Rooij. "You're working like an animal, you don't have time to piss, you wet your pants. You're riding in mud like this, you're slipping . . . it's a pile of shit."

'When then asked if he would start the race again, de Rooij replied: "Sure, it's the most beautiful race in the world!"'

Jo reaches over and squeezes my hand tightly, and gives me a knowing look, reading my real, very desperate thoughts. I think, in that moment, she realizes exactly what drives me when I ride my bike, and why I am so restless when I have no task ahead of me to aim for. It's not just about the challenge, or about the kit and equipment. I don't just want to do what cyclists consider the norm, and go for daily jaunts, or cycle to Brighton, or any other event that seems to be advertised in every edition of the London *Evening Standard* I care to open on the train home from work. I don't know exactly why, but for me to be interested, it needs to be ridiculously hard.

No more is spoken about the race and we turn instead to enjoying ourselves in the most romantic capital in the world. Jo doesn't need to say anything about cycling. Deep down, I know I have to start planning.

What follows is the tale of a rank amateur who wanted to live a dream, a middle-aged man fighting the dying of the light and trying to impress his kids, and who was prepared to cycle through hell to do it.

Two Men and a Velodrome

> One day, spectators will have had enough of seeing competitions between riders looking fresh and elegant; they need to be offered the spectacle of roadmen looking exhausted and covered in mud.

Théodore Vienne, 1898

When one analyses the year 1896, one could argue a comet must have been hurtling through the sky, such was the portent it brought for the sporting endeavours mankind would submit itself to in the coming century. First and foremost, the dream of Baron Pierre de Coubertin of bringing the Olympics back to the modern age would come to fruition.[1] Under the umbrella of the USFSA (*l'Union des Sociétés Françaises de Sports Athlétiques*), and at the movement's spiritual home – Athens – sixteen countries competed in the first modern Olympic Games.

The sudden appearance and widespread enthusiasm for the

---

[1] On 16 April 1896, the American athlete James Connolly would win the triple jump and thus become the first Olympic champion in over 1,500 years.

fledgling motorcar gave rise in 1896 to the very first city-to-city car race: Paris–Marseille–Paris. Organized and run by the equally new Automobile Club de France (ACF), the race was won by Émile Mayade across ten stages, covering over 1,700 kilometres. To a nation unused to mass transport other than the train, and with the communications industry still in its infancy (no radio, television or phones), a race like this must have been intoxicating to witness, the equivalent of seeing Martians landing in your backyard, perhaps. For an agricultural-based society, it would have been a thrilling spectacle, almost as exhilarating as reading the various new sporting newspapers that were springing up to cover such occasions. Cycling would be the next sport to receive such coverage.

By 1896, cycling had well and truly established itself as the method by which the masses could now transport themselves to work. The bicycle had taken many decades to evolve from a child-like, wooden-framed machine – a glorified hobby horse on wheels and nothing more – to the 'Eureka' moment of a Frenchman inventing the cranks and pedals that would give the rider the ability to actually drive the bike forward.

A variety of inventions (with patents) followed as the modern design we all know today finally came off the drawing board and into the high street in 1895: the 'Safety Bicycle'. This design, encompassing four key elements of steering, safety, comfort and speed, together with the invention of the inflatable tyre, was arguably the greatest evolution in transportation to date. The bike was no longer perceived as a dangerous toy (crashing head first off the top of a penny-farthing on to cobbles doesn't bear thinking about) and was embraced by young and old, male and female, as a machine to be enjoyed in safety.

In France alone, Sunday cyclists numbered well over 150,000 (including nearly 10,000 women, who labelled the bicycle 'The Freedom Machine') with societies and clubs springing up across the country. The moneyed classes saw the bicycle as purely recreational, while their working-class counterparts viewed it as a means of essential transport, as well, in time, potentially an escape route to riches through sporting prowess. This phenomenon was being repeated across the Western world from Australia to the United States of America. Human nature would triumph – like with the car, people were unable to resist racing one another on this unique and fascinating contraption. A new craze and a new sport was born, the bicycle had infiltrated all aspects of society.

As a spectacle, as we see today, a bike race is a colourful, intoxicating blur of whirring gears and wheels married to the excitement of the chase, and the terror of the crash. To French society in the late nineteenth century it must have been equally addictive, as start-up cycle clubs and associations – allied to entrepreneurs looking for the next 'big thing' to generate income – organized their own amateur and professional races across the country. The main issue to resolve was one of public safety – a great many accidents occurred with bystanders taking an innocent Sunday stroll in their local park being run down by barnstorming riders thundering around the walkways. Change was coming, however.

By 1896 dozens of velodromes had been constructed across France to house the new sporting craze of track riding, as local mayors vied with one another for the honour of building their very own modern sporting arena. A velodrome was now the must-have venue for any municipality, where every decent Frenchman with money to spend wanted to witness racing. As the price of bicycles was lowered, the craze spread throughout all sections of society. New and lighter frames and stronger wheels with brakes were all invented very quickly, which led to faster bikes, increased speeds for the riders at events and more excitement for the spectators. For locals never having witnessed human beings going at such speeds under their own volition, it was simply incredible to watch. To the man who owned a stadium, it was too good to be true, as he now had a captive audience, to whom he could also sell and advertise goods. Layer upon layer of business opportunities opened up to any man who had the vision and the money to bring forth the commercial evolution of the sport.

Usually constructed of cement banking which supported either wooden boards, asphalt or even dirt, the majority of the velodromes boasted a smooth track that rose high up at the banking, and which was surrounded by grandstands for the eager audiences flocking to see their heroes riding bikes with a fixed drive and no brakes or gears (a tradition that we continue to see today). Cycling became immensely popular as a recreational pastime, and a huge money-earner. From Nantes, Bordeaux and Toulouse, to Marseille, Nice and Caen there wasn't a weekend when one couldn't enjoy the spectacle of track racing.

In London, a new form of continuous track racing was invented: the Six Day. This was an endurance race whereby teams of riders raced round the track continuously for six days, winning intermediate sprints, and vying for the overall fastest time. This form of racing would quickly spread to America where, by the end of the nineteenth century, thousands would flock to Madison Square Garden; by the 1900s Europe would embrace the Six Day, too. However, soon a new form of racing would supplant it in the eyes of the sporting public . . .

Endurance racing had steadily built a sizeable following: now legendary races such as Paris–Brest–Paris and Bordeaux–Paris were created; and, as clearly seen from the names, all roads led to the capital, the logical place for a grandstand finish. Paris–Brest–Paris was simply a ridiculously long, arduous test of stamina and strength of mind, body and bicycle. One shudders to think of what the riders of the time were expected to race: over 1,200 kilometres on roads very rarely tarmacked, as France was still crisscrossed with badly laid roads and, in many cases, cobbles. All this on what was still a heavy bicycle, with rudimentary brakes and gearing.

The hero of the first Paris–Brest–Paris race in 1891 was Frenchman Charles 'Charley' Terront, who crossed the line first after almost three days of racing a bike weighing a lung-busting 21.5 kilograms. Of the 206 starters, only 99 would eventually make it home within the ten-day limit the organizers had imposed. It was the beginning of France's love for the absurd, heroic sporting feat; over ten thousand witnessed Terront's triumph.[2]

Also conceived in 1891, Bordeaux–Paris was France's blue riband cycling event. Riders were expected to cover 600 kilometres in a single stage, often riding through the night, to finish in the capital, naturally, and be acclaimed as heroes. The epic event across the country was of its time: man and machine versus nature. It captured the imagination and inspired a generation. Crowds flocked to the event right across the route; it was the one race all riders aspired to win, such were the rewards of fame and fortune.

At the same time, with the money now on offer, a cadre of professional riders began to emerge right across Western Europe, not only in France, but also in the Low Countries and Germany. A fully fledged sport was taking shape quickly and there were those with the resources keen to develop their own races (and profit) outside of Paris. Still, the public held track cycling in far higher esteem than the endurance events, the long-distance riders being seen as some sort of underclass of sportsmen – covered in filth, oil and whatever else the road threw at them – when compared to their flashier cousins of speed, who looked heroic on their dazzling, clean contraptions.

However, with the exploits of men such as Terront, and a young upstart coming on to the scene called Maurice Garin, the roadmen were beginning to develop their own mass following. *Le Vélo*, the

[2] Terront would later ride St Petersburg–Paris, a route of over 3,000 kilometres, which he completed in fourteen days and thus became a sporting superstar in France. He, uniquely, would be the subject of the world's first sporting biography.

daily sports paper which ran the big races, needed to expand in order to increase its circulation – and organizing or sponsoring a road race was infinitely cheaper and less of a risk than paying for events in an expensive venue given the number of track riders they'd have to employ. One such group of cycling enthusiasts was based in a small, industrial backwater near the Belgian border – Roubaix.

As the veteran cycling journalist Les Woodland dryly describes, Roubaix was 'an embarrassment, a run-down place so close to Belgium that you wonder they don't push it across the border. If an enemy again invaded, nobody would defend [it].' By the 1890s Roubaix was a town of some 115,000 inhabitants, lying a few miles outside of the city of Lille. While today Roubaix is regarded as part of the semi-industrial sprawl of Lille itself, back then it had its own identity, dominated by the wool industry, with the majority of the population working in the many mills that dotted the skyline of the town.

As one can see with the history of any mill town in the north of England, earning a living to support a family was extremely hard, with children encouraged from a young age to skip school and join their parents and elder siblings in bringing a wage home. The hooter from the mill dominated the community's working lives, telling them when to come to work, when to stop for food, and when to leave for home. Housed in tight streets of Victorian red-brick houses with communal toilets and bathrooms, and very few facilities for relaxation and recuperation, a typical northern mill town would have one thing going for it: sport.

Roubaix was no different. Henri Carette was a local politician who was elected as the town's – in fact France's – first collectiv-ist mayor. 'Collectivist' back then almost certainly meant having what we would now term communist leanings (the north of France has a long tradition of left-wing affiliation), and Carette wanted to better the lives of his constituents through recreation. By the 1890s he was just as taken with the craze of cycling as anyone else (he supported the founding of the area's cycling society, *Fédération Cyclopédique du Nord*), and thus was open to ideas to develop the sport to help his town, by generating income and recognition for the struggling populace.

In early 1895 Théodore Vienne found himself with a potential money-spinner. Born and bred in Roubaix, he was from a middle-class family who owned a textile mill on the outskirts of the town, living very comfortably from its profits. With a business associate, and fellow cycling fanatic – Maurice Pérez – he had been bitten by the commercial potential, as well as the kudos, of providing Roubaix with its very own velodrome. The pair had already organized their own races in local parks the previous year, which had been huge successes. The problem was that spectators in parks do not generate ticket sales, and the fledgling sports promoters knew they needed a safer venue to charge for entry. So, here they were a year later, having purchased 46,000 acres of land (backed by investors' capital) and a wonderful velodrome to fill to capacity. The success of the events they were staging – riders were doing fast times due to the innov-ation of banking along the track – was such that punters were coming from Lille and even the Belgian border to attend meets.

What would be the next step? Vienne and Pérez couldn't help but notice the publicity and income generated by Bordeaux–Paris for *Le Vélo* (the whole country was raving about it) and the benefits brought by a race passing through a town or city. 'But why must all the races finish in Paris?' they thought. Their Eureka moment wasn't long in coming: why couldn't a race end in their newly created velodrome?

Looking back at events, one could perhaps surmise this was a complicit plan with *Le Vélo*'s editor Louis Minart, with our pair of intrepid entrepreneurs drawing up their blueprint for a new race, starting out from the capital and ending in their sparkling new cycle track at Roubaix. They would need the newspaper to adver-tise and generate publicity in order for this to work, and so artfully suggested that theirs would simply be a 'warm up' event for the professional riders who would then undertake the established Bordeaux–Paris race two weeks later. Thus primed by Minart, they dashed off a formal letter to *Le Vélo*'s director Paul Rousseau.

Dear Monsieur Rousseau,

Bordeaux–Paris approaches: the great annual challenge founded by *Véloce-Sport* and entrusted for the past year to *Le Vélo*, has done so much to spread the word of cycling that an idea has come to us. What would you think of a training race three weeks before Bordeaux–Paris?

Paris–Roubaix would entail a course of about 289 kilometres, which would be nothing for participants in Bordeaux–Paris. The finish could take place on the Velodrome Roubaisien with several laps of the track, as for the finish of Bordeaux–Paris at the Seine [track]. The crowd would welcome each rider enthusiastically, all the more so because the people of Roubaix have never seen the spectacle of a great road race. And we know enough track riders here to know that Roubaix would show true hospitality.

As for prizes, we offer here and now a first prize of 1,000 francs in the name of Velodrome Roubaisien and we'll occupy ourselves by raising more prizes so that everyone will be satisfied.

As for the date, we think May 3 would fit perfectly because the riders in Bordeaux–Paris will already be in good shape by then and they'll have three weeks to recover before the big race.

And so, cher Monsieur, can we count on the support of *Le Vélo*, on your expertise for the organization, the start, etc? If so, announce the great event [this is in English in the letter] straight away and open your columns to entries.

With our friendly greetings . . .

Théo Vienne & Maurice Pérez

The pair sensibly proposed the race to be held on a Sunday, when workers had their day off and could enjoy a relaxing afternoon out at the velodrome. What could be more perfect than the spectacle of cycling heroes striving through extremes of weather and terrain, racing from Paris to their little town? The potential was huge, and they knew it. Vienne and Pérez both believed that by charging a fair price for entry, then stocking the stadium with food and drink as well as pre-race entertainment, they would not only cover their costs but, given the increased publicity from *Le Vélo* combined with local companies advertising their goods, would turn in a healthy profit.

First and foremost, however, Vienne and Pérez were bike fans who wanted to see their heroes race by, just like anyone else lining a road or sitting in a stadium. But, crucially they also spotted the one flaw in the racing schedule as it stood back then. The whole sport lacked a credible race where one could watch both the start and finish on the same day, during daylight hours. Epics such as Bordeaux–Paris were a great feat of strength, but those races were held over such an enormous distance that, unavoidably, a great deal of the action would take place in the hours of darkness – and with municipal street lighting still in its infancy, and yet to spread to the countryside, who could possibly witness these events?

The racers, too, had to contend with those conditions, using home-made dynamos to light their way. Naturally, the potential for cheating and saving time and energy by jumping on passing trains, or hopping in a new-fangled car, was a temptation for many competitors. As would soon become apparent, when the first few editions of the Tour de France were raced, it was the norm for riders to steal time on their rivals through devious means, often at dusk, and it was an impossible task for the race officials to keep track of everyone.

New rules were brought into play, such as checkpoints to

validate competitors – but, again, these could be dodged, or identities faked. Even if the riders finished in Paris, in the stadium, their journey to get there could be viewed by the organizers, and the watching public, as compromised. This is what Vienne and Pérez spotted, having visited many races, and why they believed their 'One Day' race could succeed and gain plaudits for being run fairly, with a winner deemed to have raced honestly across the whole course, thus ensuring the validity of the race itself and, of course, the honour of French sport.

The nature of Roubaix, with its provincial size, industrial background and not much else going for it, meant that the pair could not realistically try to organize a race starting and finishing in the town. How would that generate regional and national news, and how would they attract the best racers of the day to win what they envisioned to be a prestigious race? Roubaix to Roubaix? Not a chance. On the other hand, if the race could commence in Paris, with all the fanfare, colour and crowds that the capital guaranteed, and then proceed the 280 kilometres north towards Roubaix's velodrome with a captive audience (and the press) waiting to greet the winner, then it stood a chance of success and acceptance by the powers that be.

As the letter revealed, Vienne and Pérez cleverly played upon the fact that their race wouldn't be in competition with Bordeaux–Paris, but would serve as a warm-up to the main event. Of equal importance, the distance guaranteed a daytime finish, in the glare of the press and officials, thus ensuring a 'clean' race, which would only enhance road racing's reputation. And the juicy worm on the baiting hook: the announcement of the 1,000 francs prize money, about seven months' pay to your ordinary mill worker. Perhaps this sealed the deal? Who knows, but for whatever reason, maybe all of them, Paul Rousseau's interest was stirred and he decided to send one of his acolytes north to check out these men from Roubaix.

Le Vélo's cycling reporter, Victor Breyer,[3] was called into Rousseau's office, briefed accordingly, quite possibly scratched his head while he studied a map of the region, and agreed to find out if the race proposal was the real deal. Legend has it that he was given a ride north by the editor of *La France Automobile*, Paul Meyan, in one of the latest motorcars to hit the market – a 6 h.p. Panhard. Together the pair travelled as far as Amiens, where Breyer took to the road on his bike to see what the route was like. He soon wished he hadn't, as, under a heavy downpour and a strong headwind, with the temperature dropping like a stone, he crawled his agonizing way through cobbled roads and farm tracks towards Roubaix.

Breyer was a wreck of a man by the time he finally reached Roubaix, unrecognizable from the healthy, young reporter who had eagerly followed his boss's orders. Falling into the welcoming arms of Vienne and Pérez, the mud-spattered vagrant staggered into warm shelter, a restorative shower, a hot meal and perhaps a few glasses of local wine. Within hours, his initial outburst to Vienne of the race being a 'diabolical' idea had become an enthusiastic endorsement of the route to his masters in Paris. And so are legends born!

Breyer's official report back to Rousseau endorsed the venture for several reasons. There was the aforementioned advantage of staging a pre-Bordeaux–Paris one-day training race; the enthusiasm of the locals of Roubaix for the event to succeed and be well staged was evident; and the local train and tram stops guaranteed fans would be able to get to the velodrome. Crucially, Breyer was also clearly impressed (or perhaps he was being ironic) that while the roads leading north from Paris were well laid with asphalt, as one neared the Belgian border cobbled roads were everywhere. The

---

[3] Victor Breyer was one of the six founding signatories of the UCI and would go on to become its secretary. Henri Desgrange made him race director of the fledgling Tour de France.

pavé, honed from carved 'setts' of sandstone, reflected the wealth of the area, but more importantly to the locals (as well as any future invading army passing through) these roads ensured good, reliable transportation regardless of weather conditions. Breyer, his epic journey now long forgotten, stated that, of course, cycling on the *pavé* would be arduous, but it was only a day's racing! The race was duly endorsed by *Le Vélo*, who would promote the event and report on it. They had the stadium and a willing audience, now all they needed was a date for the race.

A lot of legends have built up over the decades as to how Paris–Roubaix was created as *La Pascale* – the Easter race. It was said that the promoters fought with the local clergy, who fiercely argued that the event should never actually be held on a Sunday, the Lord's Day. That they then forced Vienne and Pérez to move the race date and that the businessmen's idea to hold a mass early in the morning, before the starting pistol sounded, had also been vetoed by the local priests, who threatened to put up posters proclaiming the race should be ostracized. As we all know, stories can become facts through time.

In reality, the very first race was held on 19 April 1896, two weeks after Easter, and the clergy didn't object. The early morning mass was simply a PR stunt by a canny promoter in order to spice up proceedings before the riders got underway. *Le Vélo*, as good as their word, got behind the race and the news of Breyer's herculean ride through the mud, rain and wind grabbed France's attention, thus guaranteeing big crowds at the Roubaix velodrome, as well as at the start at Porte de Maillot – near the modern-day tourist phenomenon of the Arc de Triomphe – in Paris.

Perhaps the newspaper article painted too painful a picture of Breyer's journey, though, as only half of the expected one-hundred-plus entrants actually materialized on the day of the race – but there were still some track and road stars there to ensure the event was an elite gathering. Wanting a grandstand finish, the organizers also cleverly allowed the local riders from Lille and Roubaix to start first, just to ensure their compatriots would be waiting for them in the velodrome at the end of the race.

The rules of the very first Paris–Roubaix race read like some kind of *Wacky Races* episode:

1. All types of bikes are permitted to be used, even tandems and triplets.
2. Checkpoints are set up at key places along the route, such as Amiens, where riders are required to dismount and sign in.
3. The time limit to finish the race is thirty hours.
4. At the velodrome, the riders are to complete six full laps of the track, without pacers.
5. If riders reach the stadium past 7 p.m., then they are to finish at a nearby café.
6. On no condition are riders allowed to abandon their bikes along the route.

The field undertaking the race contained some notable riders of the day, including the winner of Bordeaux–Paris the year before, a Dane by the name of Charles Meyer; the Roubaix rider who would gain fame as a winner of the future Tour de France (and indeed would become a multiple winner of future Paris–Roubaix races), Maurice Garin; the Briton Arthur Linton, who specialized on the track and would go on to win that year's Bordeaux–Paris; and the top rider from Germany, Josef Fischer, who had won numerous track meets as well as prestigious endurance races such as Vienna–Berlin and Milan–Munich.

Those in the know picked Fischer as the favourite for obvious reasons; *Le Journal de Roubaix*'s reporter, who was watching the riders enter the café near the start of the race, described Fischer as 'a beautiful athlete'. One notable absentee, for future cycling historians, was a certain Henri Desgrange, who had signed up for the race initially. He was a decent track rider, but would find fame as the organizer of the first Tour de France in 1903.

Large crowds had gathered by the 4 a.m. start time on that crisp spring morning, making it difficult for those late entrants trying to sign in, but at last they were called to the start line by Victor Breyer, wrapped in a warm coat and scarf as the temperature was a chilly 3°C. The elite riders were photographed at the line standing next to their bikes, all looking anxious to get going, flat caps on, long-sleeved coats with armbands showing they were competitors, knee-length breeches and long socks. Some had planned ahead and carried supplies in leather bags draped over their handlebars, while others kept pouches hanging off the ends of the handles themselves.

Dawn was just about to break when Paul Rousseau stepped forward and ceremoniously dropped the starting flag and the fifty-one competitors got underway. The race was on! From the off, many riders – possibly geed up by the crowds and the excitement of venturing into the unknown – decided to make an immediate race of it as they sped through the suburbs of Paris. What followed was a classic race of its time, with the favourites jockeying for the lead across several hours as they vied for the many bonuses on offer for reaching various sections along the route first.

The cream was rising to the top, as the pre-race favourites Linton, Garin, Fischer and Meyer were all in the vanguard of the peloton by some distance, despite crashes, mechanical failures and cows drifting on to the road. Garin was even run over by a chasing tandem, having just crashed into a triplet that was pacing him. Newspaper reporters were staggered at how many people were coming out to witness the event, especially at the Roubaix velodrome, which was packed to capacity. Vienne and Pérez must have been hugging one another.

After setting a mesmerizing pace (for the period) of 31 k.p.h., Fischer finally arrived on the Roubaix track to the roar of cheering crowds, and a band playing '*La Marseillaise*'. The fact a French crowd gave a German any kind of positive welcome, twenty years after Prussia had crushed them in the Franco-Prussian war of 1870 and occupied Paris, spoke volumes about how close to their hearts the race already was. Fischer basked in the glory of his six laps while being given a standing ovation, then got off his bike, signed in at the registration desk and gleefully quaffed a glass of champagne while Vienne, Pérez and other officials of the town heartily clapped his shoulders and showered him with bouquets of flowers. As for the *pavé*, he seemed to have revelled on it, stating, 'It wasn't hard, I rode so that I could take the *pavé* gently, at my own speed.'

Watching other competitors come in told a different story. Garin was covered in blood having been run over, a pedal gashing his neck; Linton had suffered multiple pile-ups and was mentally and physically destroyed. The last rider, a Belgian called Theron, arrived thirty hours later having stopped on the route to sleep. It's likely that Vienne and Pérez had stopped counting their takings by then. The press, as well as the racing public – stretching from Paris all the way up to the people of the north – had all declared themselves converts to the race, thus stitching Paris–Roubaix into the French sporting tapestry.

The following year the race would actually be held on Easter Sunday. Paris–Roubaix became established as the bona fide *La Pascale*.

The Hell of the Minute

What it takes to succeed in cycling hasn't
changed. The best riders are half-born, half-
made. In other words, they're made up of a
combination of talent and commitment. That
has applied, and will apply, to everyone who has
ever made it to the top, from the first bike racer
to the last.

I lapped up every word of Michael Hutchinson's brilliant book
*Faster: the Obsession, Science and Luck Behind the World's Fastest
Cyclists*, a terrific insight into the world of elite cycling. However,
practically everything in it – from analysis of VO_2 max output
and oxygen supply, to key muscle groups, to body–fat ratios, to
the discussion of the psychology of an athlete – none of it really
applied to me. I am not an athlete. A regular cyclist, certainly,
and an enthusiastic swimmer and walker when time allowed from
work and family commitments.

The older one gets, the tighter that schedule becomes, until
one really has to make sacrifices. This was now that moment, as
I finished reading Hutchinson's book. I knew I had a modicum

of talent, or I used to when younger, slimmer and dedicated to regular training. When I had ridden John O'Groats to Land's End in 1996, it was against the prevailing winds, taking detours through mountains and windswept hills, with next to no preparation, and I loved every minute of the fortnight it took me to complete it. That was eighteen years ago, however; now it was different. I had to get fit.

I had already read many magazine articles (mainly in *Cycling Weekly*), browsed specific books, and surfed the web to see what most advanced training tips I could find for getting my legs and lungs into the best shape possible – in six months. I soaked up all the advice I could get, from whoever offered it, such as fellow cyclists at work. Svein Coulston, the digital guru of the publishing imprint I oversaw, was one of them. He embodied the type of cyclist we see heading up the Col d'Aubisque chasing after Chris Froome. With a stick-thin upper body, balanced out with wiry, toned cyclist legs, he had the gaunt features that betray hours and hours of intense riding up British hills and European mountains. He'd think nothing of flying to Geneva in order to try out a time trial up Alpe d'Huez. Svein and I shared a passion for supporting our beloved Aberdeen FC, the mighty (and wholly original) Dons. When not lionizing the latest ride by Vincenzo Nibali or Alberto Contador, we would more likely be discussing tactics for Saturday's match against St Johnstone.

Svein had been impressed by my announcement at the staff Christmas party that I was riding Paris–Roubaix; I'd actually drunkenly shouted into his ear above the music blaring out across the office. '*Chapeau!*' he mouthed above the din as he raised his can of beer, and that had been that until a few weeks into the New Year. It was then that I was beginning to scramble around for ideas on how best to get geared for the challenge.

Hence, here we were talking by his desk one Monday morning. 'Try the Olympic track,' Svein said. 'They're opening up now for

amateur cyclists like us. You can pay for a full hour and get to ride
the one-mile circuit; it's perfect for time trialling and just getting
yourself fit. Mind, they don't offer to replicate the battering your
backside is going to experience come April.' He seemed to say this
with relish.

I had seriously considered the Olympic track, but had passed on
the idea, as it wasn't offering me anything that simply riding out
on my normal ride into the Kent countryside could provide. Like
most weekend warriors, I enjoyed the early Saturday morning rise,
the sneaking out of the house without waking the family. Before
London was up and awake, I would already be out of the city,
cresting Titsey Hill on my way to Hever Castle via Toy's Hill. If
I was feeling frisky, then I'd detour and go up the monster that is
Yorks Hill, too.

Followers of the Hill Climb Classic will be well versed in what a
brute this one is, and how good it is for testing one's stamina and
sheer leg strength on a bike. With an average gradient of 12.5 per
cent which then tops out towards the end at a savage 25 per cent,
it is rightly seen as an exceptional challenge. The Classic is usually
staged on the first Sunday of October by London's oldest cycling
club – Catford CC – which, bar the exception of two world wars,
has run the climb since 1886. It still attracts climbers from all over
the United Kingdom, I am told, though whenever I go up it, the
silence of being alone up its unforgiving tarmac is only broken by
my expletive-laden sobs of pain.

But I knew this wasn't the type of training that would get my
body close to where it needed to be for the cobbles of Paris–
Roubaix. To be truthful, that hill bloody scared me anyway, and I
saw my weekend rides merely as relaxation from a mentally tiring
week, not to push me, and my bike, to the limits up Yorks Hill.
No, I needed to take advice from an expert in these matters. Best
to speak with Chris.

I had met Chris Sidwells through my day job as a publisher of non-fiction books, working with authors across sport, history, music and the outdoors. It's the perfect job, you might think. There are two major problems with it, though. Firstly, you're working in London, with all the pressure that brings as you navigate your way across town on the daily commute – an energy-sapping, stressful hour on a good day. And secondly, you're then a desk-jockey. The job involves meetings, meetings and then reading and editing, and more meetings to discuss the editing you've just re-read. But I wouldn't swap it for the world. I've enjoyed twenty fantastic years thus far in the business, meeting a myriad of fascinating and colourful characters who had books to publish. One of them was Chris.

Chris had been a detective inspector of Her Majesty's constabulary for over two decades in Yorkshire, before he decided to make his passionate hobby – cycling and training cyclists – into a full-time job. He had now been a successful cycling coach and fitness instructor for a number of years, as well as a renowned and well-respected journalist for *Cycling Weekly*, and a writer of several books on the sport he loves. He had written one book for a previous imprint I had run, and it was madness not to pick his brains for the task that now lay ahead of me. How to build myself up for the coming test of stamina, strength and pain.

So Chris and I met up in a café across from Angel tube station in north London one winter's lunchtime. Lunch was, of course, pasta. Even for a guy in his mid-to-late fifties, Chris exudes rude health. With a compact, wiry frame, he reminded me of his uncle, the late, great Tom Simpson, and he hardly had a spare ounce of fat on him. Practising what he preaches in the many training guides he'd produced over the years was his mantra, and when he talked, in between mouthfuls of delicious lasagne, I was listening. We began by me recounting to him where I was at.

'I've bought a turbo trainer, Chris. I'm thinking it's the best way of getting fit, or I should say fitter, more quickly. I just can't

afford to take the time off and do the longer rides, or get out as
often as I'd like. I reckon a turbo would get me there over the
coming months. What do you think?'

He nodded wryly a few times as I outlined my plan. I had bought
his book, *Cyclosportive: Preparing For and Taking Part in Long-
Distance Cycling Challenges* on the pretext of then getting more
personal one-to-one tuition from the great man himself.

Chris picked up his glass of wine. 'Try building some peak,
torque strength for cobbles, because you need to use a higher gear
on them than you normally would.

'So in your normal turbo sessions do some efforts of between
20 seconds and 1 minute in as big a gear as you can push, as hard
as you can push, but stay seated and don't use your upper body to
help you pedal, just pedal from the lower back and legs.'

'OK,' I answered, 'so stay seated as much as possible?'

Chris smiled. 'Stay seated all the time, Iain. Try not to roll your
body, stay in a fixed position if you can. It'll be hard at first, but
the stronger you become over the next few months, the smoother
the cadence will be. It won't be easy. You've got to commit yourself one hundred per cent to the sprint [he said this slowly in his
West Yorkshire accent, emphasizing each word]. Whether it is ten
seconds, thirty seconds, or a full minute. You have to really take it
on full bore for each repetition. That's when you'll feel the benefit.
That's what you need to do for a race like Paris–Roubaix.'

There it was. So clear, and yet so awful. Repetitions! Suffering
was now to be the order of the day if I took onboard his expert,
and freely given, advice. The man knew what he was talking about,
and I trusted him. We parted that lunchtime promising to keep in
touch via email, and I immediately went back to my office, closed
the glass door from my colleagues and, pushing a pile of manu-
scripts aside, eagerly flattened his book out on my desk, locating
what I needed to read. 'Chapter 5: Sportive Training.'

Without giving a verbatim account of the book itself, Chris's instructions were simple to follow, but were administered with a heavy dose of professional realism. This wasn't something to pick up and then put down if you were serious about improving and making significant gains in your fitness and performance. Chris broke the training down into key elements of what the body could do under duress when riding for 10 to 20 seconds; 3 to 5 minutes; one hour; and, finally, two hours. Riding these time intervals at a specific pace was the essential goal one had to attain in order for the body to feel the crucial benefits; 'they all have a positive role in making you a better cyclist' was the mantra.

I had already built up a decent level of fitness for undertaking three- to four-hour bike rides that normally covered 75 or 80 kilometres, with a few choice climbs thrown in. What seemed to be the requirement now was the need to build core strength up in order to undertake and complete what were – in essence – twenty-eight very long and arduous sprint intervals – across *pavé*. The landscape would be pretty near flat as a pancake, judging by the race notes I had been emailed by the organization running the event. Overall, across 170 kilometres, I would only cover 700 feet or so of moderately undulating hills. Of more concern was simply making sure I had the tools to get me over the long stretches of cobbles that covered almost a third of the journey. If I could target that, then I might crack this thing.

All cyclists who ride a sportive will be aware of the intensity levels one must adhere to when training. I had often heard my friends talk about these levels when we met up at an event to enjoy a coffee, post-race. I have to confess here and now that was the only time I chatted to them, as from the gun they set such a tough pace that I'd invariably ease down to a rhythm I knew I could handle for 100 kilometres. They would be on their second coffee (or in Charles's case, a protein drink) by the time I rolled into the car park, head bowed and legs shattered. They were all very familiar with the 'intensity', 'wattage output', and 'power-to-weight' jargon, and to be fair to them they trained by it, too. They were at a much higher level than me, and that was down to serious and dedicated training regimes. They had young kids and stressful jobs just like I did, but for whatever reason, they sacrificed more to make sure they had time to fulfil their ambitions. I needed some of that.

Within Chris's table of zones of intensity were the following:

Level 1: easy, just turning the pedals over, and I can speak easily, with my heart rate at 65 per cent of capacity. Level 2: a solid riding pace, and I would now only be able to speak in short sentences with the effort involved, my heart rate now at up to 80 per cent capacity. Level 3: would have me at 90 per cent capacity, with difficulty speaking – impossible to carry on after an hour of this pace. Level 4: no speech, with every sinew required to last even for 3 to 5 minutes with my heart rate well over 90 per cent. Level 5: a complete drag race for 20 seconds, or longer if I could manage it. I was worried to read my heart rate at this zone was 'not applicable'! I was to find out why soon enough.

Chris had pointed me towards Level 3 as the ideal zone to aim for on my turbo trainer in order to build up stamina. One could adjust the intensity of the pace one maintained, as well as the length of time riding at that level, in order to play around with what actually best suited my physiology. So, instead of a basic 20- to 30-minute session at 80 per cent heart-rate capacity, I would look to push it up to a full hour, and sometimes an hour and a half, at 90 per cent. I then took it a step further and kept a 25-mm tyre on the rear wheel just to increase the resistance and make the process even harder.

This was my goal throughout January and most of February, as I strove to get my legs and lungs tuned in for the coming rigours. Those long sessions were tough, especially the final thirty minutes when you're hanging on and longing to just stop and recover. I had the stereotype Middle-Aged Man in Lycra set-up (as seen on the adverts during ITV's Tour de France coverage) of a laptop perched in front of me on the kitchen breakfast bar. I usually played music, but sometimes would watch inspirational shows like *Question Time*, and Simon Schama's *The Story of the Jews* on the iPlayer. It was just noise in the background as I pounded my cadence, the deafening whirring of the thicker 25-mm tyres on the drum of the turbo drowned out for me, but alas not for my long-suffering wife (she also hated my sweaty lycra), and the neighbours (I'm hoping they didn't hear my aeroplane taking off).

The casual eye looking over my training apparatus wouldn't believe it represented to me the worst form of torture. If they'd had this in the Spanish Inquisition's time, he'd have got his confessions a whole lot quicker. It looks such an innocent piece of equipment, but the terror it imparted in me every time I geared up to train was chilling. It consisted of a CycleOps magnetic fold-away turbo trainer, with the front wheel of my bike locked into one of those ingenious plastic riser blocks (I found that even though I wasn't training for climbing, the increased resistance benefited my general fitness).

Occasionally Jo would come over, attempt to push the pedals round, once the resistance was set against the rear wheel, and laugh at the stupidity of it all. Her dad, Peter, had been an ultra-distance runner back in the 1960s and '70s when it wasn't the craze it is today. She'd endured many a ribbing at school from pals laughing at her mad father running to and from work, sometimes with a headlamp switched on in winter. He'd even run in record-breaking events, one-hundred-mile distances, he was that good. Needless to say, Peter was very supportive of my plans, if not a little envious, as I could detect a glint in his eye when he too talked about racing Paris–Roubaix. When we discussed the in-house training regime I was embarking on, he practically salivated.

I started the Garmin. My resting b.p.m. was now approximately

47, which I was told by Peter was pretty good, and I was on the right track, but could do better! With this ringing in my ears, my plan was to try to map out an interval regime that I would want to stick with – not something that I felt a macho need to try, and would ultimately put me off ever doing again. I had never tried this kind of training before, but in for a penny . . .

The original plan I had signed up to was for 10 minutes warm-up, then for the next 15 minutes I would go full bore for 10 seconds, with a rest of 20 seconds. So, in effect, you're doing two sets of sprints per minute, for 15 minutes, 30 all told. This would be followed by a five-minute warm down, and then the second and final set of sprints, which mirrored exactly the earlier ones undertaken, with a 10-minute warming-down period. A 45-minute workout of real intensity, which I was promised would yield very speedy results.

Chris's narrative in the book called it the 'On-off Switches', guaranteed to improve core strength and power to the pedals. It emphasized not taking any short cuts, and a total focus on the sprint, each one being unique, of its own, and you had to go full-out, otherwise it wasn't worth it. This was a sound plan, but you quickly know what is right for your own physical capabilities, as well as mental fortitude.

At first, to say I was dead on the bike afterwards was an under-statement. I was buggered for three days. I managed to complete the two sets, but pushed myself way above my normal b.p.m.s (181) to 190 and immediately having completed the second set of sprints, almost fell off the bike in my urge to unclip my feet, open the kitchen window and gulp as much air as possible in order not to suffer a potential cardiac arrest. I staggered back into the living room, drenched in sweat, ashen-faced, groping for the doorframe to keep me upright. 'You aren't going to have a stroke, are you?' wondered Jo.

I tried this approach for two more sessions before reading

more of Chris's book, looking for different types of interval training I could do. I had attempted one of the hardest workouts, thinking it would quickly turn me into a Wiggo-esque endurance cyclist, but it wasn't for me. The motivation to endure that kind of training was ebbing away more speedily than I was actually cycling. A new programme was required.

The 'V02 Max Intervals' seemed right up my street. I needed to increase the frequency of going out on long rides for basic endurance, and supplement these with interval training sessions where I kept the pace required for longer periods of just 10 seconds. Chris's book recommended a programme of a 15-minute warm-up, then up to six sets of 3 to 5 minutes' maximum effort, with a similar time for riding easy between each set. There was leeway, of course, to tailor this programme to suit the individual rider, and this is what I looked at. I was very keen on doing one-minute intervals, spread across a whole hour, as I knew come race day I would be completing a great many more intervals across the *pavé*.

So, with a new resolution to pull my finger out and get a six-week block of training accomplished to give me a chance of succeeding, I went at it. And here I was, staring at the machine about to inflict torture upon me for the next sixty minutes. Spinning, at whatever level for a complete amateur, is mentally taxing. If it's a one-off test of physical endurance, then that is fine and you'd want to really take it head on. When it's part of a three-times-a-week routine, allied to a four-hour bike ride at the weekend, then it takes on another dimension.

I started to look at the bike with dread, animosity and guilt in equal measures. Dread, when I was sitting at my desk at work, thinking about training that evening. Animosity, for the impact it was having on my social and family life, with everything being centred around me having enough time to train, and with all other responsibilities thrown back at Jo. And guilt, for missing out on life with happy young children, a beautiful wife, good food and wine, and relaxation from the stress of the working week.

The turbo trainer stared impassively back at me, taunting me as if to say, 'Think you're tough enough, sunshine? Climb aboard and let's see what you've got, then!' Bastard.

The intervals themselves could be merciless. The warm-up was great: I'd be plugged into some tempo-inducing song from my iPlayer (usually AC/DC, or Stereophonics), and when the sprint intervals began I'd switch to the Foo Fighters. My scientific study had proved beyond reasonable doubt that the Foo Fighters tempo was perfect for lung-bursting effort, when a wall of noise was required to forget about everything other than the seconds ticking away before it ended.

Each of the six one-minute intervals followed the same pattern. Confidence for the first 20 seconds as my legs and heart rate increased rapidly, as I hit warp speed on the final sprocket, and the Garmin was telling me I was nearing 45 k.p.h. (good for me). With the sweat stinging my eyes, and 'The Pretender' building to a crescendo – Dave Grohl wailing to screeching guitars and a mind-numbing bass – I would then grit my teeth to holding the pace for the next 20 seconds. This was the point it would get very messy indeed, depending on what number of interval I was at. For the final one, by 40 seconds into this blur of pain, I would be hanging on for dear life.

I would do my utmost NOT to look at the kitchen clock to my right, in a desperate and futile attempt to speed up time and release me from this torment. I would manage to keep my eyes tightly shut for the next 10 seconds as I put in another tremendous push of the pedals to get me over the 50-k.p.h. barrier. Could I hold it? Sometimes the whole crazy mix of audio and respiratory struggle would make me grasp at my headphones and wrench them out just so I could give myself to the final 10 seconds. With head and shoulders manically rocking, my cadence right up to the maximum I could manage, I would take one final gulp of air and just let rip, watching the second hand of the clock suddenly go into slow motion.

Believe me, it did. Time seemed to stand still as I was locked into this never-ending pain. I would want to stop – I had to – but the voice in my ear would chide me to finish. The kitchen was echoing with the sound of rubber being burnt on metal, the cats having long since fled through the door flap into the relative peace of the back garden as I grunted and gasped my way to the imaginary finish line.

And then it was over. Within a few minutes, flicking down the gears to the last one, I would spin madly, watching my heart rate drop back down to a manageable 125 b.p.m. as the burning sensation left my legs and my lungs started to recover from the dry heaving that lasted usually for a few seconds. Within five minutes of warming down it was as if it hadn't happened. I stress 'as if'. I would be soaking wet, my feet would feel like they were on fire, and I would gulp down a litre of water. It would then be a case of struggling to get off the bike, staggering to the kitchen window and gulping in huge drafts of fresh air with a few 'Fuck me's!' announced to all and sundry.

God knows what the neighbours thought.

A Promise Made

Three months before Paris–Roubaix, I got the motivation I needed to keep at the training, to accomplish the dream of completing the race. It came, as these things do, in the most tragic of circumstances.

It was a miserable winter's day, and I was sitting in a spotlessly clean private room in a hospital in Northamptonshire near where my sisters and brother live.

The respirator methodically pumped up and then down, never missing a beat, though not going as quickly as my mother's heart, judging by the way her chest was rising and falling as she lay motionless on her bed.

Her backstory is a typical, heart-breaking narrative of being married to the man you have loved since you were an 18-year-old girl and first spotted him in the local pub where you worked as a barmaid. They were both products of the thousands of Scots who had travelled south to find work and a better life. Settling in a new town with a steel works, they lived a full life with all its many ups and downs, raised four kids and managed to end their days together living in what they believed to be (and I agreed) paradise, in the West Highlands.

My father had been dead nearly six years now from leukaemia, and slowly my mum's desire to carry on life without him after fifty years of marriage had ebbed away. She was dying of a broken heart, and now we were witnessing the final days.

When I was a young boy my mother had always been there for my many accidents, whether being hit in the face by cricket bats, or knocking myself out when crashing my friend's racing bike. I must have driven her and my father crazy. I had always wanted to make them proud, whether it was doing well at school, going to university, or getting my career in publishing up and running. My mother was well known to the main bookshop in her hometown of Aberdeen as she often pulled books I had edited, or commissioned, off the shelves and took them up to the counter. Not to buy them, but merely to point out the name on the imprint page and, beaming with pride, tell the bemused bookseller that this was her son's book. I still smile thinking about that anecdote.

Both she and my father loved my cycling or walking exploits, whether it was trekking the West Highland Way, or cycling coast to coast, through the Alps, or the arduous John O'Groats to Land's End. These cycling badges of honour meant little to them; they just were pleased I had achieved what I set out to do.

So here we were. I sat next to her bed on my own, while one of my sisters talked to the staff outside, knowing that Mum would possibly never open her eyes again. By now we had asked the medical team that our mum should not be resuscitated should her condition deteriorate. The woman who had been my comfort blanket in life, and at times the rock that had kept me on the straight and narrow, and always encouraged my dreams . . . and now I couldn't do anything for her.

I was beginning to invent conversations with her in order to try to keep my mind focused on the inevitable denouement. 'I've decided to do another stupid bike ride, Mum,' I whispered into her ear. No reply, not even a flicker of an eyelid. I persisted. 'It is going to be the toughest thing I've ever done. I just signed up for it last week, it's from outside of Paris to a town on the Belgian border which you've never heard of.' And I proceeded to rattle through the long description of how famous the race is, what makes the cobbles so tough to ride, why completing it means so much to me and how arduous it will be.

'You and Dad always supported me, even when you thought I was crazy. But let's make a deal. You open your eyes for me, just once, and give me a smile, and I'll finish the route – I promise you I will. Please?'

Nothing happened. The pump still inhaled and exhaled monotonously. A nurse walked in to check on her condition, and I sat up and snapped out of my meditation.

My mum would pass away, having never regained consciousness, a few days later, with all her family around her. By the end it was a blessing, as I am sure anyone who has been in this kind of situation will agree, and I sat with her body lying on her bed for a while, just contemplating what she had meant to me, to my own family and what I could do to show I loved her and took pride in her being my mother. The shock of realizing I was now alone, without the emotional pillars I had come to take for granted, struck me to the core.

My mind was made up. Not until then had I realized what would be my motivation to do this race. Now, no matter what happened, I would get around that velodrome track, even if I had to carry the bloody bike with me.

The Hell of the North

We enter into the centre of the battlefield. There's not a tree, everything is flattened! Not a square metre that has not been hurled upside down. There's one shell hole after another. The only things that stand out in this churned earth are the crosses with their ribbons of blue, white and red. It is hell!

Report from *L'Auto*

Every time I wheeled my bike into our hallway before stepping out into the pre-dawn cold for a training ride, I studied an old picture frame on my wall. Landscape in format, it is a simple black wooden frame, about 40 x 90 cm, and most visitors to our house pass it by without a second glance. To me, it is extremely important and close to my heart. Within it are a few medals, a citation and a heraldic-like certificate, plus a burnished bronze disc plaque, roughly the size of a tea saucer, and very old. Etched into it are the images of Britannia and a lion standing over a prostrate Imperial German eagle; it's all quite Edwardian in style. The words *Freedom and Honour* are proclaimed at the top and standing out proudly beneath those words is the name Private George MacGregor – he was my great-uncle.

This is what is commonly called a 'Dead Man's Penny' and over a million of them were cast by the British government from 1919 onwards to hand out to the families of those who died serving in the armed forces during the Great War. The story of how the medal came into existence, how the government at the time decided this was the one thing the King's ministers needed to do in order to show the British public they felt their pain, is a fascinating one. But not for this book, I'm afraid. But I looked at it and touched the frame every time I went cycling – just like any other sportsman who feels they require a lucky charm (just as Liverpool players tap the sign that says *This is Anfield* before stepping out for a match) – it offered some weird sort of solace, maybe even protection. On another level it reminded me that the past is always with us.

The race I would undertake would cycle through the very heartland that my forefathers themselves travelled to a century beforehand. And, for my kin, just like millions of other working-class men, it was almost certainly the first time they had travelled abroad, quite possibly the first time they had ever left their home city of Aberdeen.

George MacGregor, who served with the 8th Battalion of the Black Watch (Royal Highlanders), would die at the infamous slaughter that was the First Battle of Passchendaele (also known as the Third Battle of Ypres) in the autumn of 1917; he was 19 years of age. He was one of four brothers from the 'Granite City' who had all joined up together.

The Ypres Salient, where the battle was fought, is some 150 kilometres north of Paris, but the whole area around the village of Busigny, where my race would start, is dotted with war cemeteries, giant memorials and commemorative walls inscribed with the names of the missing and fallen. Mons, Ypres, Cambrai, Vimy and Arras are all burnt into the Great War lexicon, their monuments representing to some visitors the futility of the struggle and its purpose, and to others commemorating the immense bravery all troops, from both sides of the wire, displayed.

Like millions of soldiers in the First World War, George MacGregor's remains were never found; it is here the name of my great-uncle is listed on the Tyne Cot memorial in Flanders, near Ypres, the largest cemetery for Commonwealth forces in the world, in any war. It contains the names of 33,783 soldiers of British forces, and 1,176 New Zealanders.[4] As with all the other cemeteries and memorials, it is an extremely moving and beautifully peaceful place, completely at odds with the horrors and suffering the men buried there endured on the Western Front.

Roubaix and Lille were quickly occupied in the first year of the war by the Kaiser's army – and would endure many years of hardship under military occupation until their eventual liberation in 1918 by the Allies. Lille itself was bombarded at one point when the locals pretended to the invading German forces that the city was equipped with artillery, when in fact it had a solitary cannon. Rationing was severe, sabotage was common, and hostages were taken in reprisal for any sign of protest or dissent. Like all French towns and cities occupied by the German army, Roubaix suffered troops being forcedly billeted in the homes of its inhabitants, who were in turn unceremoniously turfed out into the elements and ordered to make do as best they could. Before the Germans had departed in the wake of the 1918 Allied advance, the Roubaix velodrome itself had been plundered for its wooden boardings and metal fixtures, first by the occupying troops then by homeless civilians needing to build shelters and keep fires going.

The area to the south of Lille – where the race would travel north as it sped its way from the original start line in Paris (and later Chantilly and then Compiègne, famous for the railway

---

[4] 'Tyne Cot' is apparently derived from the name given by the Northumberland Fusiliers to the German concrete pill boxes (mini bunkers with machine guns) the Fusiliers were tasked with trying to destroy. In Tynecastle, north-east England, a worker's cottage was called a 'Tyne cot'.

carriage where the Armistice was signed in November 1918) – crisscrosses what was in places categorized as No-Man's-Land, as well as German-occupied and Allied-controlled territory. One is cycling through history, literally riding over terrain where millions of troops fought, and hundreds of thousands died. As a publisher of history titles, this is what attracted me to the race just as much as the cobbles. The latter was simply a sporting challenge that dripped with nostalgia and uniqueness, while the emotional resonance of following in my ancestors' footsteps towards northern France was too much to resist. The more I delved into the history of the event and the reasons why it was labelled the 'Hell of the North', the more my desire to go was strengthened.

The subsequent Paris–Roubaix in 1897 was won by the local hero Maurice Garin, who also won it again in 1898. Garin was the darling of French sport, proving himself to be one of the best track and endurance racers of his generation, going on to win, in 1903, the very first edition of a new race created by *Le Vélo*'s direct competitor, *L'Auto* – the Tour de France.

By the turn of the twentieth century, however, Paris–Roubaix was actually losing prominence in the cycling calendar as many track stars dropped out due to the unrelenting nature of the *pavé* and the multiple punctures it caused competitors. With the demise of *Le Vélo* in 1904, in the circulation war with *L'Auto* over the Dreyfus affair,[5] the event was now being promoted by the latter newspaper, edited by Henri Desgrange, who had three years earlier

[5] The Dreyfus affair related to the scandal of the French army officer – Captain Alfred Dreyfus – who was of the Jewish faith and was court-martialled for spying for Germany on fabricated evidence and exiled to Devil's Island, off French Guiana, in 1894. The case split France in two, and *Le Vélo*'s editor supported the victim, whereas many powerful companies whose advertisements his paper carried did not. Piqued by his intransigence in attacking the ruling elite in his editorials, they pulled the plug and set up *L'Auto-Vélo* in direct competition, ultimately forcing the paper to close. Dreyfus was exonerated and freed by 1904.

tried to hijack the race to set up his own paper's version. Pierre Giffard at *Le Vélo* had attempted to block this move but, with the assistance of the French government, *L'Auto* won the rights to Paris–Roubaix and, as valuable advertisers jumped ship to Desgrange, guaranteed *Le Vélo*'s extinction. So the race survived, even though the number of spectators dropped.

Josef Fischer may have been the first foreign winner of *La Pascale*, but it was then dominated by the French, winning sixteen out of the next eighteen editions until the Great War called a temporary halt to the race in 1914, with Roubaix marooned behind the German lines. Of those French riders, Octave Lapize was the shining star, becoming the first cyclist to win three editions of the race in a row, in 1909, 1910 and 1911.[6] Curly-haired, diminutive and fiery, the triple victor at Paris–Roubaix also won the Tour de France, as well as becoming national champion three times. A natural climber who soared in the Alps, Lapize's ability to therefore turn his hand to slogging his way across cobbles and mud at speed was unique. He would volunteer for the French air force in 1915, rising to the rank of sergeant, and would die in aerial combat above the Western Front (near the site of the Battle of Verdun) in July 1917, ironically on Bastille Day.

Along with Lapize, two of *La Pascale*'s other early winners stood out for me as heroes. Firstly, there was the winner of the 1914 edition, Charles Crupelandt. He would be wounded in battle and awarded one of France's top honours, the Croix de Guerre, but then mysteriously cashiered in, was disgraced and later jailed. But my favourite was an ex-teammate of Lapize's, the docker from Luxembourg, François Faber. A stocky, moustachioed

---

[6] Lapize would also win the 1910 Tour de France, but is most famous for being the rider who, summiting the brutal climb of the Tourmalet in the Pyrenees, shouted, 'You are murderers!' at the Tour officials in protest at the mountainous route.

racer who won the Tour de France in 1909,[7] he raced to victory in Paris–Roubaix in 1913.

Faber seems to have been quite a character, enlisting in the French Foreign Legion when war broke out before he was killed by a sniper while ferrying a wounded comrade during the Battle of Artois on 9 May 1915. He had just received a telegram from his wife saying she had given birth to their daughter.

So three main riders of the pre-war period, who had dominated the Classics, as well as played significant roles in the Tour de France, had perished in the conflict. Without them, who else was left to pick up the pieces and see if the race could be launched again?

With the Armistice signed at Compiègne, and a ceasefire holding after 11 November 1918, by the following year Western Europe was beginning to see the first shoots of normality, despite the massive loss of lives. France alone had suffered almost 1,400,000 dead and 4,500,000 wounded, roughly one-fifth of her total population. As would again happen in the Second World War, whole towns and villages had simply ceased to exist as a result of the fighting. The vast armies were demobbed, men were returning home, and the idea of leading a civilian life again, without bullets, bombs and bayonets getting in the way, was tangible. People would return to the jobs they had before the war, and the pattern of work, rest and play was once again evident.

Sport was back on the national agenda, with all of the traditional events starting to re-establish themselves, cycling included. Under the guardianship of Henri Desgrange, *L'Auto* was firmly in control of running major races, including Paris–Roubaix. Desgrange was eager to see if the race was salvageable and so dispatched once

---

[7] Faber actually set a record that has never been beaten: winning five stages of the 1909 *Grande Boucle* in a row, despite horrific weather conditions which saw fifty riders drop out in six days.

more the ever faithful Victor Breyer (who was now working for *L'Auto*) and Eugène Christophe[8] to see if the roads were passable, Roubaix itself was still standing, and its velodrome intact. Before national telephone networks, and more significantly before this area of France and Belgium, where the fighting had been most fierce, had its basic postal systems up and running again, no one south of the Western Front actually knew what life was like there. Were the towns and cities still habitable? What condition were the roads and railway tracks in? What had become of the inhabitants?

Even six months after the war's end, these questions still remained to be answered as the ebb and flow of returning troops, refugees and displaced populations caused endless confusion and delay. With the Easter deadline fast approaching, Desgrange needed answers.

What Breyer and Christophe found shocked them to their core. It is easy for the public nowadays, with all the modern communications we have at our fingertips, to witness the horrors of warfare, either on our doorstep, or further afield. For these two men, without recourse to accurate reports or photographs and films, the sight of so much utter destruction would have been heart-rending. Christophe had served in the French army in a cycle battalion, but Breyer had stayed working as a journalist for the duration of the conflict. Perhaps that is why his account of what he witnessed and what condition the actual route of the race was in is so visceral and shocking: 'Shell-holes one after the other, with no gaps, outlines of trenches, barbed wire cut into one thousand pieces; unexploded shells on the roadside, here and there, graves.'

Added to these obstacles would be the endless lines of humanity the riders would have to negotiate their way through, the quagmire

---

[8] Christophe rode eleven editions of the Tour de France and was the very first wearer of the yellow jersey (the *maillot jaune*) in 1919. He would gain fame for welding his bike's broken forks while leading the race.

of destroyed road networks, the lack of accommodation, food and drink. Everything was in short supply. It would be Christophe who coined the immortal phrase which Breyer eagerly worked into his report back to *L'Auto*'s editor: 'From Doullens onwards the countryside was nothing but desolation. The shattered trees looked vaguely like skeletons, the paths had collapsed and been potholed or torn away by shells. The vegetation, rare, had been replaced by military vehicles in a pitiful state. The houses of villages were no more than bare walls. At their foot, heaps of rubble. Eugène Christophe exclaimed: "Here, this really is the hell of the North."'

It was obviously a dream headline for a newspaper man, and one that caught the public's imagination; they would surely want to know more. But to the proud inhabitants of the Pas-de-Calais *département* it was a slur on their region's honour, and one they would resent every Easter for decades to come when the racing calendar arrived on their doorstep.

To Henri Desgrange, too, it was not great news. But, ever the pragmatist, after talking with Breyer he believed the race could be launched and a route created that would take the riders around the worst of the destruction. One significant problem was the state of the Roubaix velodrome itself, which was now in total ruin. To finish the race there was out of the question, so Desgrange scouted the town and decided to hold the finish line on the main boulevard, the Avenue des Villas, which was still in one piece and easily accessible to the public.

The resumption of the race certainly attracted the crowds, but there was also a definite sense of starting anew – an attempt to reignite enthusiasm for such an event, perhaps any social event, so soon after the devastation of the Great War. As for the competitors themselves, what must they have thought? Here they were, possibly after years of service in their respective armed forces, now about to ride again with little training in their weary legs, on bicycles that were more fit for the knacker's yard than to compete with. What would be going through their minds while waiting for the flag to drop and the race to commence again? Had they seen their comrades die, homes destroyed, families displaced or lost in the fog of war and refugee misery? Perhaps they were starving, homeless and desperately needed to race in the hope of earning a fee to support a family? Now they were about to ride through the very hell they had survived.

Looking at a number of photographs from the period, such as those of the infamous Messines Road, which was the main supply road running through to the Battle of Ypres in 1914, 1917 and 1918, all that's discernible is wrecked tree stumps, shell craters and a sea of mud. Nothing is living – and the road was ruined. It was hardly the venue for a bicycle race.

Yet one hundred and thirty riders rolled out from Versailles on Easter Sunday 1919, flanked by columns of French soldiers, some on leave, some on security duty, and excited civilians eager to have a normal Sunday in a metaphorical 'hell', so to speak! The contraptions (for that is what arguably most of the bikes could be accurately described as) the cyclists rode were a mixture of pre-war race bikes that had been mothballed for the duration of the conflict and given a brief service, or, if the rider was lucky (such as the race favourite Henri Pélissier, the David Beckham of his day, apparently), he was atop a newly constructed frame and wheels.

Pélissier, and his younger sibling Francis, along with elite fellow professionals such as Eugène Christophe and the Belgians Lucien Buysse and Philippe Thys, were attempting to kick-start their careers once more, and French bicycle manufacturers were desperate for results to reignite interest in their own merchandise. As with the rest of Europe, France was lacking essential raw materials that had been requisitioned for the war effort. Machinery created for producing specialist bike components and frames had been turned over after 1914 to construct weapons of destruction: rifles,

howitzers, bullets and bayonets. Skilled labour for bikes, too, had
either been lost to the casualty list, or had simply given up the craft
now that other industries had arrived, such as mass-produced car
manufacturing.

In a nutshell, those French bicycle manufacturers still in existence needed to pool their resources or they wouldn't survive,
and so a new consortium was established – La Sportive – which
comprised five well-known companies: Alcyon, based in Neuilly
close to Paris; Peugeot, who had been pumping out bikes, trucks
and artillery shells for the army, and were based in Montbéliard
near the Swiss border in eastern France; the venerable La Français
company based in Paris; Automoto, founded in St Etienne; and
another popular Parisian company, Gladiator. Cleverly husband-
ing resources to manufacture goods, as well as to retain valued
skilled staff and salesmen, La Sportive simply wanted to re-
establish professional bike racing in the French sporting calendar,
to create strong publicity through new races the public could
witness, and thus drive sales of their bikes. They collectively
created a team of the best riders around at that time – such as the
Péllisier brothers – paid them, what was for the time a good wage
of 300 francs per month, and ensured they rode the best bikes and
had the best kit available.

On a clear, dry, early Easter Sunday morning, the riders, officials
and an appreciative crowd buzzing with anticipation stood to
attention for an emotional minute's silence. Their tribute was to the
many fallen in the conflict, as well as to pay their respects to their
dead comrades of the road: Lapize, Faber and hundreds more. The
flag was dropped and it was probably obvious to all concerned –
spectators and riders alike – that they would not be hitting the
kind of speeds previous events had achieved due to their lack of
preparation, the bikes they were riding and the conditions of the
war-ravaged roads. Immediately upon leaving Paris, it is possible
that a deal was struck that the peloton would remain calm for the

majority of the route, until a designated distance from Roubaix when the real racing would begin. No proof exists, but reading the various descriptions of how they ticked along at an average speed of 23 k.p.h., one can surmise this was certainly not a breakneck, hell-for-leather Paris–Roubaix.

Approximately 70 or 80 kilometres from the finish line, the main pre-race favourites made their moves. The Pélissier brothers were joined by the Belgian Thys, and the plucky Frenchman Honoré Barthélémy,[9] as they drove a breakaway for the finish line, though Francis Pélissier would drop back due to a triple puncture. What followed then had all the makings of a classic Paris–Roubaix legend.

Arriving at a level crossing, all of the riders came to an abrupt halt as a train was stationed across their path. This was a repeat of what had happened a month earlier at the nearby Tour of Flanders. On that occasion, the eventual winner, Henri Van Lerberghe, had simply shouldered his bike, climbed through the train carriage and continued the race. Inspired by this, perhaps, all of our leaders of Paris–Roubaix did likewise, though Henri Pélissier had the initiative to decide to press on first. Indeed, his stamina and speed of thought would win him the ultimate prize.

Coming through the outskirts of Roubaix and towards the centre of town, amid the excitement of the roar of the crowd, tired minds and aching limbs, Pélissier senior was awake enough to see the finish-line banner on the Avenue des Villas heralding victory. Immediately he kicked away and sped to victory and into the arms of the throng of journalists and officials. Pélissier's winning time still stands as the slowest on record: 12 hours and 15 minutes.

---

[9] Honoré Barthélémy would gain future notoriety in the 1920 edition of the Tour de France when he crashed on the stage to Aix-en-Provence and was blinded in one eye from a piece of flint on the road but heroically went on to complete the race. The following year he would come third with a glass eye in place.

It was a reflection of not only his poor state to ride his bike professionally, but also the war-ravaged conditions he'd had to traverse.

Even though the average speeds had declined by almost a third compared to pre-1914, and with a great deal of rebuilding to be done all along the route, the organizers knew they had backed a winner. The level of public interest was huge, just as immense as in the very first year of 1896. The rebirth of the race mirrored that of the nation. France would rebuild and the good times would return. Like other professional road races, Paris–Roubaix was again cemented in the hearts and minds of the peoples of northern France. Even if they were from the hell of the North.

Fit for Purpose

From the first racing bike my parents bought for me at Christmas when I was 12, to the later more expensive model I eagerly purchased with one of my first monthly wage packets, I had never really suffered any kind of injury while riding. Historically, I have nearly always bought a Raleigh, not really because they are cheaper (and I rode a Giant when completing John O'Groats to Land's End), but because I prefer them to others within my price range. The Raleigh I now owned for Paris–Roubaix had served me well thus far and, although I'd love to weave through London traffic and climb the Kent hills on a sexy, jet-black Colnago CF12, I was wise enough to know this was my level. My legs and lungs would compensate for a heavier bike, or so I thought. I had noticed, though, that I didn't recognize too many Raleighs on my various training rides. Was I alone in thinking they were any good?

I might have been happy with my bike, but I knew I was falling into the trap of thinking there was more to squeeze out of my performance with improvements in clothes, training, food and bike technology. Reading the many articles in either *Cycling Weekly*, *Procycling* or the new kid on the block of monthlies, *Cyclist*, all of the adverts and reviews told me that what I was wearing wasn't good enough, that my shoes needed to be the best carbon, that my helmet wasn't safe enough compared to the latest model, or that my nutrition or method of interval training was wrong. I seemed to be bombarded with questions and concerns wherever I looked. Couldn't I simply have a cup of tea and a bowl of porridge pre-ride, followed by beans on toast afterwards? Should I not remain loyal to my four-year-old shoes which had been under seventy quid when I bought them? What about my bottom of the range bib shorts and jersey? The only thing I hadn't skimped on was my helmet, which I knew from experience was essential, and my lovely Garmin was on loan from the cycling writer Tim Moore. Talking with friends and fellow riders, one thing came up again and again. How did I feel on the bike? Was I getting the best performance possible without injuring myself in the process?

Granted, I did feel the odd twinge behind my right knee when I was pulling myself up to the top of Toy's Hill, or Ditchling Beacon, but I always put that down to the wear and tear of being older and tired at the end of the ride. Back in my twenties I was fitter from regular running and swimming, so to tackle riding the length of the country without specific training hadn't really been a problem. Twenty years on, it most certainly was. Beer, eating more of the wrong food, beer, less regular exercise, more beer, and less sleep from looking after young children meant one thing: I was always knackered after a ride and the painful twinges seemed to happen more frequently.

So I listened to my inner voice of concern, addressed my negativity and decided that a bike fit[10] was a 'must' in preparation for riding the cobbles. I had been in regular contact with journalist and author Richard Moore, as well as listening to the excellent podcasts he created throughout the cycling season for the *Telegraph* alongside fellow writers Daniel Friebe and Lionel Birnie – they

---

[10] A bike fit is basically being measured so that the rider's body shape is attune to the size of the bicycle he or she is riding. The size of bike frame, length of handlebar, etc, can all combine to make a rider either comfortable, or put him in agony.

were funny, informative and original. Richard always has some-thing new to say about issues or people in the pro ranks.

And he didn't hold back when I told him about my intention to undergo a bike fit. 'I'm not sure about bike fits,' he said, 'though I did have one done by Phil Burt at British Cycling, with video analysis and all that, and I thought it was really interesting. Fair enough if you're a professional bike rider, then it's essential. If you're an amateur or weekend warrior, it's a sledgehammer to crack a nut. Most [riders] look terrible on their bikes before and after their bike fits! Any coach or experienced cyclist can offer useful advice on position – most people don't need the all-singing, all-dancing bike fit with bells and whistles.'

I could see his point, especially given the prices some places charged for the service. Whatever, I thought, for the purposes of research and for finding even one per cent more comfort on my bike for Paris–Roubaix, I decided to give it a go.

There were two options open to me where I lived in south-east London: first, to visit my local bike shop, a small out of the way place that catered for our general cycling community, repairing and maintaining commuting bicycles – a very straightforward and inexpensive place but with a loyal following. The second option was to place myself in the care of a commercially slick and thoroughly professional outfit based at the top of Crystal Palace hill, on the route of a very popular training circuit for hundreds, if not thousands of local cyclists serious about their sport. In a fit of extravagance, I decided to visit both and see what they could do for me. But as I dug a little deeper into what was on offer, I unearthed some very interesting characters.

My local shop was owned by an ex-national champion, from Lithuania, whose name adorned the shop front – Vaidas Cycles. Vaidas Granauskas has the classic frame of a professional rider from the old days: stocky and muscular, he looks like a powerful sprinter. He had raced since he was 12 years of age, by 16 he was racing professionally on the road, and two years later would win his national championship and go on to represent his country for six years. At one point he was ranked number ten in the European ratings – he had quality.

After Lithuania had been welcomed into the European Community, Vaidas decided to move to the United Kingdom, and for the past five years he's owned two bike shops – one in Brighton, and the other right on my doorstep in Forest Hill. I first encountered him when the London shop opened its doors and I eagerly ventured in to check it out and buy something – anything, really – the way we all do. Along with Vaidas, there was his assistant George, a young, ginger-haired local guy with a goatee, whose gaunt, sallow-cheeked, bespectacled appearance belied a serious cyclist who raced most weekends. He was also a bloody good mechanic and the front of house salesman for the shyer, more serious Vaidas.

While Vaidas would often be silently turning an impressively huge gear on his turbo trainer in the back of the shop – without breaking sweat or being out of breath, I might add – watching the ebb and flow of customers, I chatted about all things cycling with George, and looked around the small shop, which was stylishly adorned with bikes and frames hanging on the walls; the ceiling decorated in a mosaic of vintage newspaper headlines from the past four decades. It had the feel of just about getting by with a small, established clientele, and the ambition to sell some moderately priced mid-range road bikes.

They regularly serviced both my Brompton and the Raleigh, despite the latter often being the cause of much hilarity. There is a very relaxed atmosphere there and the way they offer a service to the community is a throwback to how bike shops used to be, to my mind at least. I always enjoy dropping in and hope their business will thrive. Informing them I was going to tackle the Paris–Roubaix brought guffaws of 'seriously?' from George, and a stern lecture from Vaidas about how tough the cobbles were: 'I have ridden them in Romania . . . very painful.' Even so, I still thought it was time to stop just buying inner tubes and energy gels, so after he had serviced the Raleigh for a sportive I was undertaking that weekend, I asked George how much a bike fit would cost. 'Ah, don't worry about that, let's call it part of the price for the bike's service, shall we?' I was happy to accept their generous offer, but the fitting itself reflected why the offer was so readily given.

George respectfully waited ten minutes for Vaidas to complete his marathon session on the turbo trainer and when he had finally taken himself off to get a drink, George then fixed my rear wheel into the turbo trainer and asked me to set myself up as I normally would when riding. Clipping myself in, I started to pedal slowly while George sized my style and cadence, taking mental notes while stroking his goatee. 'OK, we need the plumb line,' he then announced.

'The what?' I asked.

'The plumb line, you know? String with a weight on it. I need to see if the angle of your leg joints aligns correctly with the pedal stroke, how high your seat post is, whether your cleats are in line, and if you are overstretching to the handlebars and drops, etc. It won't take long.'

With that he disappeared downstairs into the cellar of the shop – where the bikes were repaired – to get his equipment. Or the string, I should say. Returning within a minute, he immediately dropped to his knees and placed the string against my knee joint while I held the pedal horizontal, my knee at a 45-degree angle. 'Hmm, needs looking at,' he murmured. He then went to the front of the bike and studied my cleat positioning, taking some notes on a pad. 'OK, can you pedal and reach out to the bars for me, Iain?' I followed his instructions and once again he gave me the hard stare through his John Lennon-style glasses and gave another, 'Hmm.' After five more minutes, he seemed to have figured out what needed adjusting. Within another thirty minutes, George had moved my right cleat approximately 4 millimetres forward, my seat post up a centimetre, and installed a new higher-elevated head set for the handlebars, to make my reach to them less strenuous.

'Can you feel the difference?' he asked, with a beaming smile.

'It does feel smoother,' I hesitantly replied, 'and my shoulders and neck feel more relaxed, that's for sure – which is great, as that was becoming a real issue for me when riding for more than three hours.' This was the answer he was looking for.

'Your head and shoulders are what will take the battering at Paris–Roubaix so I'm glad you feel more comfortable. The cleats might need more adjusting, but I think I got it right. You'll know soon enough when you're out on a big training ride. Let me know how it goes and I'll adjust again if necessary. Have you thought about double-wrapping the handlebars? Just to keep vibration to a minimum?'

'That was a good idea,' I thought, so said, 'Yes, let's try that. I'm willing to give most things that prevent pain on the cobbles a go, George.' And that was it. I paid him the service fee of fifty-five pounds, which included the bars being wrapped, two new inner tubes and some energy gels. It was a bargain and it had been an enjoyable and informative experience of how bike fits were probably performed when my dad was riding bikes as a kid during the Second World War. So, I had tried the old-fashioned method; now it was time to embrace what the latest bike-fit technology of the twenty-first century could offer me.

I had discovered Cadence Performance on Google a while back, and their pretty cool and efficient website was definitely in keeping with the centre itself, which I had, by the time of my test, visited several times. A very pristine and swish two-storey building, it was in the perfect catchment area for club riders and enthusiasts as they headed out towards Kent and Surrey for a training ride. On the ground floor on the right-hand side as one enters is a boutique café serving everything the hungry cyclist craves, from pasta to cakes and the ubiquitous coffee machine offering up anything you want with caffeine in. On the left-hand side is the bike repair area, and towards the back is a spacious shopping space full of bikes, equipment, clothing and nutritional supplements. It is a very pleasurable place to wander around and spend your money as an army of cyclists grab a bite to eat, or drop bikes off for repair.

On the top floor, which one accesses at the back of the store, and can also look up to from a mini-atrium, there is a mixture of computerized bikes offering 'Ride Alpe d'Huez'-style experiences, as well as cardiovascular machines for the general athlete. It's a very sleek and athletic-looking place and attracts that kind of rider who has money to burn – either to buy the bike of his dreams, or receive the best-quality coaching and advice on training and fitness. I have to admit I liked going there, and had recently attended a talk with Sean Kelly, who was promoting his autobiography. How would a bike fit here compare with Vaidas?

For a start, once I was on the Cadence Performance website, I could choose from a range of services when it came to seeing if my body was in tune with my machine. Their promise was to make me a better cyclist by offering me a selection of three bike fits. The cheapest was the Dynamic service, which was similar to Vaidas's (but they didn't use string) and the fitter, I was told, was an expert who knew what to look out for and adjust if required. The second was the Retül service, in which an expert fitter would provide me with a cleat-alignment check, plus a physiological overhaul to ensure all positioning was accurate and pain-free, once I had been measured and the length and reach of my body taken into account. Finally, there was the Optimum service, which covered the whole package of a Retül fit, plus a footbeds check where, if necessary, a bespoke set of insoles could be created for the customer, and lastly a pedal-stroke analysis which sought to maximize the power output of the rider.

This was clearly a very professional range of services and I felt totally confident that any of them would find any deficiencies I might have. I plumped for the Retül as I had never had any kind of physiological analysis of how I performed on the bike, and it was priced right at the top of my budget.

I booked a two-and-a-half-hour slot for the week after and turned up on a dark wet, winter's evening after work. There were few people at the centre, just some customers on the second-floor balcony checking out exercise machines, a mechanic repairing some wheels, and the café assistant cleaning the coffee machine. I was told to wait for Andy, who would take me through my bike fit, so I grabbed a coffee – the assistant didn't seem that impressed with my goal to tackle *La Pascale*. Then a very tall staff member introduced himself as Andy and asked me to come upstairs to the bike-fitting room. We walked past the gleaming computerized bikes and down a corridor of clean, new rows of shower cubicles and changing rooms. This was a very professional outfit, no mistake. 'What was I doing here?' I kept thinking.

Initially we discussed the pros and cons of a basic bike fit. Andy wasn't exactly trying to give me the hard sell – as a semi-pro rider himself he was, of course, more concerned with being healthy on the bike itself. 'If the salesman is experienced,' he summarized, 'then the sort of sizing process that you can get in any bike shop over the course of ten to fifteen minutes should be pretty good. Things like seat height, and then the reach is very important, so those two things are what people are looking for. It doesn't matter where you go.'

My problems, I thought, were pretty standard for someone who bought his bike online without getting properly measured for it: I would get pain in the top of my shoulders and neck after a few hours on the bike. Andy thus gave me more detail to mull over. 'Quite often we can resolve a "reach issue" really simply by having a shorter stem or upright stem. It's very rarely solved with a longer set-up. We often find people come in for a fit just because they've got some sort of pain in one side, which is quite common for a club cyclist in general. Sometimes it's related to the amount of riding they are doing, and how their body adjusts from a few hours to much longer hours on the bike at the weekend. That's quite a common thing and our Retül system – the cameras analysing the rider – allows us to put dots on the landmarks of your body and monitor how you react. We will also check the angles on the bike and check dimensions to the millimetre as well.'

Andy then checked the tyres and up to the handlebars where he quickly noticed the double-tape George had applied. 'Do you get cramp at all in your hands, because that can be a negative side effect?' he asked. I hadn't over the three long rides I had undertaken since my first visit to Vaidas. 'I notice that they are relatively new shoes you've got on.' He was systematically going through my whole set-up, which was reassuring. 'The cleats don't look too worn, did you get them in the same place?' he asked. We then discussed whether my feet might be slightly out of line due to the fittings of the cleats themselves.

Andy smiled at my reaction to all these questions. 'I'm always fiddling around with my own bike,' he said. 'That's what bike fitters do, actually, when they're not bike fitting. They fiddle around to try to eke out as much performance as they can, really. It makes quite a lot of difference, doesn't it.' He explained that in this session he'd be making observations of me riding the bike and from there we would then go through some physical screening, checking the range of the motion in my joints, top to toe. Over the next hour, after watching me pedal a pretty nifty cadence – if I say so myself – for fifteen minutes, Andy gradually built up a picture of what potentially was going awry in my set-up and what he could do to alleviate it.

I was impressed with how methodical and detailed he was in checking my positioning on the bike, the rotation of my shoulders, hips and ankles as I put power down through the pedals, and finally my reach to the handlebars. Such was his expertise in how flexible the body should be, and how it should handle stress loads that he gradually spotted several injuries I had suffered in the past playing rugby and football, and how this had resulted in a rolled right shoulder, very tight hip movement and tight hamstrings. As we went through all these tests, he offered advice on how I could improve. This was all well and good to know, but right now I wanted the problem of a very sore neck rectified.

We discussed shoes, cleats and my training set-up at home. 'A turbo trainer's good,' said Andy. 'If you are on that quite a lot you could break it up with a set of rollers, perhaps, and what you gain with a turbo trainer in strength you kind of lose in leg speed. So a good set of rollers will give you great leg speed. And you want a good combination of both. Also, it gives you something to concentrate on as you're watching TV.'

After attaching various electronic monitoring dots to my joints he had me carry on cycling while the software analysed me. He had me sitting upright, then tucked down on to the drops, again and again, all the time measuring flexibility and how my body shape looked to his expert eye. We were now into over two hours of testing and analysis. Finally, he highlighted a major area for change. 'You look really confined. You look like you're on a smaller bike than you should be, so we are actually going to lengthen things out a little bit. I know you've had a long stem in the past so I do this with a bit of reluctance, but it might be the right thing to do today.' And with that he disappeared to the front of the store and returned with two road handlebars. 'So, I've got two bars here that might be appropriate to help you. They're the same size. This one here has a firmer and flatter finish to it and is a little bit more expensive, but might be the better one for you?'

'Yes, OK, we'll go with it. My health is at stake here, after all,' I replied.

'We'll try it. I'm not saying this is the answer, but it is marginally narrower.'

New, slimmer-width handlebars in place, Andy then put me through my paces again as before and it instantly felt more comfortable. 'Everything about this looks a bit more relaxed,' he concurred. 'The wrists are relaxed, the elbows look less relaxed now, but the shoulders look relaxed and back as well. Looks nice. How does it feel, Iain?'

'Yes, it does feel comfortable. I am not feeling that tingly pressure on my neck at all.'

'Yeah, that's a great position. I'll take the dimensions of the bike with this stem so you can use the stem at home. I'll sort that out now and we'll get the levers in the correct place for you and I'll re-tape it all up.'

And with that we were done. It had taken almost three hours, but I now felt very confident in my position on the bike, and the fear of enduring a pain-filled ride in France seemed a distant concern. The overall fee was off-putting, and perhaps this was an extravagance considering my level of ability and the amount of time I was able to put into riding. I suppose ultimately I did agree with Richard Moore's comments about whether an amateur like myself really needed to pay for this type of service, but I balanced this with knowing that in a world where people nowadays pay thousands for the bike of their dreams, it might not be a bad idea to guarantee that it actually fits them. For a few hundred pounds more, what Cadence offers satisfied this need. Whether we like it or not, this is the future. A future without string.

Here Come the Belgians!

Roubaix suits the profile of a Belgian (usually Flemish but not exclusively) Classics rider such as De Vlaeminck, Merckx, Museeuw – cobbles, wind, wet – much more than the average French cyclist. It's actually more a Flemish Classic than a French one, that's why it's grouped with Ghent–Wevelgem, Tour of Flanders, Het Volk – the kind of riders who win those tend to win Paris–Roubaix.

William Fotheringham, *Guardian*

Back in the 1980s when I was growing up, one hardly noticed world-class cycling events, especially those with any decent British participation, other than the Milk Race in which I would watch Malcolm Elliott, Sean Yates, Joey McLoughlin, Robert Millar and Sean Kelly vie for the title – usually on Channel 4.

There was one amateur club near where I lived in Northamptonshire – Rockingham Forest Wheelers – but I never quite grasped the nettle and gave cycling a proper try, thinking it was too hard and the equipment too pricey to maintain. Football was for me. I would imagine nowadays there are hundreds, if not thousands of kids up and down the country who have been inspired by Sir Bradley Wiggins, Chris Froome and Mark Cavendish to get on a bike. The big difference in 2014 is there is a strong infrastructure to welcome them in. But there has to be a spark to light the fire, and that is precisely what happened with one rider in Belgium more than one hundred years ago . . .

When one studies the winners of every Paris–Roubaix race since its inception, there is one country that tops the table, and by quite some margin. Belgium has dominated the podium for over a century of the competition; Belgian riders have won *La Pascale* a total of fifty-five times, almost twice the amount of wins by France (twenty-eight) who actually host the race, and five times that of the other great spring Classics nation, Italy, whose riders have triumphed on eleven occasions. The two most successful multiple winners of the event are also Belgian and span two different generations, both having won four times: Roger De Vlaeminck (1972, '74, '75 and '77) and Tom Boonen, who has thus far crossed the finish line first in 2005, '08, '09 and 2012, and may well add to that tally in the coming seasons. Behind them comes a mini-peloton of other legendary riders with three wins apiece: Gaston Rebry in the 1930s; George Claes in the 1940s; Rik Van Looy (the 'King of the Classics') in the 1960s; the 'Cannibal' Eddy Merckx (arguably the greatest rider of all time) in the 1970s; and the 'Lion of Flanders' Johan Museeuw, whose victories spanned the 1990s into the first years of this millennium. Then there are other famous Belgian riders – Rik Van Steenbergen, Marc Demeyer, Dirk Demol and Peter Van Petegem – all of them hard professionals of the road who built up quite formidable *palmarès*. Any national outfit would have welcomed them onboard.

How, one could rightly ask, has one small nation with a population of just over eleven million citizens (and Flanders contains just over half of that number) come to dominate an elite cycling event that isn't even in their own country? Sure, Brazil can justify its elite status in football, but it has a huge pool of talent from a population of over two hundred million. The West Indies bestrode international cricket for all of my childhood as that was *the* sport of those islands. Canada, too, only sees as far as an ice puck, and rarely a Winter Olympics goes by without their team either being in the ice hockey final, or winning gold. But why has Belgium, as opposed to neighbouring Holland, France and Germany, excelled in this race, and the spring Classics as a whole? For that we can pinpoint one man who through his racing exploits staged a revolution in cycle racing in his own country. That rider's name was Cyrille Van Hauwaert.

Belgium has always been rife with internal ethnic complexities, comprised as it is of three distinct ethnic groupings: Flemish (closely associated with the Dutch) in the north of the country, where Flanders is situated; Walloons in the southern half where French is the dominant language; and pockets of German speakers towards its eastern borders. It has been a federal democracy for almost 150 years with a constitutional monarchy at its head in order to preserve the country and maintain a harmony between the culturally divergent groups. Only in sport and politics does this divide appear so marked, and that is where our man Van Hauwaert comes in.

Before the Great War, Flanders was the poor relation of the three groupings. With the capital, Brussels, based in the richer, more industrialized southern part of the nation, the Dutch-speaking Flemish were often looked down upon by metropolitan Walloons as country-bumpkin types, only fit for laborious work in the fields, in the fishing industries or down the pit. The richer south could therefore create the image of a two-tier nation, with theirs the dominant culture and French being the accepted language taught in schools as well as administered by national and regional governments. Dutch-speaking Belgians (or 'Flandrians') would not have a say in what language they could be taught until the 1930s.

In any country, in any period of history, such treatment would cause deep-rooted resentment and a desire for heroes to emerge to tackle the 'bully boys' of the government and instil some local pride. By the time Van Hauwaert caused a cycling sensation with his victory at Paris–Roubaix in 1908, all the elements were in place for this to happen. His win stirred a nation to suddenly see a route to gain a place at the top sporting table, as well as poke the eye of their overbearing neighbour, France.

Born in West Flanders in the town of Moorslede, Van Hauwaert was only a racing professional for seven years, but in that time he managed to win a variety of prestigious races including Bordeaux–Paris, Milan–San Remo, a national championship and a stage of the 1909 Tour de France. This was a man blazing the trail for the (then) very few riders of Flanders. Within a few years of his defining victory at Paris–Roubaix, Belgium's love for cycling had received an incredible shot in the arm.

Cycling, and pro cycling in particular, now exploded with over forty tracks being built across the country, and the number of licensed racers increasing from 127 to over 4,000. Such an exponential growth would dramatically affect results of races that were now being created by Belgian entrepreneurs or, as in France, national newspapers wishing to promote their product by sponsoring new races.

A snowball effect was taking place. In 1912, a 20-year-old racer called Odile Defraye won Belgium's first Tour de France. This victory inspired August De Maeght (the director of the Société Belge d'Imprimerie) to found a weekly sports magazine called *Sportwereld*. His aim was to promote Belgian and especially Flemish interests, and to that end he would co-found the 'Ronde van Vlaanderen' – the Tour of Flanders, in 1913. The route took in every city within the Flemish territory and ended, like Paris–Roubaix, on a track, in Ghent. Again, what this did was open up professional cycling to a whole new generation of would-be racers, whose willingness to accept the aches and pains of every-day life supplied the perfect ingredient to pour out a production line of tough road men who would give their all to win these newly established races. To win one of these would set up a working-class rider for a good many years.

To them Paris–Roubaix was as significant as any other race in the area, as Peter Cossins, author of one of the best books detail-ing the history of the spring Classics, *The Monuments*, explained to me: 'Right from the early years Belgian fans would flock across the border in droves to see the finish of Paris–Roubaix and that certainly provided local riders with motivation. These riders were also very familiar with the conditions at Roubaix as their roads were – and still are to an extent – very similar. Most towns and cities still had cobbled streets, cobbled hills, etc. They were all-weather roads and so cobbles were perfect for that period. Obviously tarmac would evolve and become the norm for road building in the twentieth century, but in the farmlands of Flanders and in northern France, this was slow to happen and thus *pavé* was still the norm. There's also a cultural aspect to it, as most French riders and teams tend to be drawn more to the Tour, whereas their Belgian counterparts have always given huge significance to the northern Classics, particularly Roubaix and Flanders. You could almost class both as Belgian races given the number of Belgian fans that attend both and their importance within the Belgian cycling community as a whole.'

The need to win as much prize money as possible to support one's family was the key driver in the decades that followed, pretty much until the arrival of corporate sponsorship into the sport over the past twenty years. But back in the post-war years, right up until the late 1980s, professional riders would ride the full calendar year of events to earn money – there wasn't the individual tailoring of riders' race programmes by trade teams that we see today. It was all-out action from spring through to the final Classic Tour of Lombardy – the 'Race of the Falling Leaves' (which tells you when it takes place).

As Peter summarized to me, 'Winning Paris–Roubaix, or any Classic, was important and significant to a Belgian rider, but nowadays – with the media coverage and sponsorship involved with the Classics – to someone like Tom Boonen, if he wins Paris–Roubaix his season is made. Whereas to a French rider it depends much more on his success at the Tour de France for that to happen.'

Even though this was a real eye-opener for me, I still wondered why elite riders – Belgian, or otherwise – would put themselves through such horrors, at such speeds on the *pavé*? Peter's background in writing about the spring Classics made his the perfect brain to pick for the answers:

'I think it's the ultimate one-day race. I remember when I got into cycling, it was the one that really captured my imagination. You know, it's the images that really work on you: I remember Sean Kelly, 1984 when he won it, and I remember a picture of him at the end and he looked like a troglodyte coal miner. The mud, grime and dust were simply sculpted on his legs, arms and face – he was unrecognizable. Cycling is a sport that is very rooted to the landscape and that's kind of the whole point, and why the Belgians take so willingly to the cobbles – they ride them every day, it surrounds them. Riders are the painted figurines and the canvas is the landscaping itself. With Paris–Roubaix, that landscape is very extreme in the same way that the mountains are extreme for the Tour de France, the Giro, etc. These flat lands breed a type of rider that is suited to the conditions they throw up, hence they have a better chance of success, I suppose.'

When studying the long line of Belgian champions who have won Paris–Roubaix, two riders stand apart from the rest, mainly due to their great rivalry, number of wins, and competitive antagonism during their careers: Roger De Vlaeminck and Eddy Merckx. They both bestrode the Classics throughout the late 1960s into the late 1970s, with De Vlaeminck proving himself one of the best ever one-day racers, while his compatriot reigned supreme over professional cycling – period.

Whereas 'the Gypsy' from Flanders – as the dark-haired, De Vlaeminck was labelled[11] – specialized in the shorter events and won all five Classics across his career, the 'Cannibal' from nearby Brussels set his mind to winning every race he entered, be it a three-week stage race, a one-day Classic, a track meet, or a time trial. His appetite was insatiable, and his talent was phenomenal to the point where many sponsors of trade teams became exasperated at having no winning riders and therefore little advertising on their jerseys.[12] Their careers ran almost parallel to one another's and their commitment to beat the other man was widely reported, especially when one throws in their ethnic backgrounds with all the attendant historical toxicity. Philippe Brunel of *L'Équipe* asked Merckx if it was true that Belgian racers were out to beat him at any cost – and he agreed. Indeed, De Vlaeminck was recorded as concurring with the Cannibal, stating, 'We were all against him . . . [he] was all we spoke about . . . to work out how we were going to beat him.'

Daniel Friebe, the well-respected cycling journalist who had interviewed De Vlaeminck at length and also wrote a definitive biography of Eddy Merckx, seemed to be the perfect man to explain the history between these two riders. I managed to catch up with him, in between his reporting duties on the upcoming spring

[11] His family were travelling clothiers.
[12] In the races for the 'Monuments', De Vlaeminck would win Paris–Roubaix four times; Milan–San Remo three times; Omloop Het Volk twice; the Tour of Lombardy twice; the Tour of Flanders and Liège–Bastogne–Liège.

Classics, in a bookshop near to where I worked. He was keen to emphasize the difference between how the professional riders of today view *La Pascale*, compared to the glittering stage races we all see on television:

'What's special about Paris–Roubaix is that in every other race, in every other kind of manifestation of professional cycling nowadays, riders kind of rebel and object to anything that they see as outdated. Whether it be a super-long stage, or whether it be terrible wet weather that they see as just barbaric to ride in. So, for Paris–Roubaix they just accept everything around it and no one ever raises any objection – they completely embrace it. That's not to say everyone rides it, because they don't, but there have been very few riders in history who have actively kind of pooh-poohed it. Bernard Hinault was one [famously calling it "for dickheads"], but he still rode it and won it.

'The Classics are much more interesting than the stage races now anyway. Stage racing is often like a series of lab tests these days. You may as well stick the whole peloton in a lab before the race and you pretty much find out who is going to win – just measure their numbers. The Classics are totally different.

'Equipment absolutely is becoming more important than it used to be, because they do so much more work on that now and it really makes a big difference. The film *A Sunday in Hell* really captures the atmosphere of the whole day, really, not just the race.'

'What about the Belgian element to this race, though, Daniel?' I asked. 'Watching *A Sunday in Hell* was the first time I had ever really heard of Roger De Vlaeminck. I always thought it was Eddy Merckx and that was it as far as Belgian greats were concerned, but here was this guy who really took it to Merckx and tried to dominate him. Do you think Vlaeminck's given the credit he's due? If you park the kind of feisty character he is reported as being – he was apparently famous for not replying in French to journalists from the south of Belgium out of respect for his Flemish fans –

and you just look at him purely on his results, how does he fare compared to Merckx?'

'Well,' Daniel replied with a wry smile, 'on paper he's the best. He's the best Classics rider apart from Merckx, ever, and he did it at a time when Merckx was in his pomp with an unbelievable team at Molteni supporting him. De Vlaeminck straddled two different eras: the Merckx era and then he carried on [into the 1980s] when Bernard Hinault had already come on the scene, and he won the Tour of Lombardy as well. He won really diverse races throughout his career. He won all five Monuments. I think Merckx's record[13] is still better, just in terms of quantity of wins in the big Classics, but there's not that much in it.

'De Vlaeminck was a natural on the cobbles, too. To be good at Paris–Roubaix you have to be "parkour". You find a lot of the good Paris–Roubaix riders are quite low on the bike and just aerodynamic – and they have quite a long position – but he was very low and very smooth as well. Franco Ballerini always used to say that the best Roubaix riders, they ride like it's velvet, and De Vlaeminck was very much like that.'

Indeed he was, as I recalled watching his style as he glided along during *A Sunday in Hell*. He appeared to read the cobbles, picking the perfect lines, and never seemingly suffering a puncture – in fact, he stated he had only ever suffered one puncture in ten years of racing the *pavé*. The legend has it that at various editions of the race – and remember this is a rider who rode it fourteen times and only failed to complete the course once, in 1980 – De Vlaeminck's mechanic would find the set-up of his bike at the finish line in Roubaix just as he'd left it at the start of the race. Such was his balance and control of the bike.

---

[13] Merckx would accumulate the following Monument wins: Milan–San Remo seven times; Liège–Bastogne–Liège five times; Paris–Roubaix and the Tour of Flanders three times apiece; and the Tours of Flanders and Lombardy twice each.

Daniel continued, 'The great thing about De Vlaeminck was his character. He was just so cocksure and, in 1968, Merckx was spectating at the amateur tour of Belgium and he knew of De Vlaeminck's growing set of results. He found him at the race and said, "Do you want to ride for me next year? Do you want to attempt Roubaix with my team?" De Vlaeminck surprisingly replied, "No. I want to ride against you." Merckx was already a god in Belgium at that time and De Vlaeminck was just nineteen years old. He relished confrontation and really thrived on those kind of rivalries, especially when it got a little bit nasty.'

'That's what Barry Hoban was talking to me about, too,' I said. 'He said it was a lot more aggressive, personally aggressive, in his day[14] and that he had a couple of arguments with Merckx himself, when he got annoyed with his tactics at Paris–Roubaix. Equally he hated Merckx winning, stating after one Paris–Roubaix victory, "It's always nice to win, especially if Merckx is beaten."'

'I think it used to be a lot more tribal in a way with the fans as well,' replied Daniel. 'It's a kind of cliché, really, to witness it, but not just between De Vlaeminck and Merckx [themselves], but these riders really split Belgium down the middle and they used to have fervent support. They still have fan clubs today!'

I asked Daniel whether the race and pro cycling in the Classics is less tribal compared to the veterans of the 1970s.

'Where you see the tribalism now in cycling is cyclo-cross, and that's a Belgian sport. I mean the cyclo-cross is kind of like the Classics pro-cycling scene was fifteen, twenty years ago – because, primarily, only people from Belgium followed it in large numbers. It was Belgian spectators going to support a particular rider. They still love cycling just as much in Belgium, the crowds are still

---

[14] Even though we see the odd punch-up in a stage race – such as in 2014's Vuelta a España when two riders (Ivan Rovny of Tinkoff–Saxo and Omega Pharma–Quick-Step's Gianluca Brambilla) were ejected during stage 16 for throwing punches at one another.

massive. Paris–Roubaix is probably less tribal, though. The atmosphere isn't as good as the Tour of Flanders. It's more of a Tour de France atmosphere. People, especially along the route, go just to applaud, or "it's great, we're going to watch Paris–Roubaix", whereas at the Tour of Flanders they're really into it, I think it's a much more knowledgeable public at the Tour of Flanders.'

From my own memory of watching races over the past two decades, or reading magazines, I couldn't see any animosity or tribalism between two Flemish greats like Museeuw and the man who pretty much took his mantle, Tom Boonen. It was Pete Cossins who confirmed Daniel's view: 'There's no real tribalism now, not in the way there was years ago. Tom Boonen was seen very much as Museeuw's protégé, and I think Boonen is pretty popular in Belgium as a whole as he's so nice and clean-cut. Problems did bubble below the surface between Flemish and Walloon riders, as was shown a couple of years back when Philippe Gilbert said he couldn't understand why fans waved Flemish flags and no Belgian ones at the world championships in Valkenburg in 2012.'

Gilbert dismissed those fans who wanted to wave the famous black Flemish lion on the yellow background, which one sees everywhere I have to add, grouping them with political extremist groups who were popular in Flanders. The uproar his comments caused forced him to clarify what he had meant: he wanted to see just Belgian supporters, and not flags from either Flanders or Wallonia. 'You're riding for your country and not your region,' he intoned.

Nothing stays the same, and sporting heroes come and go, but their exploits remain as part of their *palmarès* and are rightly celebrated. As Daniel told me later, even though Merckx is still held in high esteem – not just in Belgium but globally – De Vlaeminck's star has definitely waned. His tempestuous character, and fame for always speaking his mind no matter what the cost, has coloured his reputation down the years. He has famously fallen out with various riders who have come after him, particularly Tom Boonen who, by winning his fourth Paris–Roubaix in 2012, found himself on an equal footing with his Flemish predecessor from the 1970s. But that's not how De Vlaeminck saw it, curtly dismissing his young rival's opponents as 'third-raters' in an attempt to diminish Boonen's achievements.

De Vlaeminck's outspokenness – he's a Belgian version of Geoffrey Boycott on *Test Match Special*, perhaps – has sadly seen him lampooned by the Belgian media. A Twitter profile was created to parody his regular announcements on cycling – each tweet begins with the line, 'In my day . . .' – and Belgian journalists eagerly make contact with him each spring in order to get a juicy quote they know their readers will lap up. The man can't help himself when it comes to stating an opinion, and perhaps there isn't any shame in carrying on as he was in his heyday – that was the spirit which transferred into his riding, after all. At least he is magnanimous about his great rival's ability: 'I'm happy to have ridden against Merckx. He was the best in the world, the best ever.'

He even named his son Eddy.

Chasing Sky

When the chips are down, how many times have we all heard the little motivational phrase, 'No one ever said it was going to be easy'? I was muttering it to myself as I crawled up Ditchling Beacon one cold and wet afternoon at the beginning of March, seemingly right at the back of the other 449 riders who were ahead of me. It was just over a month until *La Pascale* and my fitness seemed ominously absent. I'd spent the past five hours navigating my way around the beautiful Sussex countryside on my own, following orange signposts like some lemming who seems to have been jettisoned by the rest of his suicidal tribe.

My fellow riders were pouring down triumphant from the top of one of the South Downs' toughest climbs, an average gradient of 7 per cent with a couple of killer 12 per cent ramps thrown in just to see if you're paying attention and not getting too cocky. If you're riding up this hill straight off the bat, perhaps just after a coffee and cake in nearby Brighton, it's not a problem; just get in the right gear and pedal up it. Simple. I had actually achieved this on several occasions years ago as a twenty-something with nothing to do of a weekend, and no commitments. But, zoom forward twenty years, when it's at the end of a rather tough sportive route of 65 miles and 1700 metres of climbing (as well as your first of the year), in the breezy chill of a winter's afternoon, and you've missed the feed station because you stupidly thought you didn't need it and you wanted a quicker time – then it all adds up to a mess of trouble.

With the last gear engaged I struggled up the final 400 metres as a variety of riders sauntered past me on their way back down, sporting their club kits: the blue and black of Dulwich Paragon CC, the Italian-style green, white and red of Penge CC, the very cool reggae-style black, red, yellow and green of Brixton CC, and several, alas, in the ubiquitous livery of Team Sky replica kit. Like a swarm of lycra-clad bees on bikes, these 'Team Sky' buggers had been around me all day on this ride. It was getting a bit tedious, but I had more important matters to hand – like staying on my bike, and not being the *only* one walking up Ditchling. The struggle continued.

The final, torturous ramp arrived as I swung the bike around the final left-hand bend only to be greeted by two young kids pulling faces at me through their parents' car window as they accelerated past. As I'd seen on various Sunday sportives, drivers of 4x4s and cyclists seem to gravitate towards one another on steep climbs, the former always wanting the latter to hurry up despite the obvious sight of the rider toiling against gravity.

I looked up and could see figures dotted around the horizon watching the few of us remaining on the climb ascending to the finish line at the car park. Putting my back into it, I lowered my gaze to stare hard at the Garmin, which informed me I was flying along at 9 k.p.h. with a heart rate of 182 b.p.m. My concentration for the final push was broken as I heard familiar voices coming towards me. Looking up weakly from my handlebars, I made out the blur of two familiar figures. Ben and John were screaming past me, oblivious to my predicament as they happily chatted away to one another as they weaved their way down the road to the eventual HQ of the race some two miles away at Ditchling Recreation Ground.

We had started together that morning, but the pair of them
were sickeningly fitter and fresher than me – and within fifteen
minutes and some five kilometres – had disappeared down the
road. Mind you, my missing the first crucial signpost on the
route and free-wheeling down the hill into Lewes didn't help. Like
a dufus I only realized my mistake once I was actually on the
high street. Tears of frustration swept aside, I hurriedly sped
back the way I had come and, more by accident than design,
discovered the vital signpost. It was catch-up all the way from
there on in, as the memory of Ben's suggestion a few months back
to enter this bloody race came to the front of my thoughts. 'The
Puncheur is a great race for testing your legs, mate, you'll need to
do this if you're serious about training for the Paris–Roubaix. It's
all about doing a fast time over a rolling course before you fly up
Ditchling Beacon.'

Fly?

'John and I did it last year and we loved it, it really got us into
the training again.'

Ben and I had been work colleagues and friends, cycling
together over the years, our last epic ride being John O'Groats to
Land's End in the summer of 1996. What had started as a chat
over a lunchtime coffee on the King's Road near to where we both
worked, progressed to purchasing the train tickets and signing
on with the CTC, who organized accommodation and the route
for the uninitiated. To cut a long story short, we finished the ride
after a few heated arguments, mountains of energy gel, a lot of
painkillers for the sore knees, and copious pints as we roared to
each day's designated finish line in order to watch the next match
of Euro '96 at a local pub.

Keeping in touch over the years, girlfriends became wives,
children arrived and finally we evolved into MAMILs by our
forties. Ben welcomed the arrival of the Boris Bike with open
arms. It was a natural progression for him to then buy a new

road bike – a Verenti Insight – and I naturally followed suit in this game of one-upmanship by ditching the racing-green Brompton and purchasing my beloved but not so top-of-the-range Raleigh Comp.

The main difference between us was commitment. Ben took to training with a zealous will, all monitored by Garmin and later Strava. Much more statistically minded than myself, he studied his numbers like a seasoned professional. Power output, cadence average, heart rate . . . he knew his data like a NASA engineer monitoring one of his astronauts upon take-off. 'Good on him,' I thought to myself as I nonchalantly attempted three-hour training rides in an attempt to get as fit. I just didn't have the mathematical ability, or patience, to want to read data of my training, even though a friend had loaned me the latest Garmin. Just knowing how fast I was going and perhaps how high I'd climbed was enough for me – that was something to explain to Jo and the kids as to where I'd been for the past four hours.

The difference in data analysis unfortunately mirrored our different approaches to training. Come rain or shine, sometimes even frost and howling wind, Ben would willingly rise at 5 a.m. on a Saturday morning and spend an hour crossing London's streets before hitting the Essex countryside and covering almost 100 kilometres, mixing in some well-known climbs in the area, such as Yorks Hill. And he happily did this every weekend. Needless to say he is a strong rider and, once underway on a sportive, he's committed and wants a good time. I respected him for that. I, on the other hand, preferred to get fit on the turbo trainer watching BBC iPlayer on the laptop, and follow that up with a monthly run out into the Kent countryside to undertake hill repeats. However long this would take didn't matter. I wanted to enjoy it my way, I'd convince myself. If I am honest, however, I took it easy because the pain of the effort would ultimately lower the morale, and weaken the legs to the point of standstill. To remedy this I thought,

I really needed to try to stick with Ben and his regular riding partner John.[15]

John is easily the best of us all. A mild-mannered scientist by day – well, I do him an injustice: Professor John Edmunds is actually dean of the Department of Infectious Disease Epidemiology at the London School of Hygiene and Tropical Medicine – he is blessed with Indurain-like lungs, a thin upper body and Captain America-like thighs; he is a diesel engine of a rider. He may look like Simon Pegg but he rides like Greg LeMond. He would come to sportives, climb aboard his 'Black Beauty' as he fondly called his bike (a Ribble r872), chat with me for a wee while as we sped along for the first few miles . . . and then the brow would crease, the eyes narrow, the smile fade and he'd engage warp speed. Whether it was leg-wearying rolling terrain, or steep gradients along the South Downs, John would effortlessly spin along in a low gear as Ben hung on to his wheel and I desperately clung on to Ben's.

On this day, however, it was evident that winter training had proved beneficial for Ben, too, as he not only kept pace with John but passed him as we sped out of the starting gate. It was then I knew the game was up. Taking a wrong turn proved a blessing, perhaps, allowing me to ride the course at my own speed. The whole point of this exercise was to get fit for Paris–Roubaix, not to get into some macho drag race with anyone, least of all my friends. But human nature always kicks in, as every middle-aged guy who's ever ridden one of these races will tell you: looking achingly thin due to regular training and the cutting out of all the good stuff over the winter, riding state-of-the-art trade bikes, dressing in the replica kit of whatever team takes our fancy . . . we all believe fervently that we can, as they say, 'put the hammer down!' It normally takes

[15] Ben and John have since ridden the 'Coast to Coast' across the Pyrenees and are currently training hard (without me) to tackle Alpe d'Huez multiple times in a week in the summer of 2015. In 2016 they will take on the Marmotte stage race.

the first climb, possibly the second one, before common sense or despair finally prevails. Yet, we'll all talk a good race when we get back to the car park.

Throughout the course of the day I was passed by dozens of riders, young and old, as they looked to get into a season-long ritual of suffering and salvation. I was more than happy to let them past as I concentrated on keeping the pace up to 25–30 k.p.h. on the flatter sections, and on simply getting to the top of any climbs without having to dismount. It was the first race of the season, or, I should clarify, the first 'participatory event' of the year for me, and it was good to see where my legs were.

The Puncheur was well organized (bar that first signpost), and was evidently a popular choice with the fitter, more athletic and talented rider. But the climbs weren't too tricky and it allowed you to try to set a strong pace all the way through. A hilly time trial maybe? Yet, much to my chagrin, I was being made to look rather ordinary despite thinking indoor training on the turbo was yielding results.

Possibly I was just having one of those days. Two flat tyres, one at the midway point and the second some five miles from the Beacon, broke up the rhythm I had planned to set. With Roubaix in mind I figured I would just concentrate on a steady pace, even if there was a headwind. Tony Martin I am not, but my indoor sessions had me believing I could drive a decent enough pace on the road. A kitchen can't really replicate a winter's day on rolling hills, however. Then I made the rookie error. By trying to make up some time, I decided to forego what looked like a lovely feed station at the 35-mile marker, feeling safe with the many energy gels and bars I was carrying. But nothing beats crunchy carbs and calories, and there was my mistake. Becoming fed up with another gel I baulked at a few when I should have taken them and so here I was cresting the top of the Beacon totally spent, sweating like a farm animal and annoyed.

I was absolutely deflated that with a showing like this – just over 105 kilometres of exertion – I was a wreck. What would I be like over a much greater distance across cobbles? What if it was an even shittier day than this one, with the sort of crushing headwind not uncommon to northern France?

Once again the little voice chirped up in my brain: 'You're fucked.' Ignoring the beautiful wintry view across the Downs, I climbed on the bike and coasted back down the Beacon towards the rugby ground where the race was officially headquartered, and where the race notes had promised me delicious hot pasta was waiting. Feeling sorry for myself, I refused to join in with the happy back-slapping afterwards between the finishers and the smiling race stewards and helpers, who were all wrapped up in raincoats and body warmers. I was tired and just wanted to get home, have a bath and a beer. I refused to turn right into the ground, where Ben and John must have been waiting for me for the best part of half an hour, and went straight to my car, which was parked a little further along the country lane at the edge of the village.

Throwing my wet gilet, gloves and helmet into the boot, I dismantled the bike and angrily forced it into the back passenger seats without even wiping it down. (I'd explain the oil stains on the covers later.) Even though I was beginning to get the dreaded knock of hunger, I convinced myself I'd grab something at a petrol station on the way back; I just wanted to get out of there. Without any communication to the guys who had actually enjoyed their race, judging by the looks on their faces when they'd passed me coming back down the Beacon, I drove off for home to lick my wounded pride and think about whether I wanted to do this bloody race.

I needed to start thinking properly about training, and for this, one man could help.

The very first edition of Paris–Roubaix in 1896, as the intrepid cyclists, in armbands, get set for their voyage into the unknown. The race was won by the German Josef Fischer (**in the centre above and in portrait below**), who was the favourite owing to his having already triumphed in other early endurance events such as Vienna–Berlin and Milan–Munich.

Above: The Italian Serse Coppi, brother of Fausto, was controversially awarded victory in 1949, despite only finishing third in the sprint, before the Frenchman André Mahé and the Belgian Frans Leenen were disqualified for not following the designated *parcours*. The records now show a shared victory between Mahé and the lesser-known Coppi.

Below: In the era of the great Eddy Merckx, Britain's Barry Hoban rode exceptionally well to finish on the podium in the 1972 edition behind the 'flying gypsy' Roger De Vlaeminck, winner for the first but by no means the last time.

My favourite rider of all time is Sean Yates, seen here in 1994. Hard as nails and always riding to win, the Paris–Roubaix race was perfectly suited to his ability and mental toughness.

Roger Hammond (**right**, in the UK national champion's jersey) was so close to a dramatic win, losing out in the sprint to Magnus Bäckstedt (**centre**) in 2004. Hammond also finished fourth in 2010, but is he given the credit he deserves?

Above: My local bike shop owner, Vaidas Granauskas, at the top of the Col du Galibier. A former pro, he was a great help in getting me prepared.

Below: Tackling Ditchling Beacon shouldn't be this hard. A tougher day than expected at the Puncheur sportive in March 2014, a month before my big challenge.

Above: Chris Sidwells showing how it's done. His guidance for my training proved invaluable.

Below: There are cobbles in England too, you know. Francis Longworth (**left**), founder of the Tour of the Black Country, out with a colleague on the route he created.

The Roubaix velodrome (**above**) may not be much to look at, but it is as significant to followers of professional cycling as Old Trafford is to football fans, or the Yankee Stadium is to New Yorkers. In the main bar (**below**), famous feats and the names of previous champions are etched above the counter.

Each winner of the race also has a nameplate affixed in a changing cubicle in the stadium's legendary shower block, where countless stories of heartbreak and triumph have been told to reporters by exhausted riders. Not much reward for the effort, you might think, but you become an immortal in cyclists' eyes.

Left: William Lanigan from Pavé Cycling Classics, with his colleague Alex Voisine, gave me great advice about riding on the cobbles. It's a brilliant concept to take amateurs out onto the legendary roads of northern France.

Below: I also learned a huge amount from the president of *Les Amis de Paris–Roubaix*, François Doulcier, here seen restoring his beloved *pavé*.

The Hell of the Black Country

It was a bloody freezing, cold Friday morning, the monotonous, low, grey light set against the empty motorway turn-off of the M6 as I began to drive towards the outskirts of Wolverhampton, looking for a velodrome I hadn't known had existed until recently. Chris Sidwell's advice to research a 'cobbled Classic' right here in the middle of England had intrigued me when he first brought it up on the phone: 'It's going to be a brilliant little race: some guy has created it from nothing to try to recreate a little bit of northern France *pavé* in the Midlands. It has its own sections of rough terrain, including cobbles, some decent climbs, and you finish in a velodrome. It'll be great preparation for you. See if you can find it.'

Finally, I'd face my fear and ride over cobbles again – it couldn't be as bad as before. The last (and only) time I had tried to master cobbles had been in Edinburgh, six years ago.

I used to cross the city regularly on my trusty Brompton, despite the pretty strenuous climbs on some sharp gradients between Old and New Town, with Princes Street bisecting them. The Old Town has a lengthy section of cobbles on its famous Royal Mile, which begins approximately 300 yards past the Scottish parliament building at Holyrood and ends at the world-famous Edinburgh Castle esplanade. So, you're looking at perhaps a kilometre of

cobbled street that climbs to a tough gradient quickly, which if
you're even reasonably fit won't bother you that much. But those
cobbles are in a pretty good state; the stones are generally the same
shape, size and are quite smooth.

Despite this, throughout my time in Edinburgh I tried to avoid
at all costs travelling down the Royal Mile at any kind of speed –
except for the one time I tried getting over the cobbles quickly, just
to see what it was like. I couldn't help myself.

It was a cold autumn day and I descended confidently from the
castle's car park, thinking I'd soon be enjoying the view of Arthur's
Seat, which dominates the skyline around Holyrood. I left the
smooth and safe tarmac road surface and rolled on to the crown
of the cobbled road. Within less than 200 metres I knew I was in
trouble. The problem was the combination of the slightly slippery
road and the small front wheel of my Brompton – the two are not
a safe combination when the brakes are applied. I failed to stop at
the first crossroads, much to the irritation of a few tourists whose
photo opportunity with the highland piper was ruined by me rolling
through and bellowing, 'Watch out!' I picked up speed dramatically
and was soon roaring down the jarring road, dozens of shocked
spectators turning their heads to see what the commotion was.

The fact was, I couldn't handle the cobbles and, as I desperately tried to maintain a straight line, slamming my feet on to
the road in an attempt to halt further embarrassment and reduce
the likelihood of serious injury, this was becoming painfully
obvious. I fought for control of the bike, but the front wheel
buckled left – and over the handlebars I went.

With a sprained wrist, a sore shoulder and a jacket torn at the
elbow, I decided to give that particular trail a miss from then on,
though I did jog the route from time to time, and always grinned
wryly as I saw some madman trying his luck on a bike. 'Sod
cobbles,' I vowed. 'From now on I'm sticking to tarmac.'

Still, here I was again, excited, even intrigued to see how it was possible that someone had actually created a mini-Paris–Roubaix course, in the West Midlands. On the flip side, it was March, cold and wet, and I'd be driving seven hours in total, there and back, with a 100-kilometre ride through unknown country to squeeze in between.

Slavishly adhering to anything my satnav spoke to me (in the Han Solo voice my wife had downloaded on to it, complete with roars from Chewbacca) I enjoyed a trouble-free drive, even managing to take a break to carbo-load for the big ride. Aldersley velodrome came into view, and it was a genuine surprise. It was much like any other modern-day sports complex, but with the added twist that around the running track, ring-fenced with high boards and surrounded by a wood on the far side, was a beautiful tarmac cycle track, complete with banking. It was possibly one of the best venues I had visited for the start of a sportive.

Amid the dozen or so parked cars nearest the centre I could see a red Flandria road bike on the roof of an old Rover. The owner, dressed in black winter gear, was busy taking the bike down from the rack and fixing his front wheel on to the forks. He looked across as I started getting my bike set up too.

'Iain?'

'Hi, yes, lovely day for it.'

We were both grinning at the situation as we shook hands. The sun was starting to fight its way through the low blanket of cloud, its rays splitting across in dozens of spokes covering the car park and cycle track. Here we were, about to discover some cobbled tracks in the Black Country.

In a way, Francis Longworth is very much like me. Very much like the thousands of other MAMILs throughout the UK: professional, 45 years old, married with two young children. 'We practically have parallel lives, Francis,' I joked as he gave me a tour of the velodrome and the track itself. As we bestrode the finish line of the track he swept his arms out in a grand gesture of 'imagine this' like some mad-eyed utopian genius: 'Right here, this will be the best finish one could imagine. We'll really be getting into the whole idea of offering a mini-Paris–Roubaix with a lot of French themes. I can't take credit for this side of things, it's my wife Deborah who came up with the ideas for all of the non-route-related elements of the event – which I would have been completely clueless about how to organize. All the riders who complete the distance will get strong, freshly brewed coffee, croissants, crepes, a glass of champagne, and cupcakes branded with my cycle club colours [black and white] and logo.'

He looked proud and excited about the debut of his race in May, which he'd spent years researching and painstakingly construct-ing. We clipped into our bikes and headed out just as the morning was fully awake at 8.30 a.m. I had feared it would take a while to traverse the myriad A-roads of the area, and the traffic was stead-ily building up, but with a guide such as Francis and his intimate knowledge of the locale, within twenty minutes we were out into the rolling countryside, bikes abreast as we chatted. I had so many questions to ask him.

'Well, as you've just seen we started on the outskirts of Wolverhampton at Aldersley velodrome and I'm taking you out west, now, via Wightwick Manor and into Staffordshire and Shropshire country.' This I liked, as I knew the 'Shroppy' hills well, having lived in Ludlow for a few years in the late nineties. Attempting to climb up the Long Mynd, or Much Wenlock, with a rusty old mountain bike and dodgy gears brought the pain all too readily back to mind. I could see this was going to be a testing training ride, akin to anything the Kent hills could throw at me.

Francis then reeled off the itinerary: 'We turn southwards to Kinver, passing through Highgate Common and a huge area of forest known as "The Million", where the first sectors begin.' He seemed to say this with relish. His stocky frame and athletic physique already told me he was an experienced cyclist. 'Yes, our club – V-Sprint – is an offshoot of another, more famous cycle club, Halesowen Athletic and Cycling Club, which is a lot closer to Birmingham. There were originally about a dozen of us who are all located in the Bromsgrove area, and we just felt the time was right to head off on our own, along the local roads we know and ride regularly. That's how V-Sprint came about.

'We have our own club kit, newsletters, and a well-informed website. A lot of the guys from the club have been a great help for me in setting up the race itself. Geoff Dingley rode parts of the route with me and suggested five or six changes which I think really made it better, and eliminated a few semi-dangerous spots. Geoff is one of those older guys who seemed to have found the secret of eternal youth through cycling. Tall and slim and still very powerful, I think he's nearly sixty but looks about forty on the bike. He'd organized some events when he was younger and was a great help.

'Another member, Adam Brooks, is a decent cyclist who lived in the same street as me when we were children and now works for HSBC on project management, and he was a big help, too. It was initially dispiriting and intimidating when he basically said, "Look, there are about twenty ways in which you could screw up an event like this." I think I managed to avoid about half of them.'

All this information was tripping off his tongue; he was like a dam full to the brim – he had the pent-up energy of a complete convert to the cause – and his own D-Day was fast approaching. We increased our cadence as we started to hit some rolling hills – not too bad, but enough to get the b.p.m.s over the 130 mark, and for the talking to die down to stop-start sentences. We weren't trying to race one another, thankfully, but I was tense, thinking I needed to get my mindset sorted out for the cobbles and rough track about to come up. Francis, however, cycled with the air of a rider who knew this route like the back of his hand, as indeed he did: 'Yes, many weekends I've had my wife, and my kids, all crammed into the car as I explored the area. I would be picking over detailed Ordnance Survey maps in the office during the week, trying to piece together the route. Then someone would mention a section of off-road that might be suitable for me to include, and that was the weekend planned, so to speak. It took a few years to get it to the stage where, from a safety perspective, we were equally ready to seek accreditation from British Cycling to stage a sportive.'

We carried on into the hills and then, talk dying down again, Francis abruptly took a turn on the front and quickly signalled a right turn into a wooded lane. We rumbled downhill for about a kilometre, all the while the front end of my bike taking big hits as I tried to avoid small potholes and large stones on the gravelled path. We'd hit sector one. The unease and tension I had been feeling all morning quickly dissipated as I clung to the drops of the bars and manically tried to maintain my balance. After a few minutes, the panic subsided and the thighs took the pain as I felt confident enough to drive the bike along.

After another five minutes of huffing and puffing through gravel and the odd violent bump and grind as we climbed towards a church, we crested the assault course and hit smooth tarmac again. It had never felt so good. I was covered in sweat, and amazed the bike was not damaged at the speed required to keep up with Francis. I felt vindicated in trying out my new Continental 25-mm tyres.

Francis pulled over to one side of the road to allow a local trader to squeeze his van past the pair of us in the narrow lane, shielded on both sides by high hedging, much like the *bocage* one finds in Normandy. The clouds had now darkened and the rain was starting to fall – light at first, but as we talked the drops became fatter and wetter, if that's possible. Within a few minutes it was teeming down and the wind picked up. We threw our rain capes over the gilets, and donned our gloves. We were in for a soaking.

'If this keeps up, I don't think we'll progress on the full route, as there are some tricky sections,' Francis warned. 'The Waltonberg in particular can be very slippy and it tops out at twenty-two per cent gradient, and the state of the cobbles means it's hard to keep traction on the bike. Let's see how the weather fares as we progress.'

We headed out into the stiff breeze, the rain still coming down heavily, my morale slipping all the time. I was in a strange place, with no idea of where I was going, and getting soaked. The rain did cool you off, and I was just happy to keep up a steady rhythm and follow Francis's wheel. We took in one further off-road section, which only lasted another several hundred metres but still packed enough in it to give me a pinched tyre. The front wheel suddenly developed the familiar rumble of rim on road and the vibrations went right up my arms to my neck. Pulling over quickly to avoid losing balance while clipped in, I quickly set to work in replacing the tube, only to realize I'd left my saddle pouch with spares in the blessed car. My shoulders sagging and my loud cursing told Francis something was up.

Sizing up the problem, as only a visionary of exceptional sportives can, he quickly got the necessary tools required from his own supplies and helped me set about a quick tube replacement, talking all the time, through the rain, about the route as we knelt together over my bike.

'Why call it the "Tour of the Black Country"?' I asked.

He smiled as he helped set the tyre back over the new tube, now placed into the rim of the wheel.

'It might suggest a bleak industrial landscape of blast furnaces and coal mines, but as you can see the route is very rural and goes through several small attractive villages. I chose the name partly because it trips off the tongue in the same way as "Tour of the Basque Country", which makes it sound like a proper event, and because of the Roubaix-like connotations of the Zola-esque *Pays Noir*.'

The wheel now back in place, we rebooted, and looked down

the road. We'd covered barely 20 kilometres, and traversed two sections of the fifteen, but the weather looked like it was setting in. We were both dripping wet.

'I might not be able to do the whole route, mate, as I have to head back to London, and I'd rather not hit rush hour if at all possible.'

As excuses go, it sounded pretty lame, but my rough maths and Garmin route finder told me we had at least another four or five hours ahead of us, and it was 11 a.m. already. I was feeling a little despondent, as I had been keen to cover the whole route to get myself mentally attuned to riding this surface.

Francis studied my demeanour, and possibly was thinking the same thing anyway: 'Look, there's a junction coming up in about five kilometres, and if you turn right you're heading towards the Waltonberg and still on the route. We can turn left and cut out a big chunk of the route and still take in two more sections of cobbles, so at least you'll still get a feel for them. We'll get back to Aldersley out of this rubbish and have a proper chat and you'll make it home on time. How does that sound?'

The thought of tackling a 22 per cent monster, one that had slippery cobbles to boot, was appealing – just to see if I could do it – but time was proving against me today. Thus we cracked on, and within fifteen minutes came to the said junction. We turned left and headed back towards the start. Our speed picked up now with the tailwind and we'd soon hit section four of the original route, which was a straight gravel path, pitted with humps, bumps and bush-whacking potholes. All traversable, if you saw them coming. My gaze was never more than ten metres ahead of me as I tracked the terrain with a sniper's dedication, while the more experienced Francis sped off into the distance.

Hitting the country lanes again, we were riding across roads I recognized from earlier that morning. We soon approached a beautiful gastro-pub by a canal gate – the Navigation Inn. 'From the first feed station at the foot of the Waltonberg [section ten], we have the majority of the unpaved sectors located in the final thirty kilometres,' said Francis. 'This here will be the final feed station as the riders recover before heading back to the finish at the velodrome.'

I watched as a barge came into view further down the canal, a woman walking alongside it with her dog, chatting to the boat owner. A very picturesque site for a final break at approximately the 85-kilometre mark. Francis pointed down the canal: 'The route follows the flat valley of the River Smestow. We're skirting a few of them with this shortcut.'

Again, I felt a tinge of regret at having to cut short the day. It certainly was a very well-thought-out route, and the country-side was beautiful. The climbs, such as they were, hadn't been that difficult for me, but I knew the Waltonberg was the one I would owe a visit to, one day soon. Getting underway once more, I followed Francis through the final two sections of Black Country *pavé* – the final section, Castlecroft, bisecting a modern farm complex before skirting over a long rise and descending (at not too steep an incline) through a pretty parade of trees and a vast expanse of ploughed fields. The view was breathtaking, to the point where I had to return my gaze to what lay ahead of me – just in case. I may not have completed the first ever *pavé* route I'd ever undertaken, but it was a joyous experience to glide through this scenery.

Soon, the boundaries of Wolverhampton came upon us, and within a few more miles of riding hard, the familiar brick shape of Aldersley stadium came into view. Coasting down the hill, through the car park, I followed Francis on to the track itself. 'This is where it'll finish,' he said. 'They'll get to ride a full lap around the track, we'll have the French bunting and flags out, all the frills. It will be quite an experience for the riders.'

I loved his enthusiasm. We headed out of the rain towards the centre to dry off. Grabbing a drink from the café, we sat near a window overlooking the track.

I still had questions to ask about what was probably the most unique event in the country. 'What section of the route are you most proud of, Francis, would it be the Waltonberg?'

He leaned back and thought about the question. He'd probably been over this with countless people as they planned and constructed the race for its coming launch.

'I don't think that there is any particular section that I am "proud of" in isolation. I was happy that it proved possible to string together a series of unpaved sectors in a way that gives you the intense sensation of speed you get from riding a bike. This required that the roads be rough, or cobbled, and also taken in a slightly downhill direction so that you can ride down them at about 24 or 25 m.p.h. – but without being too steeply downhill to prevent you from being able to pedal down them.

'The idea is that you are simultaneously creating *and* experiencing these sensations of speed, rather than just experiencing them in a passive way (as you would in a car, say, or when downhill skiing), and that you're able to increase this sense of speed and excitement by pedalling harder. There is some element of risk and danger, but this can be reduced by pedalling harder in a bigger gear and increasing the stability of the bike. This, for me, is the unique appeal of this sort of cycling – as a kind of *aesthetic* experience, which is maximized by cycling fast over rough or cobbled roads. I view it as being as much an aesthetic experience as an athletic one: an aesthetics of speed. Being able to ride quickly over these kinds of roads, while keeping control is exciting and also satisfying in that, if you are fit and strong, it makes you "aware" of your power in quite an interesting way.

'It was quite difficult to create a route which did all of these things in a safe way which made sense and had a good overall "flow" to it. At first I had six or seven sectors, which were good, but it wasn't at all obvious how to link them up. It felt a bit like trying to write a song where you have an idea for a chorus and a bit of a verse but are finding it hard to put everything together in a coherent way. Without wanting to be pretentious about it, putting the route together felt more like an interesting creative or artistic exercise than just a matter of logistics and planning.

'I suppose that finding a cobbled climb of the quality and novelty of the Waltonberg made me feel that it really might be possible to stage a real event – with the Waltonberg as an obvious centrepiece. Before this I had just envisaged using the route for training either alone or with a few riders from the club, without any thoughts of it becoming a ride that people would actually pay to come and do.'

His eyes gleamed as he described the pièce de résistance to his master plan. He took his Ordnance Survey map and marked the Waltonberg with his finger: 'It's a pretty hard climb. The first hundred yards are not too steep and it feels like Roubaix. But around the first bend it really steepens up, and in contrast with otherwise similar cobbled climbs, like the Koppenberg, the cobbles are not in great condition. The surface is quite variable in nature, with bricks and random bits of stone at odd angles. There are large gaps between some of the cobbles, a bit of moss, and such like, so that the extra grip (which is usually the purpose of cobbles) is not really there. It's quite easy to spin the back wheel.

'The hardest thing is concentrating all the time and trying to push the gear smoothly, even when it feels like you are going to lose it. It's not really possible to control your line one hundred per cent, so you have to let the bike bounce around and guide itself a little bit. If you lose concentration for a moment, the bike will either stop or keel over into a ditch. When you get about two-thirds of the way up, you know you're going to make it, which feels good. It feels like an achievement to get up it. Ironically, given that it is the centrepiece of the ride, the Waltonberg is a bit out of character with the Roubaix theme. All of the other sectors are about two, to three per cent downhill.'

He pushed the map towards me to emphasize the point he was

making, a look of validation etched across his weathered face. I gazed down at the indentation on the map where his finger had been prodding. All the close contours on Walton Hill told their own story. A steep bugger. Much like my own 'White Whale' back home – Yorks Hill, a vicious climb outside Sevenoaks. Included in various local races, the road is rough and in the autumn strewn with forest debris, all the way up its 25 per cent incline. It is easy to become obsessed.

'The date we've chosen is the fourth of May, so we should hopefully enjoy a sunny day with a nice mixture of colours as the peloton rides through the area: wisteria, oilseed rape, bluebells and rhododendrons. It will be close enough to Paris–Roubaix for people like yourself to still be enthusiastic about it. We're hoping to get a full field of three hundred entries. If it goes well we will look at increasing that to perhaps five to six hundred the following year. Ultimately, if we could have a well-organized sportive that could handle a thousand competitors, that would be fantastic.'

He then gave me a knowing smile, 'And there's the White Roads Classic, of course.'

The look of confusion on my face turned his smile into a broad grin. He clearly wanted to get this secret off his chest.

'Well, we want to recreate another legendary continental race, here in our own backyard. The Strade Bianche.'

I almost dropped my bottle of water. 'What? In the Black Country?!'

He stopped leaning back on his chair after dropping this bombshell and leaned in to let me in on the project: 'After thinking up the idea of the "Tour of the Black Country" in 2011, I was also considering trying to replicate other professional races that I thought were interesting. The Strade Bianche and Tour of Flanders were top of the list, races that bigger, stronger riders like Fabian Cancellara could win. A friend of mine had also suggested doing the Eroica in Tuscany at some point, but I felt that it was too far away and I didn't really want to ride an old bike with toe-clips, so it was natural to try to find something similar in England.

'The underlying principle of the White Roads Classic is basically the same as that of the Tour of the Black Country with regard to the heightened sensations of speed that you get from riding over rough roads. The majority of sportives are built around climbs as the central focus, which just makes you go slower. I also like the way that unpaved sectors break the route up into separate "units". This makes an otherwise very long route more manageable psychologically and builds in a sense of anticipation, I suppose.

'The Ridgeway was an obvious candidate for the location of what became the WRC. I knew of the Ridgeway since I had walked some parts of it with my mother when I was young, and had cycled around there a bit when I was at university. I had ridden my road bike on parts of the chalk Ridgeway itself in 1998 but found it very rough and rutted – in an unpleasant way. But I thought it would be worth going to have a look at it again. I went down in July last year on a very hot day and cycled from the White Horse at Uffington to Streatley-on-Thames on the Ridgeway the whole way, about forty miles, and then back again on the road that runs along the base of the Ridgeway. This, in fact, was pretty close to what became the final route of the WRC.

'Ninety per cent of the Ridgeway wasn't really suitable – either too steep, too rutted, particularly where the bare chalk is exposed, or too grassy. But there were some really good bits which had more of a white gravel surface. So, as with the Tour of the Black Country, the task was then to string those sections together in a way that flowed and made sense. Again, the majority of the chosen sectors of white gravel had to be either flat or slightly downhill, to enable them to be ridden in excess of 25 m.p.h.! Much of the Strade Bianche, on the other hand, is quite hilly and requires very good bike-handling skills to take the downhill bends safely. But I didn't want anything that required using the brakes or freewheeling, so I eliminated any very steep bits from the WRC.

'The Strade Bianche finishes in Siena, and I had thought

of starting and finishing our own WRC in an equally iconic setting – Oxford. I had actually mapped out a hundred-and-five-mile route in detail that started and finished on Christ Church Meadow in Oxford and then returned via Boars Hill, which has impressive views over the city's university spires. The route came back through Wallingford, Abingdon and Kennington following the Thames. So, a rider of the route would enjoy an impressive start and finish in a classic medieval town, riding on iconic white roads and all besides the country's most iconic river – the Thames. It was a great route, but it was just too long and hard.

'The WRC sectors, while not as tough as cobbles or the sectors in the Tour of the Black Country, are still tiring, and there is a lot of climbing up and down the Ridgeway in order to access the best bits of white road. So Oxford had to go, and it was then a case of deciding where to start and finish the event. Starting at Streatley and finishing in Goring-on-Thames was good for two reasons: there is a spectacular stretch of the Thames there and it would mean that the route could finish immediately after the best white road sectors, with the climax being the long section of white road which descends down to the river.

'There are some spectacular views from the top of the Ridgeway over the Oxford plain. The route goes through the village of Fawley [from where Thomas Hardy's young Jude the Obscure looked longingly at the dreaming spires] and you can see the six gigantic cooling towers of Didcot power station from about ten miles away, which get closer and closer as you move east towards the finish. There is also a somewhat sinister "nuclear" atmosphere in the area; a lot of nuclear research goes on at Appleton and Culham laboratories, and the huge faceless buildings are a bit unnerving. There are a lot of racehorse gallops up there, too; in the Lambourn Valley you often see the horses training. There are also several Neolithic, Iron Age, and Bronze Age sites, including forts, large burial mounds and white chalk horses, some of which can be seen from the route.

There's a slightly strange, mysterious and mystical feel to the place, which I really like.

'What makes it feel really authentic to me is that it's often very hot up there in the summer – it's pretty exposed in places – and the white roads get really dusty – just like in the Strade Bianche. A beautiful, perfect race, which we hope to recreate to some degree here.'

I sat back and scanned the velodrome again through the reception's panoramic window, watching the rain run down the panes in rivulets. I was trying to picture the finish line, the sun out, a spectacle of red, white and blue bunting, and relieved and happy riders. It seemed a long way away from where we were now, but I believed Francis could make it happen.

'Don't worry about not riding the course today, Iain. You've done the training. I could see for myself the way you were powering along. You'll be fine in Roubaix.'

Francis's words were a comfort. Part of me was annoyed at not attempting to tackle the whole course. One month to go and I still wanted to put a lot of miles in. I felt I needed to.

After a few more minutes of discussing the intricacies of his ambitions for the race, and seeing that the rain was easing off, I decided to get back to London. We exchanged numbers and wished one another well. Seeing someone so up for the challenge of setting up a race like the Tour of the Black Country, not to mention his home-grown Strade Bianche, geed me up, to a degree. As I drove out of Aldersley Stadium car park a wave of optimism and determination washed over me.

'I will do this,' I swore to myself. 'Can't tell Chris I didn't ride the whole course today, however.'

Even Hitler Couldn't Stop It

Ironically, it would be the year the world was plunged into a second global conflict that Paris–Roubaix embraced modernity. The famous cobbles may still have been there, particularly as one headed north towards Lille, but the gravel that lay across the many main roads outside of Paris was rapidly being replaced by tar and concrete. As one director of the Highways and Bridges department predicted, as the route's first kilometre of cobbles between Forest-sur-Marque and Hem was resurfaced, 'In six years, all the roads of Paris–Roubaix will be modernized.'

Unlike today, the pre-war French authorities embraced the coming of modern road surfaces to the countryside – smooth, navigable routes to rural towns and villages would only aid the burgeoning car-owning class, as well as improve agricultural transportation and, ultimately, be beneficial to the overall economic livelihood of the area. Cobbles, on the other hand, were seen as an archaic throwback to Napoleonic times. France, having won the war, would now win the battle for modernization. It was a pity they didn't realize they were about to be engulfed by the German *blitzkrieg*.

On 10 May 1940, Germany launched its attack on France with Hitler's panzer divisions slicing through the Allied defences in a surprise encirclement further south through the Ardennes.

Roubaix's valuable textile industries, by now the lifeblood of the whole region, were seen as particularly valuable by the German high command – so capturing the town intact was a prority for the Wehrmacht. This duly happened, when the offensive was just two weeks old, on 24 May. Five weeks later the whole country would be under German rule, with Hitler chauffeured through Paris in triumph, and the railway carriage in Compiègne that had been the site of German embarrassment in signing the terms of defeat in 1918 blown up on his orders.

The owner of *L'Auto* and organizer of its races, Henri Desgrange, would die very soon afterwards, and the mantle of keeping the public informed through newsprint, as well as trying to maintain some semblance of a sporting cycling calendar, fell to his successor Jacques Goddet.

Many books have covered the theory that Goddet may have collaborated with the Nazis, and only when Paris was certain of liberation did he decide to come down on the side of the French Resistance. The fact that his newspapers gave favourable editorial space to the German occupiers, and that his velodrome in Paris was used as a holding camp for French Jews who were later transported to the death camps,[16] pretty much makes up my mind about the kind of patriot he was. But, as one contemporary of his summarized of his legacy: 'Jacques Goddet, during the war, ran his business, kept the shop open. In a way, yes, he was passive towards the Occupiers. But no more so than ninety-eight per cent of Frenchmen in 1940.'

France was now split into zones of occupation overseen by

[16] Henri Desgrange and Goddet had bought the indoor Vel' d'Hiv arena, a popular Parisian venue for roller skating and track racing, thirty years previously. With the assistance of French police, the Germans rounded up over 13,000 Jewish men, women and children and imprisoned them within the arena for five hot summer days before they were sent to the gas chambers of Auschwitz. Goddet handed the authorities the keys to the venue. Fewer than 500 French Jews would return.

the Military Administration in France (*Militärverwaltung in Frankreich*) in the north and west of the country, labelled the *zone occupée*. In the south there was the legitimized puppet government of Vichy, which was administered independently by the French under the rule of Marshal Pétain, the hero of the French victory at Verdun in the Great War. Goddet may have wanted to resist the Germans by refusing to run an official Tour de France, but he did agree to produce a year-long racing calendar called the Grand Prix du Tour de France, which was really just a series of one-day races. By this method he could include existing races that were dear to the French public, Paris–Roubaix being one of them. The Germans were equally keen to stage the race, as for them it was an indication that life in France could continue normally despite the hardship of occupation – sport being an excellent way to keep the populace happy and sedated. Since their victory in 1940, the Germans had seized approximately 80 per cent of French food production, while French farm produce fell by an alarming 50 per cent due to a lack of manpower and fuel for equipment and vehicles. The French population was expected to survive on less than 1,300 calories per day, a starvation diet. The need to make them forget this servitude was uppermost in the minds of Hitler's overseers.

By the end of 1942, German forces were occupying all of France, despite the Allies surging to victories over Erwin Rommel's Afrika Korps and enjoying success by landing in Vichy-held North African territory. France was now renamed the *zone nord* for the north and west, and the *zone sud* for the area that had been Vichy-controlled. Hitler didn't want any nasty surprises of an invasion force coming up through the underbelly of France, so the Atlantic Wall was further strengthened around the coast.

All this led to a slight relaxing of the German grip on the borders between Belgium and France; in terms of restaging Paris–Roubaix, what had seemed impossible to the occupiers in 1940 and 1941 – due to the administrative headache it would cause – was very much back on the table as a project to pacify and control the French.

Goddet was on board; the German High Command had previously assured him they would provide all necessary assistance in terms of food, equipment, transportation and fuel for both riders and officials if he could put out an official Tour de France event. He had of course declined, there being no Tour between 1940 and 1946. But when the Paris–Roubaix edition of 1943 got underway, this was indeed the scenario: the riders were fed; had their bikes fully reconditioned; and the race officials managed to find from somewhere enough cars with fuel to patrol the route. (All paperwork from *L'Auto*'s archives disappeared in the war, so we have to judge for ourselves as to how they managed it.)

So, on 23 April 1943, the forty-first edition of *La Pascale* took place. One hundred and twenty riders took to the road, of whom thirty-four were Belgians, their number including the world champion Marcel Kint (known as 'The Black Eagle'). Belgium was suffering just as much under the yoake of German occupation as France, but its racing calendar had not been as badly affected, so their riders had the edge over everyone else in terms of physical conditioning, and Kint duly powered to victory in a five-man sprint in the Roubaix velodrome. Such was his fitness – although this was perhaps more a reflection of the state of the war-time local transportation network – that he then cycled the 25 kilometres home after receiving his trophy. Bizarrely, it took locals reading the following day's newspapers telling of his victory before anyone would believe him.

The race was deemed a success by the powers that be, and the following year's edition was organized along similar lines. By the spring of 1944, the German army was still in very good shape. In the east, they were gradually being pushed back by Stalin's Red Army, but were still being held along the boundaries of Ukraine. In the west, Hitler seemed to hold the upper hand: his Atlantic

Wall had not been breached, and the Allied advance through Italy had become bogged down in a Great War-style slog in the rainy season. Both D-Day, and the not so well-known Russian offensive Operation Bagration, clearing German forces from the modern-day region of Belarus and eastern Poland, were months away. Long enough for the authorities to feel capable of organizing a simple bike race, at least.

So, once again, at Easter 1944, two months before the Allied invasion of Normandy, the 172-man peloton prepared itself to race to Roubaix, only this time starting from Compiègne for the very first time, rather than the capital. And once again a Belgian cyclist, Maurice De Simpelaere, would take the victory, heading a six-man sprint to the line with Jules Rossi (a previous winner himself in 1937) second and Louis Thiétard third.

The bitter irony of this beautiful race being run amid the horror of war came home to roost when several cycling journalists, who were returning home after the race in their car, were seriously injured when bombed by Allied planes. The tide of war was turning, though, and by April 1945 France would be liberated once more, and the Nazis driven back to Hitler's final reckoning in Berlin.

As some kind of benevolent sign that France was now at long last free, all three podium places of that year's Paris–Roubaix race were filled by Frenchmen (the victor being Paul Maye) – the first time this had occurred in thirty-three years. Now the tarmacking of the *pavé* could begin again!

Stranger in a Strange Land

The Eurostar is easily the best way to travel to France. Unless, that is, the train engine catches fire and you're left stranded for three hours at Ashford International watching other Eurostar trains – seemingly fireproof – cruise through on time, with a compliment of happy passengers gawping at you through their windows. My first foray to the Continent in order to catch up with some experts of the race, and also to recce Lille and the Roubaix velodrome, hadn't exactly gone to plan.

The tour company Pavé Cycling Classics, however, were a godsend to meet and gain motivation for being able to ride the cobbles. I had heard of them from a friend who had signed up the year before to experience the 'Hell of the North' without the stress and fuss of organizing it himself. I had then read a great article in *Cyclist* magazine by Henry Catchpole which brought the company and what they do to glorious full colour. With the idea of picking the brains of an expert of the *pavé*, and perhaps actually visiting the velodrome or sections of *pavé* itself, I thought the expense of a train ticket that would deliver me to Lille in under an hour and a half was well worth the time and effort. So, there I was, finally standing outside Lille Métropole station, waiting for my meeting with William from Pavé Cycling, until I felt quite conspicuous.

My mobile buzzed and a hybrid Flemish–Irish accent came

online to announce his imminent arrival. 'Sorry I'm late, Iain, I've got the kids with me today as their school is closed, is that a problem?' (Cue young kids' chatter in the background.)

'No, not at all, I'm standing outside the Eurostar station if you're nearby?'

'We're actually parked by the McDonald's around the corner; do you want anything?'

So lunch was sorted as I greeted a very athletic William Lanigan carrying a large bag of takeaway Happy Meals and Big Macs and smiling broadly as I jogged up to his car. We shook hands and quickly got underway, his kids watching me from their car seats in the back, silent as they tend to be when a total stranger comes into their world.

William looked like a pro racer on a day off. As he drove through the back streets of the city centre, he gave me a short biography, of how he'd moved to France in the late 1990s, following a long line of talented amateur racers, hoping to make his way in the professional peloton. Life takes strange turns, however. He married a local girl, settled down to a full-time career as an engineer, and raced cyclo-cross and road in his spare time. I was intrigued by his accent. Depending on the background noise of traffic and the kids – shyness now being replaced by boisterous chatter – he would initially sound straight from a Dublin street, but this was then littered with classic Gallic mannerisms and shrugs. I imagined he spoke French pretty much all the time, and only English-speaking clients forced him to trawl up his mother tongue from the memory banks. It was a great combination, though.

After ten minutes of driving along through the suburbs, we eventually parked in front of a pretty three-storey house with a built-in garage, which I assumed housed his apartment. Wrong, he owned the whole thing. Walking through the garage, I saw that it was lined with road bikes. Some were parked against the far wall, others in various states of repair, and all were built for riding on cobbles by the looks of them. We ascended the marble staircase, where the walls were decorated with large-framed, stunning mono-chrome photographs of cyclists in action, looking like they were riding through the Arenberg judging by the forest surrounding them. The photographs lined the walls all the way through the living room to the first-floor kitchen, where William introduced me to his business partner and friend, Alex Voisine.

The kids happily went off to the living room to settle down to eat and watch some TV. We eased ourselves around the kitchen table and tucked into the Big Mac meals. For three relatively fit-looking guys it did seem weird to be eating this stuff, even funnier when William offered me an afternoon aperitif: 'You drink a Martini?'

'No, I'm not drinking.'

He clocked me suspiciously. 'You don't drink?'

I felt embarrassed. 'No, no. I'm not drinking until I've done the race.'

I tucked into the Big Mac as Alex directed a rueful smile towards William across the table. William went to the fridge and pulled out a few brown bottles of beer. 'It's a duty free, organic beer. Go on, have one, it's our own Belgian beer – Malteni!'

Again, I declined, explaining, 'I actually had a bit of a publishing event last night for an author and there were eight glasses of wine on the table and I never touched a drop.'

They both shook their heads chuckling, 'You must be mad.'

I raised my hands in mock admonishment. 'I am mad. It's one of those things that you'll never forgive yourself if you're drained by the end of it. If I just hadn't had a drink. But, you have one.'

William took the top off his bottle, raised it to me in salute and enjoyed a long swig. Placing it down on the table in triumph, he smiled at me and announced, 'I'm riding Flanders tomorrow.' We all laughed. 'So, what do you want to know about the *pavé*?'

'Well, like I said to you over the phone last week, I'm doing

Paris–Roubaix in a few weeks' time, so I'm trying to get as much background information on the race itself – what to expect, and tips on how to handle the *pavé*. When I've been talking to people, I've asked them, "Say one word that sums up Paris–Roubaix to you," and one word more than most keeps coming back to me – "brutal". So, it would be interesting to see what you think, because you guys know, obviously.'

William looked across at Alex and raised his eyebrows as if to acknowledge they'd be giving away trade secrets. 'The first thing I would say about Roubaix, it's . . . erm, it's not as hellish as people expect. You expect really to have a killer ride, but when I remember the first time I rode the cobbles, I was thinking, "This isn't so bad."'

My perplexed look made him continue quickly.

'I remember a friend of mine back home in Ireland who raced Paris–Roubaix in the 1990s. He rode it for a good amateur French team at the time. I remember talking to him a couple of weeks afterwards, when he came back to Ireland for the area championships, and he was saying, "Yeah, I don't know what's the big deal." He didn't actually finish the race, but he said, "I got to the brink and I was riding on the cobbles and, you know, I broke my bike and I had to wait ten minutes for the team car to come, etc., so physically I personally didn't find it difficult."'

I was stunned by this revelation and looked across at Alex who was nodding in agreement. William continued with his analysis in his Dublin/French brogue: 'I'm not telling you it's easy. It is hard, but it's more a case of, it's a lottery. It's always a lottery scenario for the pros. You are trying to keep out of trouble for as long as possible. You're trying to save energy for all of the *pavé*. You know, when you look at the race, Paris–Roubaix kind of plays out over a pretty short space of time.

'Let's say, between the start and finish of Paris–Roubaix, is a two hundred and sixty kilometre race, with the first kind of selection at the *troué* of the Arenberg section. Then it's more attrition, so people will be going out the back, just running out of energy, so then the decision for victory may be between thirty or forty riders. This final selection takes place more or less on the last ten to fifteen kilometres, where it is intense *pavé*. So, it's horses for courses.

'You know, if you take a look at the television, you'll see this summer, when Froome and his skinny friends come here to ride the Tour de France, that I'm sure it's going to be hellish for them.[17] They are not used to riding it and they're twenty kilos lighter than we are. They're designed to go uphill and suddenly you give them something that's totally different. It must be really bad. Just like taking a fat guy to the mountains.'

Part of me agreed with what William was saying about weight, balance and the experience required to ride the route. But there was an advantage in riding these roads every week of the year, in all weathers. Maybe that explained part of the bravado, or casual loftiness of William's verdict on this majestic race. 'Well, it'll be interesting to see what Wiggins does,' I countered. 'He has to put on some weight, too, I guess?'

William could probably tell I was still pondering his earlier declarations of how easy the cobbles were for him. 'He is accustomed to handling a bike now on the *pavé*. He's riding Flanders tomorrow, too. Equally, just look at David Millar. David Millar, who is merely a Tour rider in the past. He became a good *pavé* rider in the end through practice.

---

[17] As we now know, Chris Froome withdrew from the race on Stage 5 of the 2014 Tour de France, from Ypres–Arenberg, Porte du Hainaut, in atrocious conditions before he even reached the cobbles. Suffering three crashes in twenty-four hours of racing, Froome fractured both wrists. However, another contender – the ultimate winner, Italy's Vincenzo Nibali – who's just as light as Froome, gave a master class of riding the *pavé*.

'It's a way of life. *Pavé* cycling for us is— it's, erm . . . well, we think we're privileged living here. Alex is from Brittany, and I'm from Ireland. By chance we ended up working together in northern France, but I didn't realize I was coming to heaven when I came here.' He pointed out the window towards the countryside in the distance, 'Because here is heaven. For a bike-racing fan from March until mid-April, you've got loads of the best races in the world. The racers are living here. You see the Italian teams coming here and staying for two weeks, three weeks at a time, so it's a really interesting period, a very intense period. These races have a lot of history. They have a lot of stories, so we set up Pavé Cycling to share that and to make it possible for anybody to come and jump on a specific bike and to be able to get out on to the *pavé*. We've been going three years now and it's funny how, although we never said it would be a breadwinner for us, it sort of has. We have riders coming from as far away as Japan, the USA and Australia to book a ride with us on the *pavé*.'

Their excitement was palpable around the kitchen table. I was impressed by their élan, nonchalance and passion for these ancient races. They were clearly living the dream. But I still had plenty of questions I needed answering.

'How many bikes do you have? Do people bring their own?'

Alex chirped up for the first time: 'Eight bikes. So people have the choice to rent our customized ones, or if they want to use their own bikes they can.'

'And you organize everything else for them, too, such as accommodation?'

Alex nodded. 'Yes, it's going to be an exciting period coming up this summer. We will ride the Tour de France route a few days before it arrives for the official stages, and our guys will ride the same sections, so it will be more interesting for them, as they can see the Tour de France covering the *pavé* they have just ridden.'

I was excited just thinking about it. However, I was in for another assumption being corrected. 'It must be good for business, that ASO have opened the race to amateurs?'

William shot me a serious look. 'We're actually not fans of it, to be honest. The "original" Paris–Roubaix race for amateurs is actually run by the Roubaix Cycling Tourist Club. It's run every second year in the month of June. For me this is the real one, because it goes from Compiègne to Roubaix, the real route. It doesn't cost a lot, the original one. It costs fifteen euros or something like that and it's very traditional. Then ASO have come along and prices have dramatically increased.'

Alex raised his bottle of beer, staring into the reflection of the brown glass. 'It's not a race any more,' he murmured wistfully.

William continued his analysis of what he clearly felt was a serious issue affecting them: 'I find that it's a kind of unwritten rule that you don't infringe on other organizations. It's really a tradition thing. The traditional race for amateurs was running for fifty years. It had been raced for thirty years before I pitched up. I think it's a little cheeky from the side of the ASO, and they've turned it, really, into a money-spinning thing.'

'So you think it's "buy the T-shirt, buy the hat, buy the video"? Buy everything, really?'

William nodded. 'That's how it is. Everyone said to me, "You guys charge to bring people on the *pavé*, too," so I suppose it's more or less the same thing. We're all celebrating it in the long run. The demand isn't high enough to have a lot of people doing it, though. It's not like Mallorca, or Tenerife, or the Alps, where a lot of people go on cycling holidays. This place attracts a certain kind of bike fan and bike rider.'

Ah, now we were talking about the main subject, I knew they'd have good advice for me. 'What's the perfect set-up on a bike for *pavé*?' I asked.

Alex gestured towards the stairwell. 'Look at our bikes.' William cut across both of us to get his point over, 'Honestly, the most important thing are the wheels. Don't look at the pros. The pros are riding wheels, disposable wheels. These wheels they are riding on Roubaix, they're not adapted by the manufacturers.'

'A waste of money,' chimed Alex.

William continued, 'I'm sure that they are less efficient with some of the wheels they are using. Not all of them, but some of the guys are riding wheels that aren't set up correctly, but they have them because the manufacturers are saying it's OK.'

I nodded in agreement with him. 'You feel you've got to have them because it's great marketing to say the pros ride them at Roubaix, too.'

'Well, the only advice I was given,' Alex said, taking over, 'was if you've got your comfortable saddle, you don't have to worry about that. Just make your wheels bombproof. Well, make your wheels bombproof and make them comfortable. For me the element on a bike that makes a bike more comfortable, the dominant element, is the wheels, because they have such a heavy filtering aspect. You can take a frame that is less rigid, or more rigid, but compared to a big section – I would compare it to a car – if you have a car with fifteen-inch steel rims and high-profile tyres and you have the same car and you put a pair of seventeen-inch low profiles on, the feeling of the car is completely different in terms of comfort. It's more or less the same sensation on the bike, and that's amplified when you are on the *pavé*. So, our bikes, we're riding low rims, for the rims they can deform circularly around the hub. Lots of spokes allows you to have lower spoke tension. When you have only twenty spokes in a carbon ring you've got to tighten those spokes a lot. We ride tubulars, 27 millimetre. Every now and again I ride a bike on the *pavé* that's not adapted for the *pavé* and I say, "What? That's hard," and you come back and you ride the other one and it's like, "Aaah . . ."'

'That's what I've been discussing with many people back

home, Alex. The amount of people I have had tell me to take more weightier tyres than 25 millimetres. Even 30 millimetres? What do you think?'

'Twenty-fives, for me, not less. Twenty-five is the minimum. I remember the fifth year I rode Paris–Roubaix, I rode with 23 millimetres. It was very hard. Madness!'

William concurred. 'For me, you ride bigger tyres and lower pressures, because if you have a small tyre and you ride normal pressure, you'll puncture, for sure. You pinch the inner tubes, so for me that's the basic thing. Other than that, I would say, don't look too much at what the professionals are doing. The pros are putting on two layers of tape on the handlebars and stuff like that. The tapes are so good today, compared to when I was a kid. You've got gel tapes on the bikes and so there's no need to put two layers on. If you put two layers on, your hands are like, "Booophh!" Too big! So, I always say the bike you set up to ride the *pavé* should be the bike you ride every day. What kind of frame do you have, then?'

I thought I was on a winner here: 'A carbon.'

They both shook their heads again.

'I'm sceptical about carbon,' said William. 'For me it's more the geometry you need to think about. We work with people from Cyfac, a famous French bike brand from the nineteen eighties, who were making bikes for most of the pro teams of France and Italy when everyone was riding steel, or at the beginning of aluminium design. They had a lot of know-how on what they were doing on the steel bikes for the pros at that stage for *pavé*. They were making specific geometries, twenty or twenty-five years ago, for bigger tyre clearance, as well as for the capacity of the frame to absorb vibration and just take up the impact of the *pavé*. So, when Alex had already worked with them on a fixed-gear bike project, they said, "OK, we'll show you what we were working on a few years ago."

'Honestly, it's crazy when I see the bike industry today. We as consumers are constantly being fed stories: "Your bike is more comfortable lighter, more rigid." It's all bullshit and the magazines feed it to us. When I test a modern bike with technology from more or less twenty years ago, the seal we're using, it's a seal developed decades ago, and the geometry information that we're using was developed twenty years ago. These bloody old-style bikes work better than a new bike. Jaysus! So, that's why I say carbon frames and all this new "technology", it's just following a consumer programme like everything else we buy.'

As with his view of riding the *pavé* itself, William was very, very sure of his footing on the type of bike to use. I couldn't argue with the man due to his knowledge based on actually riding the routes many times. I started to feel guilty about selling my old Cougar-designed, Reynolds-steel-framed bike in order to purchase the carbon beauty I now had: 'The tyres, I've sorted out, William, and I've got a carbon seat post, because I thought that would be OK. But, it's a Raleigh bike as well, but it's a good bike. It's a sportive bike, basically, but that's the only worry. I thought, "I wonder what kind of strain I'm going to put this frame under?" I want to finish this race.'

I got the feeling he thought he'd spooked me as he seemed far more consoling now: 'Honestly, if you are filtering with the wheels, if you've got good section tyres, and you look where you're going . . . the biggest risk you have on the *pavé* is to hit a hole and crash. That's where you can damage your bike. But, in general, if you avoid that on the sportive, you've just got to keep your distance from people; if you're going to keep your eyes open it's not going to be a disaster. In general, stuff comes loose, so make sure everything is tight. Even with us, we'll take our bikes out and on the first section a pair of handlebars will come loose, or something like that, because our bikes might have been hung up for a month in the garage. Basically, all the peripheral stuff on the bike suffers, because it's being vibrated. Check your bottle cages are tight, really clamp your bottles tight.'

It seemed like we'd been talking for five minutes, but my watch said half an hour. William's two children wandered in looking for drinks. Once he'd supplied them with their juice bottles he boiled the kettle and made some espressos for Alex and me.

'What about all this advice that riding on the crown of the cobbles is the best and safest place to be?' I asked.

William handed me my coffee. 'Yeah, ride the crown on the *pavé*. Look in front of you. Look what's coming up, that's the best way to survive.'

Alex decided to add some chilling advice, the one subject that was the elephant in the room: 'Not in the Arenberg. There is not a best way to look. Perhaps it's better on the right, from the middle it's better on the right. I often say to our customers when they come. Be careful in Arenberg. Everyone wants to ride the Arenberg. Arenberg is just hard. For me it is the place that represents best what you told us Barry Hoban said – "brutal" – it physically hurts riding it.'

Sitting down with us at the table, William joined in. It reminded me of the scene from *Jaws* where the hunters are all recounting their battle scars from fighting sharks. 'It can be dangerous depending on the weather,' he offered. 'It's downhill for a while, where you can pick up speed, and then it's a full-on two kilometres of flat track through the forest. So keep your powder dry.'

'At least I had been doing something right,' I thought. 'Well,' I announced. 'I've been practising doing intervals on the turbo trainer.' I was now fishing for praise.

William nodded again: 'That's what I tell people. They ask, "What kind of efforts should I be doing?" and I say, "Just do long intervals," because you will come off a section in the race, and five minutes later you come to another one, so ride a bigger gear, too. If you're comfortable on the normal paved road, let's say a 52 x 16?

Well, on the *pavé* you should be riding 52 x 15. So, the *pavé* will slow you down somewhat, but the fact that you are pushing a bigger gear is just more efficient, and the *pavé* doesn't come to you as much.'

'So would you guys say that this is the "Queen of the Classics", as all the media would have us believe?'

William instantly replied, 'I'll ask you a question. Who won Paris–Roubaix in 2011?'

I guessed, 'Was it Boonen?'

William shook his head. 'No, Vansummeren. I would always associate Vansummeren with "surprise winner of Roubaix". Until the day I die I will know that he won Roubaix. But, the surprise winner in Liège–Bastogne–Liège? I don't remember. I know who won the Liège last year because it was an Irish lad – Dan Martin – but who won Liège the year before that? I have no idea. Who won the Tour of Flanders in 2011? I can't remember, even though I love Flanders. For me, Paris–Roubaix is the main race from an international point of view; from the "common man" point of view, let's say.'

'But isn't the Tour of Flanders a big event for amateurs now?' I asked.

'Sure, tomorrow is the Tour of Flanders Cyclosportive. It's the biggest sporting event in Europe; it's seventeen thousand people. I was looking at the site last night. It's sold out. It's huge. But, it's a Belgian thing. Seventeen thousand people. That's fifteen thousand that are Belgian and the rest are a couple of French guys, a couple of English guys and some Italians. From a television point of view I think maybe Roubaix is the most spectacular race, though.'

Hearing what they were saying about the strong national identity associated with Flanders made me think about the national antagonisms between my own home countries, especially England versus Scotland. 'Is there any nationalistic antagonism from the French towards the Belgians?' I wondered. 'They seem to win Paris–Roubaix quite a lot.'

Again, they both raised a smile. 'I find that's more present in Belgium,' replied William. 'The Belgians hate a Dutch guy to win Flanders. They would prefer a Belgian guy to win Flanders than a French guy. I remember when I was racing myself in Belgium, and you'd puncture. If you're a French guy, the neutral service will just drive past you and leave you on the side of the road, and if you're a Dutch guy the neutral service will try to run you down!' They both laughed.

'The Belgians and the Dutch, they don't see eye to eye,' continued William. 'So that's the way it is. From a nationalistic point of view a lot of Belgians come to the *pavé*, and there's more trouble between the Belgians themselves on the *pavé* than with the French. There was a period, two or three years ago, when there was a lot of football supporters who were coming to the races and drinking and using it as a kind of showdown. The first time we went to Arenberg with one of our cycling groups we were thinking, "Christ, why did we come here?" because you could feel the friction. There were two groups of supporters and they were shouting. There was banter between them, but you could feel that it could kick off really easily.

'Usually, the Belgian police would be lenient with fans getting rowdy. They'd put you in a cell for the evening to cool off and then you could go, but now on the *pavé*, on the Flemish *pavés*, you've got the Belgian police present as well. They've got jurisdiction, so if you break the law, you'll start breaking the law in Belgium, which ensures people keep it peaceful. They used to be pretty heavy handed with their truncheons, just to get their message across. But, when they weren't there, I recall riders were getting spat at and their team cars were getting pelted with stones, because some of these "fans" were doing drugs. They were arriving on a Friday evening, in the middle of a field, and staying there until the Sunday. What do you do in the middle of a field for two days, then?'

Alex joined in again. 'Carrefour de l'Arbre – it was full of big balloons with drunken Finnish people. I guess they like cycling, but they are more here for the party than for the cycling.'

As interesting as this was, and clearly a cause for debate, I wanted to steer the subject more towards the troubles I'd be facing myself as a rider. 'What condition will the *pavé* be in when I race, do you think, Alex?'

He pondered this like a mathematician working out a tough calculus theory. 'The condition of the cobbles – at the moment they are easier than in the summer.'

I shot him a quizzical look, as I thought it was always the winter and spring rains that would make them far more dangerous.

'We notice that it's easier when some sections of the *pavé* have mud covering them due to the bad weather before Christmas. But in the summer it all turns to dust in the heat and dry winds, so you have some very big, huge gaps between the cobbles. So the summer months of July and August are far worse.'

'How many punctures do you think I'll get, then?'

Again, they looked seriously at me as if imparting some religious mantra. 'Keep your eyes open in Roubaix and you won't puncture,' said Alex.

'Well, I've got a 27-millimetre tyre on the front and a 25-millimetre on the back.'

'Put a 27-millimetre on the back as well, then,' he suggested. 'That's where your weight is. Every time we puncture, we always puncture at the back. A puncture is always linked to the pressure, and if the tyre is pinched. In general, you'll manage to get the front wheel over safely.'

I was now almost chanting this information: 'So, sit at the back of the saddle, light hands on the top bars, and keep the cadence high in a big gear . . .'

'Honestly,' said William, 'we were talking about this to Johan Museeuw, and he was saying that he developed a pedalling technique on the *pavé* where he reckoned he was sitting in a recumbent position. He was telling us his pedal stroke on the *pavé* wasn't the same as when he was riding on the normal tarmac when he was at home.'

'Wow, the "Lion of Flanders", how did you get him involved in your operation?'

'I met him at my work,' said Alex, 'because he used to drive his brother to where I work, and so I proposed to him that he ride with us, with our group, with some customers, and he said OK. It's not free, we pay him, but when you have a big group it's worth it, and he's very friendly. He's a bit strict at first, but after that he's a very friendly guy. Even though he's been retired a long time, he's still a real pro on the *pavé*, he's incredible. On the cobbles, when he accelerates, he's gone. You can't see him. I did one section just behind him. Pheewww!'

'When are you arriving for Roubaix?' William asked.

'The Friday evening before the race,' I replied.

'It would be suicide to go and ride on the *pavé* the day before riding the Paris–Roubaix. Don't go wrecking yourself. You'll be grand. You've got to ride at a pace you can hold on. When you go on to a section of *pavé* you know you can hold that pace until the exit. When you blow on the *pavé*, you stop. You grind to a halt, so it's not like blowing on a tarmac road. On a tarmac road you'll drop from 40 to 30 k.p.h.; on *pavé* you drop from 35 to 20 k.p.h. When you go slow on the *pavé* it hurts, so bear that in mind. Try to be a steady diesel engine all the way along, so you're keeping your powder dry as long as you can. The problem sometimes I see is that the first sections of *pavé* are not the hardest. They're quite fast, quite smooth and a lot of people start thinking they are Cancellara. So, you kind of get to the 100 kilometres mark, and you start feeling not so cool, and there's a lot of hard *pavé* to come, in and around the Arenberg. Tough sectors, long sectors. Wandignies-Hamage – it's very long.

'Pace yourself. Be careful of the middle section and you know that after, let's say 100 to 120 kilometres, you'll be able to "smell the stable", but let's say maybe the 10 kilometres before Arenberg, and maybe the 15 kilometres after Arenberg, I find there are tough sections there too. Afterwards, you get on to the Pévèle, 40 or 50 kilometres from the finish; they're hard sectors, but they're doable.

'There's some rest zones in the race as well. Some areas where you've probably only got one section of *pavé* for perhaps 15 kilometres, and it's an easy sector, so you can almost say, "I'm going flat out." But when you're talking to Museeuw, asking him what he does in this period, he replies, "OK, in this area my biggest aim is – I turn off. During the whole race I try to save energy, because I know what's going to happen in 20 kilometres. It's going to be hell for leather to the finish."'

I asked one final question of them both that related to where I was going for my next meeting. 'Do you think there's any more stretches of *pavé* to find, or are they just happy the route they have now is . . . well, that's *the* route?'

Alex brightened up again. 'I know of a lot more cobbled sections. They are more on the north of the route. Sometimes they are covered by the mud. When you're riding the route, you can sometimes just see there are some cobbles here.'

'I read that they did tarmac over lots of it, didn't they?' I replied.

'That's right,' Alex said, 'there is an association: *Les Amis de Paris–Roubaix*.'

I smiled at the name. 'I'm seeing them in an hour.'

'You're seeing them? Oh, great. They saved the race in the eighties, because at that time, all the mayors of the local towns and villages were saying, "The cobbles are dangerous, get rid of them." And they were covering them. But *Les Amis de Paris–Roubaix* said, "Stop. We have to save our heritage." They did a good job.'

Time was against us, and William's kids had finished their lunch. You never mess with seven-year-olds and their soft playtime. So, with Alex's best wishes and a slap on the back, I bade him goodbye and jumped back in the car, and William was kindly driving me back to the Lille Métropole station.

From there I caught the local service to Roubaix, which took twenty-five minutes, and then a short taxi ride dropped me at the top of the famous boulevard, Avenue Alfred Motte, otherwise known as the 'Road of the Giants', which is now the final section of cobbles. It was specially laid down in 1996 as a tribute to all the many champions the race has had, their names forever celebrated on plaques embedded into the *pavé*.

At a café near the actual Roubaix stadium I had agreed to meet François Doulcier, the current president of a very famous society.

The Man from the *Pavé*

In the North, people have always worked hard,
and the cobblestones represent that work ethic.

François Doulcier

Les Amis de Paris–Roubaix, for me, had always conjured up images
of the French Resistance in the Second World War for some reason.
I could see them, all dressed in black, at the dead of night, out on
the *pavé*, fighting modernity and the need of officialdom to tarmac
over their beloved countryside. In reality, their name simply translates as 'the friends' of the race. They are a profit-free group of
enthusiastic volunteers whose dedication has only recently been
recognized by the cycling media. It seemed obvious to try to meet
them in order to understand what is so special about these cobbles
for the cyclists who traverse them.

The society was founded in 1982 by Jean-Claude Vallaeys, with
a variety of local cyclo-cross and road cycling clubs that regularly
used the *pavé* for recreational events. Several local mayors, anxious
to show northern France as a modern-facing region, had been
busy routinely covering the miles of cobbles dotted throughout

their neighbourhoods with modern asphalt. *Les Amis*'s goal
was to thwart this drive to destroy what they saw as the region's
heritage, and to research and locate new sections and try to incor-
porate them into the race.

Vallaeys was succeeded by Alain Bernard, who was keen to
progress the preservation role of the society, but equally to educate
others in why they were doing it, and why the *pavé* and the races
held upon it were so essentially linked to the region and should
not be cast aside. He worked closely with the local authorities and
ASO, who run the professional road races that take in the *pavé*, to
promote exhibitions and run tours of the route itself. Bernard was
the man I most recognized when reading and watching commen-
tary of the race during the 1990s. So when I began researching this
story and for preparation for the 'Hell of the North' itself, I was
surprised to see a new president at the helm of *Les Amis* – François
Doulcier.

François and I had been communicating via email for a few
months before our actual meeting. I confess at this point that I
had been leading a double life to dear old François. The beauty
of the internet allowed me to don the clothes of anyone, I guess,
and in my case I had started to convince myself that I was fluent
in French. The French one speaks via Google Translate, that is.
Equally, being the cosseted, metropolitan luvvee some would
have you believe, I had this image that a man of the soil would be
standing before me, with the bulk and the appearance of a tough,
agricultural type. Nothing could be further from the truth for both
of us on this blind date.

I had told François I would have my trusty *Étape du Tour 2013*
rucksack on my back – its garish yellow a guaranteed beacon for
anyone trying to locate me in the throng of a busy railway station or
restaurant. So there I was, wandering about the bustling, spacious
café when I finally noticed, tucked away in the far corner, a middle-
aged, bespectacled, bald man rising from his table and waving in

my direction. I walked quickly over to him and hesitantly offered my hand, 'François?'

'*Bonjour, Iain. Comment allez-vous?*'

'Well, might as well confess now,' I thought. 'I am well, thank you,' I said. 'I should admit that my French is very poor. I have been using a translator on the web to make sure we could speak to one another.' I feverishly hoped he understood what I had just said, feeling half-ashamed at my ignorance of not sticking with Mrs du Pré's French classes (even though she was a bad-tempered old boot), and half-embarrassed at my skulduggery to get the man to meet with me, thinking I was bilingual.

'It's a little bit difficult for me to answer in English, but I will try.' Bless his heart. We sat down and I ordered coffee for both of us. 'Are you only in Roubaix for one day?' he asked.

'Yes, it's a flying visit. I just needed to see a few people, and for my own confidence in tackling this race in a month's time. Right now it seems so huge in my mind, and the more I think about the *pavé* and the Arenberg, and Carrefour de l'Arbre, it builds itself into something insurmountable.' I blew my cheeks out in mock despair.

François smiled and drank his coffee, obviously constructing a reply to my child-like grumbling. He put the cup down and gestured to a book in his hand which he had just brought out from under the table. An English–French dictionary: 'I need it just so my English is better. I practise with it a lot. I hope you can understand me better?' I nodded in astonished glee. 'No wonder he's president,' I thought to myself. 'I think you will be OK on the cobbles if you have trained tough enough?' he continued. 'I was working on the *pavé* yesterday nearby here, the Willem to Hem section.' He gestured behind him to the window. From my research I recalled Hem was on the doorstep of the Roubaix velodrome. 'The *pavé* is in good condition right now, and if the weather holds for you . . .' He said this in hope more than certainty, I thought.

'How are the cobbles looking anyway?' The essential question. François seemed to be a man who treated every question with the same degree of importance. He took a sip of coffee and thought carefully about his answer.

'This year? Oh, they are really good, because one of the aims in our group is to preserve and fix the cobbled sectors. So, as you know, every year we have some hard work on the cobbled sectors and this year in 2013, it has been a very wet year. We are known as *"les forçats du pavé"* – "the convicts of the road". Our aim is to avoid ruts. "Ruts"? We say *"ornières"* in French. Potholes, we say *"de poule"* in French. We also clean the cobbles to avoid the mud. Our aim is to avoid a crash for the riders. We are very pleased if we've created a good selection on the cobbles, with the athletic qualities of the riders showing who is the best, and not a crash, nor a flat tyre. So, our aim is to make the cobbles more suitable for motor vehicles, too. It is very important for us, because we usually say cobbles are hard enough. It is usual to repair the ruts, potholes, and clear the mud. So, we are very proud of our work this year.'

'For fans of the race like me, François – and I am especially thinking of the ex-professionals, or the local amateur riders, such as the guys from Pavé Cycling – do they speak with you and share their feelings about the cobbles? Do they put pressure on you to not touch the *pavé*, or to not make it easier for races coming through, such as when the Tour de France arrives in July for stage five?'

He became almost animated at this question and shook his head. 'No, no, because in the past it was too difficult. It was a little bit like cyclo-cross. But today it's not like cyclo-cross at all. I think it is a very good race on clean cobbles and the cobbles are suitable for motor vehicles, too. So, it is very important they are in such a condition. It is for that reason the Tour de France agreed we could have a stage on the cobbles for this year, so many team cars will be able to navigate their way along the *pavé*. So, we are very proud that the Tour de France has recognized the good work we do all year long, not just in the spring and summer months, because we work from January to December.'

I was captivated by his passion for such laborious work, undertaking back-breaking restoration and preservation of sections of road that date back to Napoleonic times. But it was François's calm and matter-of-fact description of how his very small team undertook this voluntary work that impressed me most. Being out in all weathers, especially the wind and rain of northern France, can't be much fun in winter time. 'Does the Tour provide financial assistance for you?' I asked.

'Yes, the organizer helps us to preserve and fix cobbled sectors. Local councils also help us, and we are lucky to have two hundred members all over the world. We have American members, Australian, Belgian, Canadian, Italian, German, South African, New Zealand and, of course, you lovely English. Their contributions are all highly valued. Why are you shaking your head, Iain?'

'No Scots?'

He smiled and gestured to the waitress to order two more coffees. 'We would be very proud to have the first Scot in our society. You wish to join?'

'Absolutely. Sign me up!' I felt like I was handing over life insurance now. But I still had a few serious questions that I thought were fundamental to understanding the local perspective on the race becoming international. 'Do you think it's a good thing that amateurs like myself get to ride the *pavé*. Is it safe for them to ride the route?'

The waitress arrived with a new tray of drinks and some biscuits. François smiled at her. The way he slowly stirred his coffee around with his teaspoon, obviously pondering what to say, reminded me of George Smiley from *Tinker, Tailor, Soldier, Spy*;

in fact, the whole conversation seemed like a scene from the film. Again, he took a sip and looked at me as if to impart some crucial piece of news, 'Yes, I do think you amateur riders will be very safe. Yes, the cobbles are hard, but it is not dangerous to ride on them. In the past it was very dangerous, because there was a lot of mud, a lot of ruts, and crucially a lot of potholes. It was very, very difficult, even for the professionals – and we have all seen the crashes some of them suffered, like Museeuw – when the weather made conditions dangerous. It was, I think, too difficult.'

'And now?' I asked.

'Now? Well, it is easier than in the past, but it is still a race that tests you, as it should. It's the reason why we have cobbles on the Tour de France this year, and it will be interesting to see how the great riders handle it. Just like other tests they will face in the mountains, our cobbles will hopefully provide excitement and determine who might win, or lose. We are very proud of this. It is great for northern France. The cobbles are our heritage and we have to preserve them as much as we can. It is one of the aims of our group and I want to stress that we do it all for love and pride. Not money. Ever.

'In the past, many believed it was a bad image for northern France, that we were not modern enough for the new Europe. But now, it is exactly the opposite. Our cobbles are . . .'

He was struggling for the right word. 'Celebrated?'

'Yes. The cobbles portray a good image now. We, the northern people in France, are very proud of the cobbles. So, things change for the better and it is great for the area, because with no cobbles, there would be no Paris–Roubaix race.' He became animated. 'And *it is* the hardest one-day race in the world of professional cycling. I believe it is the most beautiful one-day race there is, but that is just my opinion.'

Swept up in his enthusiasm, I nodded my agreement vigorously. Time for the obvious question. 'What would you say are the

hardest sections I'll face, François, seeing as you know exactly
what condition they're in right now?'

The serious face hove into view again. 'Trouée d'Arenberg is
very hard, but Mons-en-Pévèle is a very hard sector, as is Carrefour
de l'Arbre.' He held up his left hand and picked off the names
one by one on his outstretched fingers. 'Yes, the three most
difficult cobbled sectors for me are Arenberg, Mons-en-Pévèle and
Carrefour de l'Arbre.'

'And those last two are after the Arenberg? I was assuming
if I get through the Arenberg intact then I have a great chance
to finish.'

'Yes, they are the key to the final parts of the Paris–Roubaix
road, but they are very, *very* difficult. In Mons-en-Pévèle you have
to climb a little bit, usually into a headwind. Carrefour de l'Arbre
is equally very, very, very difficult. Maybe the same difficulty as
the Arenberg.'

'Is that because it's right at the end of the race? And I noticed it
was a long stretch of *pavé*.'

François nodded eagerly in agreement. 'It's very long and the
cobbles are very bumpy. The gap you will see between two cobbles
is very important. It is not very thin. It is very difficult for the
riders to cycle on this kind of cobble.'

'On that section, do you get a lot of riders going into the gutter,
rather than going down the middle?'

'If it is dry, yes, but if it's raining that's impossible. You would
never get your bike through the mud. I am sure you have seen many
pictures of those conditions?'

I had, and recalled flicking through the brilliantly evocative
book *Paris–Roubaix: A Journey Through Hell*, a gem of an illustrated title; a love letter to the passion and suffering generations of
riders had endured since the start of the race. The picture of Sean
Kelly navigating his bike through a sea of mud on his way to secur-
ing his second win in 1986 was one that grabbed me at the time. I

couldn't comprehend anyone trying to ride, let alone win a race, in such conditions. Glorious madness.

François snapped me out of my daydream. 'The race this year, if it's dry, will be more difficult for the riders, because of the speed. But I do prefer a dry Paris–Roubaix rather than the rain. The setts are not protected from the rain and snow and the cobbles are made from sandstone, which will be eroded by water seeping into them. When winter comes, the water freezes, expands and cracks the cobbles. That is why we have so many damaged, and these can really ambush a rider. I don't like the rain, because we always have crashes on the cobbles and it's not a good thing to see, nor for Paris–Roubaix's image to the world – [Philippe] Gaumont was terrible to see [see footnote 27 on page 200]. In dry weather we have a good race, with a good selection of cobbles to decide who is the strongest, and perhaps the luckiest.'

I decided to throw him an easy question. 'Who is your favourite for this year then, François?'

'I like Boonen, Cancellara and of the French riders I like [Damien] Gaudin of Europcar, and Sébastien Turgot of AG2R, who was second in the race two years ago. Gaudin, and Turgot, and maybe, this year, your Bradley Wiggins.' He shot me a knowing smile, as if this was preposterous. 'Why not?'

This final choice surprised me. Wiggins? Really? 'He's put on some kilos. He would need to put on weight to do it, to have the staying power. You never know, François. I would love it. But, I am more interested in knowing who inspired you when you were younger. Who was your hero when you were a boy racer?'

Again, the gleam in the eye returned. 'Ah yes, Bernard Hinault, Francesco Moser and also [Gilbert] Duclos-Lassalle, I liked him very much. They were passionate racers, and very determined men. Hinault didn't like the cobbles at all, but he knew he wouldn't be judged properly if he didn't try to win it. And, of course, he did.'

'I know Hinault thought Paris–Roubaix was "shit", even after he won it. But many people I have talked to always come back to words like "brutal". Would you agree with this?'

For once, François seemed perturbed by this description, but he was honest enough to want to talk about it and not dismiss my question. 'Ah, brutal. Yes, yes, OK. Well, that was the case in the seventies, perhaps. Now, it is not so brutal, or hard. I should say hard, but not too hard. Paris–Roubaix today is maybe easier than in the past, but I think it's better.'

'Do you think, as the president now, the race gets the respect it deserves, as in all the best riders come to test themselves? I ask as you do see some favourites for the Tour de France, or Giro, not wanting to risk their season by cycling the *pavé*.'

'Yes, I think so. I agree we now have some specialists with the Tour de France who avoid it. I am very happy that Bradley Wiggins will participate in Paris–Roubaix. It is very important for us that a recent Tour de France winner participates. I'm very, very happy to see Bradley Wiggins back on the cobbles. Maybe he can win.'

'For someone like me, just a complete amateur: what should I be careful of when riding on your *pavé* then, François?'

The serious look of a father imparting life advice to a wayward son returned again. 'You have to be careful with the ruts. This is very important. I would advise you to cycle on the top of the cobbles. It's more comfortable overall, and you have less risk to have a flat tyre on the top. But ruts and the potholes are very, very dangerous for a crash, so watch your speed, as some of the down-hill sections can be tricky. You think you might be in control, but you can easily fall. It's the main difficulty, so you have to see what is in front of you. And keep your hands loose on the top of the handlebars. Don't grip them.'

The table was now covered in half a dozen coffee cups. The conversation was naturally coming to an end. Walking out of the café, we stood in the doorway as the clouds darkened in the late afternoon sky. I had one final question to ask him about his beloved society: what were its future plans for any more undiscovered cobbles?

'We want to preserve eighty-five kilometres of cobbles overall. Paris–Roubaix each year uses fifty-five kilometres of *pavé*, and to me that's enough. So, our aim is to preserve all of the eighty-five kilometres of cobbles for the area's heritage. Our volunteers repair approximately five kilometres a year, and we have big plans to refurbish the sectors at Orchies and Bersée, but these are all expensive jobs. If you think about it, we repair each year 900 square metres of *pavé*, at a cost of €35 per square metre. So, just on materials, we are needing over €30,000.

'For the race itself, we have a new project: that within two or three years we will create a new, final part of the Paris–Roubaix route with three new kilometres of cobbles. It is a great, exciting project for us, but we need money. More than one million euros. We are working on this project with our local government. It is a great plan which we hope will happen. We are also planning a new museum next to the velodrome. We purchased the existing building last November, so that is in the planning stage, too. But we need money and, as you see' – he patted his trousers – 'my pockets are empty.

'All our members are volunteers and are doing their work for free on the various sections that need restoration. We have them, and also students, or apprentices. And then local companies provide some assistance. Overall, perhaps two hundred members and twenty fellow members usually work on the cobbled sectors with me. For example, tomorrow we will work on Saint-Python cobbled sector. Last week we cleaned the cobbles on Mons-en-Pévèle sector, and two weeks ago it was the Ennevelin–Pont Thibaut cobbled sector.'

I pulled the collar of my coat up to shield my face from the wind. It looked like rain was coming on. François did likewise and

offered to shake my hand in *adieu*. 'It is a patient commitment. It
is a work, but it is a pleasure.'

'Your heritage, you might say?'

'Yes, yes. We have to preserve this heritage. It is very important.
Good luck with your race, Iain. I hope you enjoy it. It is the most
beautiful route. *Bonne chance!*'

We shook hands warmly and I watched him walk quickly up the
road, a man on a mission with plenty to do, things to organize. I
thought the *pavé* was safe in the hands of someone like François,
hewn from the very stone he so loves.

The rain was intermittent now. With my train not leaving for
another two hours, and the station easily within reach, I wanted
to recon the one thing I thought about every single day as the race
loomed up in the not too distant future – Roubaix velodrome. It
was approximately 400 metres further along the boulevard, past
some council football pitches and a kids' BMX track.

I walked down the middle of the final cobbled section created
for champions past. The nondescript entrance, through a white
iron set of gates, led me along a winding road to the stadium, the
famous arena surrounding a grassy field, with high banking at
either end for the fans. I looked through the fence that barred my
entrance on to the track like an eager kid viewing the best sweet-
shop he'd seen in years.

The place was silent save for a few workmen banging around
in the bowels of the old wooden stadium on the opposite side
of the track. I studied the banking and tried to picture myself
coming round the final bend, high up on the uppermost
boards, the fans cheering my every pedal stroke, the raindrops
stinging my muddy face as I charged down towards the finish line
and glory. 'Well, you have to get there first mate!' I thought, smiling to myself as I turned to view the two-storey museum behind
me, and the famous shower block further back at the end of the
car park.

The white wooden doors of the museum were ajar, they were taking delivery of supplies for the bar and café that was housed within it. An overweight, middle-aged man, dressed in a smart white shirt and blue jeans, appeared at the top of the small flight of steps, looking for the supply driver I imagined was ferreting around in his truck for whatever was being dropped off – it looked like cases of beer, fizzy drinks and bags of crisps. I gingerly walked up to him and asked, 'Are you open, *monsieur*?', my pidgin French to the fore once again. He looked relaxed as he leaned against the doorframe. 'I'm sorry, not possible today, we are cleaning and taking stock, so we are not open to the public.' I must have looked too crestfallen, and even though he probably had thousands of bike fans descending on this little place all year round, he suddenly gestured for me to come in.

It was a pretty ordinary place, a small bar in one half of the room, with bar stools and a few leather chairs further back. On the opposite side of the room was a glass counter, where I imagined they would sell memorabilia of some sort. I looked around the walls and immediately spotted a large glass case housing model cars and trucks, as part of a diorama of what the Tour de France caravan would have been like in the 1950s. A cyclist, much like Fausto Coppi – or our own Tom Simpson – led the peloton of several toiling figures, while a classic Renault saloon and various vans followed, with two motorbike outriders leading the whole circus. Various figurines of cycling fans lined the stage, waving and cheering on their heroes of the road. It was a lovely scene, and yours for only €300. Much as I would have loved to surprise my kids with this thing of beauty, turning my attention to the bar across the room, I decided on a quick espresso.

Tucked away in the opposite corner was a basic red-brick counter, complete with a few beer taps, racks of glasses on the back shelves and a coffee machine with stacks of cups and saucers. The vibe was very much of a motorway café. Above the bar was wooden boarding with what appeared to be a menu, thus creating a kind of service-hatch look. Upon closer inspection I could tell the menu was in fact a white plastic tribute board to the various winners of Paris–Roubaix, all in strange, difficult to read, longhand script in blue ink. One could identify names, listed in four columns like some Great War cenotaph, of *vainqueurs* (winners) stretching back from the very first race to those heroes who had died in the Great War, and on to the 1970s. Walking round to the right-hand side of the bar, the names carried on right up to the present day: Stuart O'Grady, Fabian Cancellara.

On the left-hand side were those champions who warranted special mention due to their extraordinary deeds. Obviously Tom Boonen was there, heading the first line with his four victories, followed on the next line by the ubiquitous Roger De Vlaeminck (I was sure he'd hate that!). Then there was Gilbert Duclos-Lassalle as the oldest winner at 38 years of age in 1993; Eddy Merckx as the youngest (naturally) at 22 years of age in 1968; Peter Post with the fastest speed recorded across the course of 45.129 k.p.h. in 1964; Eddy Planckaert with the smallest winning margin of 1 cm in 1990; and, finally, Eddy Merckx again with the biggest winning margin of 5 minutes and 21 seconds in 1970.

It was marvellous to view. The bartender was busy stocking up his shelves for the evening session of regulars. I gestured to see if he spoke any English. He stopped what he was doing. 'How can I help?' he said, in a heavy accent that was still much better than my French.

'I am just here on a day's visit before going back home to England and was wondering if I can look around the place?'

Gauging my plea for assistance, he held his arms wide open as if to say, 'Who's going to know?' 'It is free to look around the track,' he went on, 'this museum and the showers, of course. We only charge entry for VIPs on race days, or for the main seating area across the track.' He pointed out of the window towards the large wooden stand, a relic from the 1950s. 'Everything else is open to the fans.'

This felt like being given a golden ticket to Hamleys! I quickly sank the espresso in one gulp, grabbed my rucksack and gave a thankful nod as I rushed out of the door, trying not to look too excited.

Turning right, I followed the signs taking me to the fabled Roubaix changing rooms. Now, if anyone other than a bike fan heard me say, 'I'm off to take pictures of a men's shower room,' I wouldn't blame them for raising more than an eyebrow. If you know cycling, though, then this is what Madison Square Garden means to boxing, the Long Room at Lord's represents to England cricket fans, and the Nürburgring means to Formula One fanatics. It is the inner sanctum of the hardest bike race in the world. Where the greats have retreated to – often surrounded by a frenzied pack of reporters – to celebrate a victory, or recount endless tales of bad luck, terrible crashes, or outright treachery from opponents on the *pavé*. Walking across what resembled a municipal gravel car park, I pushed open a metal-wired gate and on entering the 1960s-style glass-fronted building was immediately transported back to being a teenage schoolboy again, having just finished rugby practice on a cold, miserable winter's day.

The shower block is not a magnificent tribute to the legends of sport, nor is it a tourist-friendly attraction where you'll take a never-to-forget selfie or buy a treasured memento of your visit. It is, rather, a very bleak set of shower rooms, with rows of cement changing stalls lined four abreast with a prison-like shower section at the end of each room. It reminded me of *The Shawshank Redemption*, with chains hanging down to pull on for hot water. The changing stalls were basic: no doors, a wooden seat built into the cubicle, and a simple black metal hook for the rider to hang his sodden clothes on.

It is not an understatement to say this truly is the home of the 'convicts of the road' – in the modern sporting world of professional cycling, where the elite teams are cosseted in their state-of-the-art team coaches and finest accommodation, their every need taken care of, this shower block is a throwback to another age. I tried to imagine this cheerless place, as dank and quiet as it was that day, full of the noise and excitement at the end of an epic race. What must it be like to be sitting there, covered in the filth that the *pavé* of northern France can kick up in your face, knowing you've given your all. Your bike could be a wreck, tyres shredded, you might have crashed and injured yourself or, worse still, come close to winning the biggest race of your career and failed. What must it feel like? Images of Coppi, Hoban, Merckx, and riders of my own generation – Stuart O'Grady and George Hincapie[18] – flashed through my mind. Shaking my head, I smiled, knowing I was soon going to find out.

A lovely touch the powers that be had added to this totalitarian scene were brass nameplates attached to every changing cubicle – maybe just to encourage the riders of what fortunes awaited them should they win the thing? Downplaying such a feat with so tiny and symbolic a gesture seemed perfectly in keeping with the whole place and, indeed, the ethos of the race as far as I could tell. On the row I looked down towards the showers were some prestigious *vainqueurs*: BOONEN T., RAAS J., and BEVILACQUA A.[19] Then, however, my eyes blinked as I came across two names on the

[18] Yes, both these riders have now admitted taking performance enhancing drugs at certain times in their careers. How much this detracts from the bravery and skill they displayed tackling some of the worst conditions Paris–Roubaix can throw at a rider during the 1990s remains to be seen. You decide.

[19] Boonen's deeds the reader may be aware of. The Dutchman Jan Raas was a legendary rider of the 1970s, who won stages of the Tour de France, and also the Tour of Flanders, Milan–San Remo and the world championship of 1979. The Italian, Antonio Bevilacqua, was a strong time triallist who snatched an incredible win in 1951 from the pre-race favourites Ferdinand Kübler, Louison Bobet and Rik Van Steenbergen.

one plaque: MAHÉ A., and, COPPI S. Next to Mahé's name were
the Latin words '*Ex aequo*'. I was perplexed. What did this mean?
I didn't realize there had been some kind of draw between riders
contesting the greatest race in the calendar. The plaque only stated
those words with the year of its occurrence: 1949.

A few youngsters came into the room and the noise level
increased dramatically with their running around and hollering to
one another. 'Time to go,' I thought, 'and catch that train home.'

For the rest of that afternoon, sitting comfortably on the
Eurostar watching the countryside fly past, all I could think
about were those two names on the one plate, wondering what
had happened.

The Wrong Coppi

I was alone. I would have won alone.

André Mahé, interviewed for
Procycling magazine, 2007

A beautiful illustrated book came out a few years ago, based on the cycling career of Fausto Coppi, one of the true greats of post-war cycling. *Rouleur* magazine commissioned Herbie Sykes to produce some superb imagery detailing every stage of Coppi's spectacular career – a journey that encompassed winning the Giro d'Italia five times, the Tour de France twice, and many, many Classics. He was a complete one-off and his early death in 1960 from malaria is on a par, to some Italian bike aficionados, with the murder of John Lennon to Beatles fans.

The iconic pictures in the book are accompanied by interviews and quotes from Coppi's fellow cyclists, his comrades-in-arms, so to speak. *Coppi: Inside the Legend of the Campionissimo* is a truly brilliant piece of publishing. Herbie has also produced other books on Italian cycling; he's something of an expert on the genre, and I'd read an article he had penned for *Procycling* magazine on the

'Queen of the Classics' a few years previously. For these reasons I wanted to track him down for a chat about this peculiar result at Paris–Roubaix that involved a Coppi. Namely the *Campionissimo*'s younger, less-talented sibling, Serse.

Serse Coppi didn't have a startling career up to his win at Paris–Roubaix. He was your typical *domestique*, carrying out the instructions of his team in order for his designated leader to perform to the best of his ability in any given race. *Domestiques* remind me of worker bees, making sure the queen is kept alive. It is leg-weary work, constantly on the lookout for breaks, attempting to stifle attacks, launching their own team's riders up the road; carrying food and drink from the cars at the back of the peloton to the front, even donating a wheel, or a bike, in order for their main man to carry on to the end. In the baking heat up mountains, barrelling along at breakneck speeds on wintry flat country roads, the rain driving into one's face and freezing arms and legs . . . all this Serse did, but the one thing he had going for him was who he was working for – his legendary, world-class cycling brother, Fausto.

As William Fotheringham described in his biography of Fausto Coppi, *Fallen Angel*, 'Serse had some of the qualities needed by a *campion* – the charisma, the personality, powerful legs – but he didn't have the necessary application.' I am sure this scenario between siblings active in the same workplace has been played countless times. Serse was talented, but nowhere in the same league as his elder brother; while Fausto relied upon him to be riding at his side, otherwise he felt he couldn't ride to win. Fausto may have even felt guilty that his little brother was forever in his shadow. Such are the frailties of the human condition. The younger man put his brother before his own needs, always. But in April 1949, he would have his day in the sun, in a race, ironically, where the sun very rarely shone – Paris–Roubaix.

Three men had made the vital, final breakaway as they streamed

towards Roubaix, including André Mahé. The great Fausto Coppi
was far back with the chasing group and, realizing he wasn't in a
winning move that day, consented to Serse attacking and trying for
the win himself. Mahé was the sole leader by now, having attacked
his own leading group, and was looking likely to solo to victory at
the velodrome when fortune, bad luck, call it what you will, intervened on Serse's behalf.

Coming up towards the entrance to the velodrome, against a
backdrop of frenzied noise and excitement from the crowd, the
press and race motorcycles, the riders, having raced through hellish conditions, were typically mentally shot. All three race leaders
– Mahé and Jacques Moujica of France, and the Belgian Frans
Leenen – were attempting to pump themselves up for the coming
track sprint that would decide the winner. Serse was still some
distance away, chasing frantically, but thinking his chance had
passed.

In the chaos of the chase, the race vehicles were signalled by
the gendarmes to turn right, away from the entrance the racers
would head into and on to the track. The trouble was that the three
leading riders were flying along at 50 k.p.h. right behind the cars
and simply followed them away from the entrance. Pandemonium
ensued as officials, gendarmes and reporters all manically tried to
raise the alarm and bring the riders back.

Knowing that the main peloton would be thundering down on
them at any minute, Moujica turned sharply, fell and snapped one
of his pedals. He was gone. Mahé and Leenen rode around the
wall of the stadium, desperately trying to find a way in. Suddenly,
locating a side entrance, they scrambled through on to the opposite side of the track from where they should have entered, to wild
applause from the waiting, confused spectators, who then watched
Mahé beat Leenen in a sprint to the line. The bunch rode in with
Serse winning the race for third place. A frenetic finish, but Mahé
was a worthy winner, one would assume.

But then fate, politics, or corruption intervened, and we had two men on the winner's plaque.

To find out why I found myself dialling the number of an office in Turin in order to speak to Herbie. A grizzled, Yorkshire voice echoed down the line. I nervously introduced myself and outlined my stated aim of riding the race that coming April, to which Herbie could be heard murmuring his approval: 'I love the atmosphere on race day. There's so much around Roubaix. There's just the magic of Roubaix. It has no equal, really. I used to ride quite a bit in Flanders, but Paris–Roubaix is special. And the Italians have a great affinity for the race, obviously. You mentioned you wanted to ask me about the winner who never was, eh?'

It was good he got straight to the point; it could prove an expensive call otherwise. 'Yes, I went to Lille to research my book on the race itself.'

'God, that's good preparation!' he joked.

'But, obviously, I wanted to check out the legendary shower block as well. It was a "hairs on the back of your neck" moment. When I was there I noticed all the champions have their names on brass plates in the changing cubicles, but there was the one for 1949 where there are two names, André Mahé and Serse Coppi. I wondered whether you could enlighten me? How come Serse got the nod when he only finished third?'

'It's interesting as regards the politics of the whole thing, and the clout that Fausto had, obviously,' said Herbie. 'Because Fausto Coppi was the greatest cyclist in the world, but the whole context in which that race was set was very interesting. It's one more myth to hang around Roubaix, I guess.'

The reply hung in the air some seconds as I digested what he said. 'Well, my main question is, was it mainly politics that got Serse the win, do you think? Was it mainly Fausto saying, "Well, that's it, I'm never coming back unless you give him the win"?'

'Yeah, it was mainly. I think he said he wouldn't ride the Tour de France if Serse wasn't given the win – and he [Fausto] was box office, you know. What had happened is, they had introduced the "Challenge Desgrange–Colombo"[20] the previous year. That was, if you like, a forerunner to the Pro Tour we have today, and so they were all racing for points across the main races of the calendar year: in the spring Milan–San Remo, the Tour of Flanders, Flèche Wallonne, Paris–Roubaix, Paris–Brussels; then in the summer the Giro d'Italia and the Tour de France; followed in the autumn by Paris–Tours and the Tour of Lombardy.

'There was a national competition between the Belgian and the Italian trade teams, and the French weren't in the same class. They all needed points from these races in order to win, to be the best nation. Very nationalistic. Equally, on a lower level, there was the individual competition between riders and the big showdown was between Coppi and Rik Van Steenbergen.[21] The pair were the two biggest draws – the best riders in the world. Fausto decided he wanted to win it and Van Steenbergen decided he wanted to win.

'No foreigner had won in Italy for fifteen years – the French tended to ride in France, the Italians in Italy, and so on. There was very little commercial interest for an Italian bike manufacturer to ride in France, because they didn't generally market the product, and vice versa. The Challenge Desgrange–Colombo in 1948 predicated upon this and so the Italian greats started racing regularly in France to gain points.'

---

[20] The Challenge Desgrange–Colombo was a season-long road race competition invented by the two sports newspapers – *L'Équipe* of France, run by Desgrange, and *La Gazzetta dello Sport* of Italy, overseen by Emilio Colombo. The competition ran from 1948 to 1958 and, like with all the early races, was a great tool to advertise and sell the respective newspapers.
[21] Rik Van Steenbergen (1923–2003) was rated as one of Belgium's greatest cyclists, a three-time world champion, as well as victor in several Classics, including Paris–Roubaix in 1948, where he would also triumph in 1952.

'OK,' I said, 'but how did this affect the result at Paris–Roubaix in 1949? All the riders would have been competing for points. How could they fudge it in such a massive race when so much was at stake?'

'Well, the key to it, I think, is what had happened a few days earlier at La Flèche Wallonne.[22] The Italians had sent a team and Coppi thought he had been robbed of a potential win by the antics of the Belgian press cars who had towed Van Steenbergen back to the lead group he [Coppi] was heading. To cut a very long and complicated story short, Fausto couldn't sprint and Van Steenbergen was by some distance the fastest man on the planet. Van Steenbergen won the sprint and Coppi was left very far from happy.

'The upshot of that was points for Van Steenbergen, which meant points for Belgium, fewer points for Italy – and Fausto was left feeling pretty pissed off about this. You have to understand we're talking about post-war Europe now, so everything was deeply politicized. Attitudes towards the Italians weren't great, they were perceived as perhaps not possessing quite the right moral fibre. Then there was the collateral effect of the war itself – all this led towards what happened at Paris–Roubaix that year. You know what happened?'

I eagerly took up the story: 'I know a three-man break went up the road and then Mahé, the French guy, stole away from them. What I was going to ask was, basically, was Fausto not feeling too great that year? Or did he just say to his brother, "I want you to win and you go up ahead of me"?'

Herbie interjected quickly, 'No, no, no. He would never say that. He would never say he wanted Serse to win, because Serse wasn't capable of winning. It was essentially Van Steenbergen and Coppi

[22] La Flèche Wallonne is a major Belgian race, created by another newspaper *Les Sports* during the inter-war years; the first race ran in 1936.

marking one another. Fausto probably wasn't great that day, and he certainly wasn't that accustomed to riding the *pavé*. I think he'd probably ridden it once or twice before, but the Italians were heavily marked as they had all the best riders – but essentially they kind of marked each other out of the race. I think, actually, Van Steenbergen abandoned ultimately . . . but no, it was unthinkable that Serse Coppi might win Paris–Roubaix. He was Serse – he was a decent *gregario*, no question – but he wasn't a potential winner by any stretch of the imagination. Just the way it played itself out, I guess it became, you know, a kind of a stand-off between the Belgians and the Italians as regards Van Steenbergen and Fausto.

'The three riders got away and seemingly amidst the bedlam they got sent the wrong way. Cars everywhere, and typical chaos. And again, bear in mind this is a few days after what had happened at Flèche Wallonne. A journalist – Albert De Wetter of *L'Équipe* – seemingly found them some kind of a service entrance to the velodrome. The irony of all this was, of course, that they rode further than Serse and his group. Because of the cock-up over missing the turning – in fact they were compelled to ride five hundred metres further than the peloton. Not only did Mahé win the race, but he actually rode further than Serse and his group.'

'Ah, I didn't realize that,' I finally said after taking this all in.

'Yeah, they did, but then it all got bogged down in the UCI rulebook – Article 156 – which stated "the original itinerary must be regularly followed". While Mahé did his lap of honour, the Italians issued an appeal, and the race was given to Serse. Then the French federation overturned the result in Mahé's favour five days later. It was all open to interpretation, but by the same token Article 156 also says "the racers must conform to indications given by the agents of the race and of law enforcement". You've effectively got this one article and the Italians interpreted it in a certain way, ergo they must follow the itinerary, and for Mahé and co, they interpreted it as simply that they were sent off course. But this is where Fausto exercised his own influence.

'He was colossal, a superstar. And he was also a superstar in France, and that was quite interesting because the French had quite a bad relationship with Gino Bartali.[23] Perhaps it was because [Coppi, Bartali's great rival] was from Piedmont, which is very close to the French border, but for some reason the French liked Coppi a great deal. He was extremely popular, riding a lot of track meets in France, whereas Bartali was perceived as a bit snooty and a bit truculent.

'In layman's terms, Fausto put bums on seats and so obviously to the point at which he said, "I ain't riding the Tour de France," and so the Tour had a big problem, and the thing rumbled on, and, ultimately, I guess, the final decision wasn't reached until November at the UCI conference in Zurich. But I suspect that in the meantime Coppi would have been assured that he would have a favourable outcome, because that way they got him at the Tour, and they needed him at the Tour. And, of course, he did the double. That was the year he was the first person to do the Giro and Tour double.'

'And what about Mahé, Herbie? What happened to him?' I asked.

'I think probably Mahé was short-changed, and he remained quite angry about it for many years. He was the rightful winner of that race. Good on him, he won the sprint and all the rest of it, but . . .' Herbie grew silent.

'He didn't win the race?' I answered for him.

'Yes . . . he didn't win the race. In fact, initially, I think they classified him fifth, behind the four other riders. Again, politics

[23] Gino Bartali (1914–2000). Possibly one of my all-time favourite riders. He was Italy's best cyclist either side of the Second World War, winning the Giro three times, and the Tour de France twice, and was a constant thorn in the side of Fausto Coppi in the post-war period.

comes into it. The head of the UCI [Achille Joinard] was up for
re-election that autumn, and he needed the Italian votes, as they
had a bigger sway than the French delegation over other countries
who would also vote. A voting bloc, if you will. He wasn't going
to jeopardize that. And Fausto applied pressure by telling some
journalist, "I want Serse given his victory."' So the Italian stall was
definitely set out. A little while later they made their decision and
fudged it by giving the win to both riders. Mahé and the French
federation saw it as treachery, but they had to swallow it. For years
Mahé was bitter and always claimed he won Paris–Roubaix, fair
and square.'

'It's an incredible tale, full of intrigue, sure enough. Would
you say Paris–Roubaix is the best of the one-day Classics, then,
Herbie?'

'Well, what happened to Serse and Mahé informs the Paris–
Roubaix legend and ultimately that makes it the most dynamic
race in the calendar – it's such a great bike race and in this context,
you never get beyond that, because it is resolutely Paris–Roubaix.
It's never not a great race. You might get lucky and win Lombardy.
You might get a sterile San-Remo, or a dreary Flanders, but Paris–
Roubaix just . . . purely on a sporting level, it just works. Every
single time.'

Eurovision

I think where you've a growth of the sportives, it has to be a good thing, because everything which makes sport grow is a good thing. I think what's all very good about events like the *Étape* and events like sportives that are based around various great races is that you can go and ride those roads. You can go and ride along the roads that the pros ride where the great races take place. It's one of the great, great qualities of cycling. So to be able to do that in an organized way on closed roads in safe conditions, that is a huge thing. You know the link between being able to participate and being able to spectate is one of the great things about this sport.

These were William Fotheringham's final words to me when we chatted. He had also undertaken various sportives in his time, including the Giro d'Italia a few years back. This passion for wanting to go into the unknown, to take on a severe challenge, was something I could understand. But deciding to train and then actually travel over to France for the race was one thing – it was like booking yourself for an appointment at the dentist: it sounds OK in theory until you're actually in the chair and he's siphoning out globules of mucus and blood – actually going and not chickening out! One day to go until setting out on my own for Lille, and I was apprehensive . . .

A friend of mine, Kevin, who worked in television, had recommended an article online that he thought might cheer me up and instil some backbone – he could tell my resolve was faltering. It was on the *Financial Times* website, written by their travel editor – Tom Robbins – who headed the article 'Paris–Roubaix: cycling's toughest one-day race – for the cyclist in pursuit of "glorious suffering", this race is unrivalled'. Complete with short videos of Tom riding various sections of the route during the previous year's race, it also covered his entrance into the hallowed velodrome and featured a poignant interview about how he felt afterwards. He looked totally spent and in some pain as he conveyed just how bad the cobbles had been to ride. One line really struck home: 'Amid the brawl you think of self-preservation, not self-discovery. My hands go numb and I struggle to change gear; electric-shock pains jab at my neck.'

Is this supposed to inspire me!? I thought.

'Why not drop the guy a line, then?' Kevin said. 'Get the word from the horse's mouth and it might show you how much of a monkey you've been making for your back. What harm can it do?'

He was right, of course. Last-minute nerves were natural, but I was becoming convinced I'd crash, wreck the bike, or injure myself to the degree of not completing the course. I found Tom's email address and sent a quick note introducing myself and describing what I was doing. And would he mind a quick chat? With the beauty of cycling fellowship, he replied minutes later, congratulating me on my grand plan, even more that I was doing it completely on my own whereas he had undergone his baptism of fire with an 'experience' holiday company who had looked after him the whole weekend, all on *FT* expenses. 'Let's grab a coffee near my office this afternoon and I'll try to allay any fears.'

Hours later I was sitting in a Pret near Cannon Street station when the familiar bearded figure from the *FT*'s Paris–Roubaix video marched into the café. He had a classic cyclist's frame. I waved recognition as he scanned the busy venue, queued for his drink and came across to the booth I had requisitioned for us to chat in. We quickly got down to business as he had to get back to his office to make a deadline for copy.

'I think we're very similar people when it comes to how we have arrived at the place where we think riding Paris–Roubaix is the next step,' he said. 'I've done a few sportives for about, I don't know, maybe the last six years or something. I was kind of just doing normal cycling, and I then wrote about doing the Marmotte.[24] I actually started writing about cycling when the Tour de France came to the UK in 2007, when it went from London to Canterbury. It was Mark Cavendish's first attempt at the race. For me that was the start, when a lot of people started getting into road biking, so I did a story about doing that stage.'

'But what about Paris–Roubaix?' I asked him. 'How did that come about and why did you think it was a good idea, Tom?' Why is it that veterans of the cobbles always smiled at me when I asked them about riding it, as if I was about to embark upon some "rite of passage" journey?'

'Well, I am the travel editor, Iain!' Tom smirked. 'I work for a paper where travel is, you know, quite a left field, so I am allowed quite a lot of freedom to do what I want. Cycling is booming and a lot of it is amongst our readers, city people like you and me.

---

[24] A popular but tough sportive, named after a squirrel found on Alpe d'Huez.

I'd written a few times about doing mountain adventures and I actually liked doing the Marmotte race. The trouble was, I also completed and then wrote about the *Étape*, but those kinds of things are very similar, and I was finding I could easily write the same story over and over again. Whereas with Paris–Roubaix there is so much more to it. There's so much history to it. In a way it kind of writes itself, and it's not just about you sweating up a mountain.'

'But you looked remarkably fresh in the film, and I was thinking, "God Almighty! Look at him, he looks fine." When I finished the *Étape* last summer I was wrecked, and I trained really hard for it. It was the heat more than anything else that got me, but I was done in by the time I'd finished it.'

He leaned back in his chair as he drank a mouthful of coffee. 'Well, I mean, I did do a lot of cycling last year to prep for it. But I've done none this year at all, as my wife and I had a baby in September.'

'But how did you find it? Honestly.' I sounded desperate now.

'I won't lie to you, it's pretty unpleasant. The thing is, with mountain sportives, I would definitely do more of them in the future – whether that be *Étape*s or cycling the Dolomites – but I don't think I'll do another Paris–Roubaix.' He said it like he was confiding a deeply held secret.

'Oh, really?'

'Yes, because, it's not like the sort of pain – as in endurance pain, as in can I do it?, a mental test – it's actually like immediate, physical pain. Can I keep holding on to the handlebars for another second, because it's . . .'

'Going right up your arm . . .?' I completed his sentence, practically hanging on to the end of my chair.

'Yeah, that's right. And it's mainly just all about the cobbles – although I was surprised how short the sections are, you know. Most of them are short. I think the longest one is three kilometres, so you're actually not on them for very long. You're on them for a couple of minutes at the most, but the group riding is just terrifying. Everyone's moving around and, for example, one guy in our group got knocked off by someone else on the Arenberg and went into the barrier, and that was the end of it. He had to go to hospital, but he was OK. So, it's terrifying being around those other people, and I didn't realize that some of the sectors are not flat, they're undulating through the fields, and when we all started going downhill, I was like, "What the fuck?!" You can't, for a second, move your hand to the brakes and if you're on the tops when you go into it you'll be in trouble. I just hadn't really thought about that before, so be mindful of that.'

I tried to be detached in my analysis, after Tom had portrayed this vision of hell. 'So, you basically get, say, three to four minutes of cobbles, and then you probably have what, a ten- to twelve-kilometre stretch of road?'

Tom waved to interrupt me. 'That varies quite a lot, actually. I think there's a break for a while. Basically, it's impossible to get a rhythm and it's impossible to get in a group with people. It seemed like one minute a lot of riders would be around me, and then no one, and I found myself on my own a lot, going through many sectors on my own – and the wind is crazy, hitting you from different angles depending on where you are on the course.

'You will definitely see a big difference when you're going along the cobbles, and they say, "Stick to the crown where it's less rutted," and on the wheels. You see you're doing that religiously and then sometimes there will be a section that's more than the size of this table, three or four feet apart, that's just disappeared. It's like a pothole. If you went over it, there's no way you could ride it. You couldn't bunny hop it, there's no way. So if you're on your own you can slow down and swerve, or whatever, but if you're in a pack, it's just like, "What the fuck?!" But the whole technique of riding is quite interesting: you've got to keep the power on, and you've got to not grip the bars hard, you've got to let your legs do the work, and the steering, too.'

'Is that how you did it?' I interjected. 'Or did your bike handling evolve on the day?'

'Well, the group I was with had been talking about it the evening before the race, and it kind of de-evolved actually. The first section I was totally up for taking on, but the problem was I was going way too fast. Then I would control my pace in a group, but then the more tired I became the harder it was to do that, and I found myself wanting to just grip as hard as possible, but as a result of that you take it more in your arms, and that's when I suffered real pain, a sort of RSI jabbing pain in the wrists. By the final third, I'd started to go on to the verges and on the grass instead of the cobbles, which obviously is slower and you are in danger of hitting loads of crap – I was even more worried about punctures. In retrospect I wasn't putting enough power down through my legs to take the pressure off my shoulders. The faster you go the less vibration you feel and the quicker it's all over anyway. It is the accumulative suffering that gets you.

'But the other thing is like – if you've watched *A Sunday in Hell* you'll have seen it so many times in films – the traffic. Most of the time on the course it's fine, you're in these non-residential places, but then towards the end you come into Roubaix and, of course, it's Saturday lunchtime and everyone is shopping. It is totally mental! You're really mentally drained and physically ragged by then, and on the nice tarmac, finally, you want to race but there are all these cars and traffic lights – you're back in civilization, basically. It is a very weird sensation.

'And the scenery.' He smiled as he relived it. 'You would *never* go to seek out that kind of scenery for a bike ride. It's completely grey, industrial, with closed-down coal mines, pitheads, machinery. It's really quite depressing, and a lot of the villages seem shut up. But, at the same time, all the Belgian fans are coming, setting up their motor-homes and flags alongside the route for the professional race the next day. They're all getting drunk already and you realize that for them it's the mainstream working-class sport – in a way that everywhere else it isn't. I mean in Britain it is now a more middle- and upper-class niche sport, whereas in Roubaix it was everything to them. Over a million fans turn up along the roads to watch the Tour of Flanders. That all those people are there in this grim area, to stand on the mud and the grassy bank, tells you something about cycling over there, I think. It is a real passion.'

'Would you do it again?' I asked him, just to double-check.

'I wouldn't, no,' he replied adamantly. 'It is actually painful. A lot of cycling is about internal pain and managing it, whereas this feels like it's you against something else rather than you against yourself. It's something you have no real control over.'

Tom's matter-of-fact honesty didn't faze me. On the contrary the chat had re-energized my enthusiasm, to a degree. The journey back home had me concluding several salient points. Tom was very much in my mould as a cyclist, in that we liked the physical nature of endurance cycling. We equally did the same kind of training regime, and we fitted this around busy family life. I knew I was fit enough to handle a one-hundred-mile-plus race, and the terrain was pretty flat. It was just the cobbles that had been boring into my consciousness, every single, waking day. Like a difficult maths test at school – you know you can do it, and you have done your revision. I was completely up for it, but it was possibly a case of the legend overtaking common sense.

Tom's experience, and his candour in telling me how hard it would be, without dressing it up and bullshitting me, crystallized the whole thing. What was the worst that could happen? It might be 58 kilometres of cobbles but, on the plus side, it was also over 120 kilometres of tarmac! 'Focus on the positive and deal with the barriers,' I told myself. As Chris Sidwells reiterated, 'It's twenty-eight interval-training sessions, with boulders thrown in for good measure.'

*

No more talking now; it was time to catch a Eurostar. I tiptoed out of the house at 6 a.m., having kissed Jo and then looked in on the kids, taking care not to disturb them. (As every parent of a young brood will tell you, "DON'T DO IT!!! That will be them both up and about straight away.") Manhandling the Gore-Tex bike bag that was protecting my trusty steed, I managed to get out of the door as the darkness of the street was giving way to the dawn's early rays. The benign weather cheered me up and I wished it would hold for a further forty-eight hours across the Channel.

On the concourse waiting to get through the security checks at St Pancras station, it was immediately apparent that an invasion of MAMILs was occurring. A variety of forty-something, very athletic men, with rucksacks or holdalls, milled around, looking anxious but also excited about the trip we were about to undertake. All were strangers, but eager to acknowledge one another with a nod and a smile.

After I found my carriage, I couldn't help but smile at the sight of a fellow rider scratching his head, wondering how he was going to store his shiny penny-farthing onboard the train.

'Going far?' I jokingly asked. 'You're not doing Paris–Roubaix on that thing, are you?'

The giant front wheel had a modern, aerodynamic carbon disc inserted into it, and in the yellow pantone of the Tour de France organization it proclaimed that the Tour would be hitting Yorkshire on the 5 July. The rider, about 40 years of age, and just under six foot – judging by how he measured against the giant bike seat of the contraption he was leaning against – was accompanied by a photographer who was helping him load his belongings. He smiled at my question, in that way of being proud of the task he'd been set and happy to talk to anyone about it. Introducing himself as Jeff Summerfield (where had I heard that name before?) he proceeded to tell me his biking history, which sort of dwarfed my own *palmarès* by some way.

'Yeah, I'm tackling Tour of Flanders, Paris–Roubaix and Liège–Bastogne–Liège,' he said. 'I've covered the world on one of these.' He had been an engineer for a Formula One race team and now made ancient bikes for a living. 'Paris–Roubaix is one of the biggest Classics there is, and obviously Wiggins is riding it, so it makes sense to try to get maximum exposure.'

'You're riding the *pavé* on it?' I asked incredulously.

He laughed and, patting the front wheel, replied, 'Yes, we're covering the shorter circuit of seventy kilometres, but we'll still have to get over several sections of cobbles, including Carrefour de l'Arbre. After I have finished with these three Classics, I'll go to Belfast to see how fast one of these can cover the Giro d'Italia time-trial route, then after that we're riding against the clock at a race in Berlin.'

I was amazed, perhaps too visibly. 'Are you kidding, on this?' But I recovered my dumbstruck look to wish him well and hoped to see him at the finish. The encounter had really inspired me. 'If he can do that,' I thought to myself, 'what am I worried about?!'

But I was still worried, and all throughout the train journey, through the tunnel and on to Lille, I simply stared out of the window, alone with my thoughts, going over what Tom had said the day before. I really hoped I would do myself justice, and that the bike would hold together. What would the weather be like? Part of me wanted the worst conditions, just to say I'd ridden it like my heroes of the past. In reality I wanted sunshine and tarmac.

The hotel was easy to find as it had been recommended by Kevin, who had ridden the shorter circuit the year before. A little like a Premier Inn but, judging by the decor, dating from the 1980s, it was situated just a few miles from the Roubaix velodrome. It was the perfect base. Checking into my room, I lovingly parked the bike by the armchair next to the bedroom window, and unloaded all my gear, taking care to prepare everything I would need for the early rise the next morning, at 4 a.m. The floor by the bed resembled a crime scene as a lycra body, complete with overshoes, gloves and helmet, was ceremoniously laid out on the carpet, ready to be quickly attached to my skinny body once I staggered out of a deep sleep. I really didn't want to forget anything vital. How stupid would it be to forget my bike pump?

The dinner in the restaurant was a quiet affair as groups of riders again eyed one another across the large dining room, efficiently tucking into copious plates of pasta, chicken, salad and plenty of pudding. But no alcohol. Well, at least I didn't have any. I wanted to get back to the room and chill out. As is usual when nerves get the better of me, I couldn't get to sleep quickly and spent the hours until midnight watching very bad French and German programmes until the butterflies finally surrendered to nervous exhaustion. Not the best preparation I've had, but I remember dreaming about penny farthings!

The Best of British

While I had my meeting with the Hell of the North the next day, there was, of course, also the small matter of the professional edition of the race on the Sunday, and I would have been lying if I said I didn't want Sir Bradley Wiggins to triumph. Born in Ghent in 1980 where his pro-racing father, Gary Wiggins, earned a crust on the many tracks of Europe in the late 1970s and early 1980s, he had surprised many people by publicly stating his desire to try to win Paris–Roubaix.

Over the past two decades, there have not been too many winners of the Tour de France who've believed their best interests of preparation for the main event in July lay in a buffeting over miles of potentially deadly cobbles. Granted, from the post-war era, the likes of Coppi, Bartali, Jacques Anquetil, Merckx, Hinault and LeMond have all taken their chances on the *pavé*. And where some just wanted to test themselves, a fair few of them actually won the race. But in the modern era, Lance Armstrong would never risk his health for the sake of one day of glory, when he was certain to gain three weeks of it come the *Grand Départ*. Which is why Wiggo stood out for me. He not only wanted to try his luck, but he relished the challenge and portrayed it almost as a 'duty' to attempt the seemingly impossible feat of winning Paris–Roubaix. Which is why we all love him, I suppose.

Was Bradley the sole Briton we could peg our hopes on for a first historic victory in the racing calendar's toughest event? The more digging I had done, the more I wanted to celebrate those pro racers from Britain who had ridden *La Pascale*, not just once, but numerous times. All had the aim of seriously trying to go for the win, such was their skill and their form, suited to the conditions. So I wanted first-hand accounts of the thrills and spills of riding Paris–Roubaix at the top level.

I decided to concentrate on three riders who spanned my lifetime: from the 1960s and 1970s, Barry Hoban; from the 1980s through to the 1990s, Sean Yates; and, finally, a rider who was of my own generation and one who I had followed avidly throughout his career, especially when riding this race – Roger Hammond. One rider was simply a name and a grainy image from the past, the second was my boyhood hero when I discovered cycling as a sport, and the final entrant was a guy I envied for his talent and the many victories I'd read about in *Cycling Weekly* – then there was also the day Hammond almost pulled off the shock win at Paris–Roubaix.

Chris Sidwells had been good for light-hearted banter about the life of a cyclist back in the day. As mentioned, he was a nephew of the legendary racer Tom Simpson, who had met his fateful end climbing Mont Ventoux during the blisteringly hot summer of 1967, and a childhood fan of another great British rider, Barry Hoban.

Born in Wakefield in 1940, Barry was a contemporary of Simpson's, having raced against him as an amateur in the 1950s, who then turned professional in 1964 and spent the next sixteen years racing and living in Europe. He would be with Simpson when he died in the 1967 Tour de France, and would marry his widow, Helen, two years later. He raced mainly for the Mercier–Hutchinson–BP team and was one of the key support riders for the more famous and talented Frenchman Raymond

Poulidor – the modern terminology for Barry's role in the team nowadays would be '*super domestique*'.

Saying that, Hoban was a great sprinter, and not until the arrival of Mark Cavendish at the Tour was Barry's record of most stages won by a British rider (eight between 1965 and 1978, including two stages in a row in 1973) surpassed. This was a guy who could hold his own with the greats, even when in direct competition with the one rider who almost dominated the race calendar during Hoban's heyday – Eddy Merckx. Indeed, once I managed to contact Barry, it was this name that came up more often than not when discussing his memories of Paris–Roubaix.

I called Barry just a few days before he was heading across to Belgium again to attend the start of the major one-day race he won in 1974, Ghent–Wevelgem. The locals still fêted him as a hero, as one of their own, because he'd lived amongst them for so many years. I could sense the excitement he felt about the trip as we chatted, and I asked him if he was envious of how big these events had become.

'It is like going home,' he explained eagerly. 'You see, when you ride these races – even forty years ago – it was exciting. But it's changed enormously, as all sports have changed over the years. The commercialization of things – with hospitality here, hospitality there – and the French and Belgians look after me as only they know how.'

I hadn't realized until I studied his career that he had lived on the Continent for over two decades. It wasn't like today, with riders travelling around the world from a home base – possibly somewhere exotic like Monte Carlo, in the cases of Chris Froome and Geraint Thomas.

'Oh, yeah, well,' said Barry. 'I mean, as a young sprog I left Britain when I was just twenty-two to go to northern France. Helen lived there longer. She was living in Belgium then, with Tom, but I was in northern France for four years before moving to Belgium.

So, we are almost what the locals of my old town [Eeklo in East Flanders] call "*Eekloms*".'

'But what are your general thoughts on Paris–Roubaix both as a rider and, nowadays, as a fan, Barry?' I asked.

'Well, Paris–Roubaix is the greatest race. If you were Belgian you would think Tour of Flanders was, I suppose, and want a Belgian rider to win it, too. But, on the whole, internationally, Paris–Roubaix is the ultimate race. Why? Because there are races where you get an opportunist winner. With Paris–Roubaix you can't. You do not get opportunist winners. It's like the cream comes to the surface in Paris–Roubaix . . . it is a war of attrition. It's the greatest of the one-day races to win. Even Jacques Anquetil, who in this day and age would be like a Chris Froome (who would never attempt to ride it), rode it because he said to himself, "Well, I'm going to ride the greatest of the great races." The same applied to Bernard Hinault. He was as hard as nails and a great rider, but, I mean, if you can win five tours you don't have to ride Paris–Roubaix, do you? But he did, and he won it.'

'Well,' I replied, 'that gets me to my second question, which you've kind of answered: do you feel it's the toughest one-day race in the pro calendar?'

It went quiet down the line as he mulled over the hundreds of memories he must have of tackling each of the Monuments, the Grand Tours, and all else in between. Eventually, he answered, categorically, 'It is the toughest race they have. My first professional *directeur sportif*, Anthony Mann, who had been a great rider himself in the 1930s, would say, "In Paris–Roubaix, only the weak riders puncture." And I used to think, "What the hell does he mean?" It was almost like, "You do not puncture on the cobbles." But that's providing you've got the right pressure in your tyres! If you've got the right pressure, which is not as high as you'd have on a beautiful tarmac road, and you have a bit of section tyre . . . [you should be OK]. When I was racing we had special tubulars for Paris–Roubaix, which were twenty-eight millimetres. When you're talking about riding normally on tarmacked roads, then a twenty-three-millimetre thickness of tyre is fine. For Paris–Roubaix a twenty-eight-millimetre tyre is what you require due to the very rough terrain you'll be traversing.'

'I've got twenty-fives,' I stammered, 'but I'm thinking of getting bigger ones.'

'Twenty-five's not big enough for you. What's your build?'

Quickly calculating, I answered, 'I am six feet one inch and I've put weight on to bulk up, and am now almost thirteen stone.' I tried to sound impressive, as if weight had anything to do with little old me actually managing to finish, let alone compete in a race like this.

Barry's answer seemed unequivocal. 'Twenty-eight, Iain. Definitely, you'll need a twenty-eight tyre. You don't want much of a tread on them either. A slick [smoother] tyre could be all right. You know, it's not the tread or anything like that. It's the amount of air in them that counts. Too much and you'll suffer a compression puncture when hitting the cobbles, with the rim pinching the inner tube. For a professional racer that is one of their key concerns: what pressure for the tyres. [This is the] ultimate race for endurance of body, endurance of mind and endurance of machine, especially.'

Valuable advice from the master, and who was I to argue with a man who had seen off both Eddy Merckx and Roger De Vlaeminck to win Ghent–Wevelgem. But, it was the personal history of what life would have been like as a neo-pro in the sixties that really intrigued me.

'Well, you've got to realize that I went over to northern France,' Barry recalled. 'I was living not a million miles away from Roubaix itself and I was riding races which had sections of cobbles, too. I was just a rider who had an aptitude towards the *pavé*. I knew how to ride it. And they also had an amateur event – not the amateur

Paris–Roubaix they have now, but a race called Circuit Franco–
Belge, which traversed around Roubaix, utilizing sections of *pavé*,
so ultimately it held no fear for me.

'I started in thirteen Paris–Roubaix's but I only finished nine,
because you have mishaps – whether mechanical or fitness. You
never went into the Arenberg forest with the team cars in front of
you: there was a feed station just in Valenciennes, before Arenberg,
and if the team cars had gone by already and you were on an off
day, then you'd say, "See you, boys," and climb off. You would see
the *soigneurs* with the *musette* bags at the feed station, stop, and
put the bike on the roof. So, I finished it nine times, but I rode it
many occasions without getting a puncture.

'The first year I rode, in 1964, is still the fastest race time
today. It was just short of twenty-nine miles per hour, or forty-six
kilometres per hour. Peter Post won it, and I was in the break with
him.[25] I fell with twenty kilometres to go and suffered a damaged
nerve in my back. I really went down with a bang. I finished, but I
limped into the finish. Post won the race and recorded the quickest
time, no one's beaten it yet.'

'That leads on to another question,' I said. 'What would you say
is your best ride?'

'Seventy-two was when I finished third. I punctured in the
Arenberg forest and, of course, the teams weren't organized
around any individual in those days and the team cars were miles

---

[25] As mentioned earlier, the fastest ever recorded time by a winner of Paris–Roubaix is by
the Dutch rider Peter Post who, in 1964, completed the 265-kilometre run at an average
speed of 45.131 k.p.h. A fast pace from the start meant a decisive break occurred early, with
Post in it, leaving the favourites such as Rik Van Looy, Raymond Poulidor and Rudi Altig
back in the chasing peloton. Five riders entered the Roubaix velodrome with Post winning
the sprint. The course back then had far fewer cobbled sections and more tarmac, plus the
mild weather ensured a fast circuit. Post was also awarded the *ruban jaune* for the highest
speed in any Classic. He would go on to become the director of several major cycling teams,
and died in 2011.

behind and I lost over two minutes before a teammate eventually gave me a wheel – and then you're talking about chasing down the likes of Merckx, [Felice] Gimondi, [Frans] Verbeeck and De Vlaeminck – the greats. Two minutes fifteen and I closed the gap and got back to them. I had taken risks doing this and so my back wheel, which had previously punctured, was all over the place, and I was desperately looking behind for the team car to come and help me. It eventually arrived, so I had to jam to a halt and get another wheel, and that was the point when De Vlaeminck attacked.

'When I managed to close the gap again, De Vlaeminck was up the road and [André] Dierickx (who finished second) was just leaving. I couldn't follow as I had to get a breather. But by the time I'd recovered I attacked at Hem, with about eight kilometres to go. And I got clear and I know, I know that if I'd not punctured and if I'd been in that bunch when De Vlaeminck went I would have gone with him. And Roger would never have beaten me in a sprint!'

He said this with a touch of pride, as though reliving the moment. It made the hairs on the back of my neck rise. 'You've mentioned some big names to me, Barry. Who did you respect most at Paris–Roubaix? Was it Eddy Merckx?'

'Merckx was the ultimate. Merckx was the best because he had a voracious appetite for winning. I mean, in 1967 I'd been in the break in the Tour of Flanders from the first ten kilometres, and there were seventeen of us up the road from the peloton. Over all the hills, we were slowly whittled down, with me the first rider over every climb. By the time we got over the last hill there was only twenty kilometres and we were down to three riders, who I could have beaten with one leg! With about fifteen kilometres to go there was a claxon and noise coming from behind. I looked back and there was Merckx, like some demented demon, closing fast.'

I was on the edge of my seat listening to this cycling tale, but Hoban made me feel as if I were there in the break with him. 'Why was Merckx chasing you down?'

'He was young, of course, riding like he had gone berserk, but the idiot had got two Italian riders from the same team on his wheel too!'

'Oh no!'

'And he brought Felice Gimondi and Dino Zandegù with him, and once they had caught us they had a little bit of a breather and then, with ten kilometres to go, they started doing the "one-two" sequence of attacking. Gimondi would attack, Merckx and I would chase; then Zandegù would do the same and we would chase him down again, with Gimondi hitching a lift on the back. In the end Merckx couldn't collar all of them and Zandegù went away to win and I finished fifth behind Merckx, who was third.'

I was hoping that when I talked to giants of the road like Barry, I could glean some valuable 'must have' information, or tips on riding. My initial inclination had been, 'Don't be daft, how can you ask that question of an ex-professional? They are completely different criteria to an amateur donkey like me.' But the way our conversation was relaxed, simply talking about the race we both loved, it seemed natural to ask, 'How would you ride the *pavé*?'

'Well, I'll tell you what: it's simple, really. You ride the *pavé* like you're climbing a hill. You sit back on your saddle, grip the centre of your bars and you ride the centre point of the cobbles – the crown. Now the only way you go over cobbles good is to ride a bigger gear, so you go faster, which uses energy unfortunately. On the crown of the cobbles, if you've got the right pressure for the tyres, you will not puncture. In Paris–Roubaix they slit the wall, because the ride in the gutter and the edges of the cobble slit the walls of your tyre. Watch out for that, Iain.'

'What about the Arenberg then, Barry?' I asked.

There was silence down the line for a few seconds, which felt like at least a minute, before Barry spoke again: 'The Arenberg is a long straight centre. Actually, it was a friend of mine, Jean Stablinski, who discovered that, because he used to work in the mine, which is

Above: One man and his penny-farthing. Jeff Summerfield at St Pancras station with the ancient contraption that he would ride over the cobbles.

Below: On the night bus from Roubaix. I couldn't fault the logistical operation of ferrying hundreds of cyclists and their bikes more than one hundred kilometres south to the start line at Busigny.

Right: And they're off! Setting out into the dawn mist and a cycle back in time through the bleak northern French countryside, and its memories of war. What perils would lie ahead?

Below left: 'Hell' was the answer, of course. I came a cropper on the very first section of *pavé*, at Troisville, but when we hit the dreaded Arenberg, I managed to ride across at speed and not get a puncture. Relief is hardly etched on the other riders' faces (**below right**).

I was too tired to sprint
to the line, but managed
to raise one hand in
triumph.

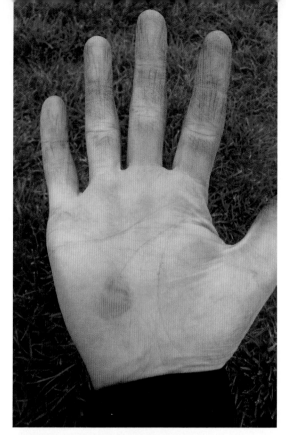

Evidence of the hard day's riding on my hands (**left**) and bike (**below**), although I did manage a manly show of bravado. You are told not to grip the handlebars too tightly, but I defy anyone not to cling on for dear life when you tackle cobbles, at speed, for the first time.

Iconic photographs such as this are one of the reasons why Paris–Roubaix has achieved its legendary status among cycling fans.

Right: The great Sir Bradley Wiggins expertly negotiates a treacherous corner in the pro event the day after mine.

Middle: Crashes are, of course, inevitable – and often brutal.

Bottom: Team Sky's Geraint Thomas hot on the heels of four-time winner Tom Boonen. It's non-stop action in this race.

Above: Cheering on Wiggins and co (**above**) at the velodrome was an amazing experience for me and my fellow amateurs.

Below: Unfortunately it wasn't to be in 2014, with Wiggo finishing ninth and Thomas (**centre**) seventh, but they and Luke Rowe (**left**) look suitably knackered!

on your left just before you reach the Arenberg forest. He worked there as a fourteen-year-old boy and there's now a monument to him just at the entrance. The Arenberg forest is actually a private road. It's not a normal thoroughfare. Even though there are walks you can do, it's actually privately owned and Jean was off hunting, as the French do in the forest, and he saw this cobbled road and he said, "Wow, this could be for Paris–Roubaix." He returned home and telephoned the race's director Jean-Marie Leblanc and said, "Hey, Jean-Marie, *j'ai trouvé la route* [I have found the route] Paris–Roubaix." And that was it.'

'But do you think the race is potentially dangerous for amateurs like me? Or is it just chance that people crash?'

I was instantly put in my place by his firm response: 'It's your own responsibility. Listen, it's not dangerous at all. I mean, if you ride on your own through there at ten miles an hour you're definitely going to hit every cobble. Other tips I'd give you are, tape your wrists to keep the shock from the cobbles to a minimum. Also track mitts are fine, and don't grip the bars tight, give yourself some freedom and go with the vibration, otherwise you'll be giving your wrists, arms and neck one hell of a hammering! And, as I say, more often than not you ride as though you are climbing a hill.'

And with that the conversation naturally came to an end, as Barry wished me well and I said I hoped he'd have a good time in Ghent. Somehow, I thought he most definitely would – he'd earned it.

I have to admit I was nervous about talking to the next British legend of the *pavé* – Sean Yates. As a teenager I had been gripped by the Tour de France in the early 1980s – shown as it was then, on *World of Sport*, and later when it first appeared regularly on Channel 4, fronted by the ubiquitous Phil Liggett. Before I got in touch with Yates, I talked to cycling journalist William Fotheringham, who had worked with me years before on one of his books, and was kind enough to go over his Paris–Roubaix memories, with particular reference to the three men I wanted to track down. Who was his favourite British rider?

'Probably Sean Yates, it would have to be Yates, I think, because he was pretty consistent in the early nineties and then, in 1994, he did very well in that really hard one. Ninety-four was far and away the best Paris–Roubaix I'd ever seen. Just the most amazing racing. This is the one where they came out of the start and it started snowing. It had rained the week beforehand, but they came out of the start and the snow started falling and you just thought, "My God, this is going to be the best race ever." Anyway, it was just fantastic. There was a moment when all the TV motorbikes crashed, so there were no TV motorbikes for quite a way. All you got were helicopter images, and you had Johan Museeuw and Andrei Tchmil ten, fifteen, twenty metres apart in a key stage of the race. A hundred kilometres from the finish it was all happening. Just the pursuit match between those two guys on a stretch of cobbles, and the images of the guys absolutely covered in mud were amazing. It was back in the days before helmets. So, it was just that little more romantic: the images of the finish, where Yates had no helmet, nothing visible apart from the mud and his eyes, just pronounced. Yeah, Sean at the top by a short hair from Roger Hammond, really.'

'I have been talking to Barry Hoban, too, about his Paris–Roubaix experiences. Do you think there's any difference between Hoban and Sean Yates? Or is one's better placing only because of luck on the day?'

'Well, no, I don't think so. Sean was consistently targeting the race year after year. I think it's also quite hard to compare the two eras, because Sean probably got better support from his team than Barry did. I think it was probably more a case that Barry turned up and did Paris–Roubaix because that was what they did, year in year out. It went well for him in 1972, whereas Sean, it was becoming a little bit more specific and a little bit more targeted when he did it. So that would be the difference, I think. Probably a bit more random with Barry, and a bit more specific with Sean.'

I was still keen to know more about whether luck plays a significant part in winning, competing and even finishing the race. With the excitement of Wiggins riding Paris–Roubaix, how did William feel his chances measured against the previous British riders I was focusing on?

He was crystal clear in his analysis of what it takes to win: 'It's not a lottery. It's a race where you make your own luck. It suits two types of riders who will do well. The first are the guys who ride cyclo-cross, so the likes of Roger De Vlaeminck, or our own Roger Hammond – they are the riders who can really handle their bikes well, jump about in the wet; and a lot of the Belgians and Dutch come into that category as they cyclo-cross when they are young.

'It also favours the big sort of brutes who may not be quite as good at jumping about on the cobbles, you know, dodging potholes, but they do have pure horsepower. That's Fabian Cancellara, Sean Yates . . . and that's where Brad comes in – and I've discussed it with Brad – and his view is, it's basically a time trial, because when you're on the cobbles you can't ride on the wheel. You're riding between two and four legs off the wheel, depending on the conditions, in order to see where you're going. It favours the rider who can basically produce the horsepower. If you're a rider who can produce the power output and you have the cyclo-cross element in your arsenal . . . well, I think Roger De Vlaeminck would be the absolute case in point there – Eddy Merckx too, and Bernard Hinault obviously rode cross as well. [Whereas] Francesco Moser [who won Paris–Roubaix three times] is a horsepower rider, so Moser comes into that sort of Cancellara/Wiggins/Yates bracket. But I really don't believe the cycling is a lottery: the strongest guys will be at the front and they will be the ones who'll avoid the crashes and punctures, by and large, and the better bike handlers will be at the front and they will avoid the crashes and punctures too, so I don't view it as a lottery. The element of luck comes in if you are already good and you are at the front and some guy falls off in front of you – well, that's chance, but it's not that much of a lottery as it's made out to be.'

It was time to call Yates himself. As well as his riding style and general toughness on terrain like Paris–Roubaix, his demeanour on the bike, as well as off it – nothing flash, just a dedication to leaving every ounce of energy on the road as he either strove to deliver his team leader to victory, or set the fastest time trial – always struck a chord with me, as well as thousands of other bike fans. He was an honest and clinical athlete. Anyone who can intimidate Lance Armstrong has to be taken seriously. He was a *super domestique* par excellence. His career took in twelve Tour de France editions (he completed nine of them), as well as a dozen attempts at the Queen of the Classics. His best result was fifth place in that infamous winter edition of 1994.

As a simple bike fan, I was just thrilled to be talking to him. It was fortunate that he not only trained on the same Kent and Sussex hills as me, but was also now *directeur sportif* of my local Catford CC Equipe–Banks under-23 team, which included his own son Liam on its roster. I regularly noticed these guys out on training rides of a Saturday morning, and knowing Paris–Roubaix was the one race he consistently targeted, I was keen to know his view of it.

'Well, I think, obviously it's got its own particular niche, being over cobbles and there's no other race that has that same amount of cobbles. You know, I think we celebrate the Tour of Flanders but, to me, Paris–Roubaix is possibly the toughest and the hardest and the most spectacular race. It is the one that really connects with the fans the most, so obviously it is up there with the biggest of the Classics. Paris–Roubaix has obviously been going for a long time, and it's a very social event, with the commencement of the Classic season. For the riders who target the Classics – from Milan–San Remo through to the Tour of Flanders – this period is, in a way, the culmination of their racing year. They will obviously ride other stuff through the year, but, really, guys like Tom Boonen, it's pretty much based around this two-week period.

'As an individual rider, you know it's flat, free from the hills one tackles in the races in and around the Ardennes, and you need to be very skilful to ride the cobbles well. Obviously, positioning and such like and technique are vital in this event, as they are in the flat in the Tour of Flanders.'

What Yates was saying mirrored exactly the advice Barry Hoban had given me, but, again, it was the personal stories I was after.

'How hard is it to ride on *pavé*, Sean? Is there a specific skill, or is it just a case of having to be on your mettle on the day, you've just got to watch out for things?'

'Well, I think, obviously the first time I rode the cobbles in 1983, I thought, "Bloody hell, what's this all about?" And, obviously, you need to be a certain character to ride in that shit weather all day. It was shit weather in our day, definitely. I think it's more of an attitude and clearly a certain body type that rides those kind of races. You certainly need to have the right equipment. The bigger tyres, the twenty-eight-millimetre tyres, the low pressure. Not many atmospheres, five atmospheres or so. My best performances were pretty much all done with Rockshox,[26] which obviously absorb the impact. You can't really feel the cobbles much compared to if you rode it with twenty-three-millimetre tyres and seven, eight bars,

[26] Rockshox first came to prominence in the peloton at Paris–Roubaix in 1992 when veteran French rider Gilbert Duclos-Lassalle finally triumphed at *La Pascale* using this innovative suspension system over the cobbles. The following year he won again on the same suspension, becoming the oldest winner of the race at 38 years of age. Duclos-Lassalle was denied a third straight victory in the infamous 1994 edition when atrocious weather conditions reduced the race to a test of survival. The race was won by the iron man of the Ukraine, Andrei Tchmil, who was also using Rockshox.

and then Rockshox. The downside of having no pressure is you're prone to impact punctures, which means you have to really choose your line carefully.'

My choice of tyres seemed to be now confirmed. 'I was going to ask you about that, actually, as Barry Hoban was saying something similar, as that's the conundrum I've been having on tyre selection. I was going to use twenty-fives, but then I thought, "Well the pros would probably use twenty-eights, because they're going at a much faster speed than I'm going to be." Would you agree with that, or is it a safer bet to have twenty-eights? You might as well just "bomb-proof" them?'

'Definitely have twenty-eights, Iain. I mean, pretty much everybody's using twenty-fives now, and previously one thought that the narrower the section the better it was, in that the rolling resistance was lower, but in fact there is little or no difference between the rolling resistance of a fat tyre and a skinny tyre, and with the advent of deep dish wheels, damaging an actual wheel is much more frequent. Give me a strong tyre – when a wheel has hit the ground you can't just rebuild a deep dish wheel. You wouldn't chuck away a thousand-dollar wheel every two seconds, would you? Definitely, the fatter the tyres, the better, in my opinion – and that, in turn, enables you to have a lower psi, which helps you to ride the cobbles better.'

'I was also going to ask, if you were riding the spring Classics, was there a specific type of training that you did? Or were you doing your normal training and would simply just rock up to a race like this?'

'Well, as I said, guys who ride the Classics were following a programme from the start of the racing calendar, and built up fitness as a result. The first Classic is Milan–San Remo, but already before Paris–Roubaix you would have ridden Omloop Het Volk and Ghent–Wevelgem, which'd give you a taster, and then you'd go into E3 Harelbeke and then the Tour of Flanders. All the time you'd be building fitness and getting accustomed to riding the cobbles before Paris–Roubaix itself.'

Having talked to several people within the biking fraternity, I was getting mixed signals as to how the amateur events, or 'mass participation races', were viewed. Some riders and pundits endorsed them, to a degree; others dismissed them entirely as a joke, which shocked me. A man steeped in pro racing like Sean, who had gone on to stellar success as a *directeur sportif* with Team Sky, would, I was sure, fall into the latter camp, but what he said both shocked and encouraged me.

'Certainly I think it's good having it. It's a free world to that extent, and I think people should be able to do what they want unless they're hurting someone. I'm all for it. Millions of people watch it, both on TV and out on the course. To get an experience of what the pro guys are doing and how they prepare themselves – and ride fast, or slow, or whatever – it's a fantastic opportunity for every individual.' He let out a laugh. 'It's not something I would do myself for the hell of it, but I think it's a great opportunity to have fun. Obviously the *Étape* was very well organized, as are most sportives, so it's all in a controlled and safe environment.'

(Good on you! Finally, bona fide endorsement from one of the greats!) Seeing as he was in a jovial mood, I wanted to know what his own ambitions for the race were when he was a rider, and what he thought about the current crop.

'For me the races like Tour of Flanders were always too early,' he admitted. 'I seemed to take a long time to get really fit, and Flanders has got lots of climbs which require peak power over two- to three-minute periods. I just didn't have that kind of fitness. I went much better at the Tour de France and later races in the calendar. Whereas Paris–Roubaix is much more than just strength. You don't have to push out a thousand watts for a minute to be up there, unlike the Tour of Flanders where you go up so many climbs. The more progressive power over long periods really suited me. And I could ride the cobbles, but it required positioning. You need to be able to position yourself to save energy through-out the race and also mind the cobbles when it's wet, when it's really slippery.

'In the 1994 edition the conditions were really bad the night before. Come race day there were only ten guys in that race who could ride the cobbles in those conditions, and most of the others were letting wheels go, guys were crashing off, you know. They were just totally out of control, but the fact that I'd got Rockshox suspension, plus flatter tyres with really low pressure, enabled me to ride really, really easily on the cobbles. That year, coming into the Carrefour de l'Arbre, I was second on the road; Tchmil was up the road and he won the race. I never felt like I could win it, but I think that's one of the highlights of my career, coming on to that last bad section. Second on the road, having just overtaken Museeuw, and dropping the champion, Duclos-Lassalle – and the crowd screaming at you was special. That really was one of the highlights of my career and a great feeling.

'My progression over the years went from actually taking a long time to finish Paris–Roubaix, to then, finally, getting placings: I came fourteenth, then eleventh, then eighth, and, of course, the highlight in 1994 of fifth. So I was getting better each year. That really gave me incentive. Ninety-nine per cent of the time I rode for others, but in that particular race, in my team, I was pretty much the best. I was kind of motivated to ride for myself, whereas the rest of the year I didn't, really. I felt I rode good and it suited to me, going up a gear; sitting back gave me extra motivation.'

'Do you think Cancellara will win it this year?' I asked him.

'Well, certainly he's the favourite. He's won a lot of races, and the law of averages may play against him, but, all things being equal, certainly he is the favourite. I wouldn't be surprised if Spartacus won it: he's a beast, he's a legend, and I'm sure he'll be pretty deter-mined to add to his tally.'

'But what about Wiggins, can he become our best British rider?'

Yates took his time thinking about this one before committing. I thought he was going to dismiss his chances, but, again, he surprised me with his answer.

'Top twenty. I think Bradley's suited to it, but he's not very good at fighting for a position. Every time you have to make your way back – obviously, it also depends on what the conditions are. I think the forecast is for drier weather, which makes it easier. There will be crashes, and you will need to get past riders to stay in contention. You have to overtake guys who are getting constantly dropped as the race intensifies. You're using extra energy and every time you burn a match the box gets emptier and emptier, and seeing the likes of Cancellara, super, super strong . . . but at the same time they ride clever to conserve that strength for the right moment. We'll have to see what happens.'

I had been given two unique perspectives of the race. Barry's was a vision of the past when riders were expected to compete for every single race in the calendar, wages were low and to survive, to simply continue as a professional, meant making incredible sacrifices. Sean started out during these days, but his career slowly came to a close as a new, more modern way of mapping out a rider's ability – targeting individual races where he could do well and support a team's overall strategy – was becoming the norm.

This was mirrored by the steady growth of media interest in professional cycling, which now brought Paris–Roubaix to millions of fans in places where cobbles were completely incomprehensible, but all the more fascinating for that. From Australia, South Africa, Scandinavia and America, more riders would develop and come through the ranks and carve their names in the annals of the spring Classics. And the internet age would ensure their deeds became even more renowned, and the sport itself cemented in the global calendar of 'must see' events.

The final British rider I spoke to enjoyed a career that epitomized how cycling came to be viewed in the new millennium. Roger Hammond has graced many a cover of *Cycling Weekly* from the 1990s onwards. He was British road champion on two occasions, as well as cyclo-cross champion seven times. He rode for elite trade teams, including Lance Armstrong's Discovery Channel, T-Mobile and Garmin–Cervélo. More specifically for me, he was the rider I clearly remember being thrilled to watch on television coming third at Paris–Roubaix in 2004.

I had been trying to speak with Roger for months and he finally consented after I outlined what I was planning to do. Again, I wanted his perspective on how he viewed the race and the cobbles themselves; did they hold any fears for him, even as a highly experienced cyclo-cross champion?

'I don't think it's a difficult race, actually,' he admitted, matter-of-factly. 'That's the funny thing about it. When I look back at the races I did as a bike rider, the ones that were really difficult, or purgatory, were either the ones I knew I couldn't win, or ones where I felt like I was putting myself through a lot of pain and misery for no reward, really – or it was up a mountain that I was totally not suited to doing. Whenever I looked at Roubaix there were massive ups and downs – the downs were more through the disappointment of not performing how I knew I could, or getting so close and not winning.

'In terms of physical difficulty, though, I didn't feel it was the hardest race. It was the one I went deepest into my reserves for and pushed myself, but it was a different kind of pushing, if you know what I mean? It was a comfortable pushing, and there was a reason – at the end of it there was something worth going for. You sort of ended up pushing yourself deep and then wondering about it, only knowing about it a couple of days afterwards . . . because, actually, I used to love it. I used to enjoy pushing myself in races I knew I could do well in.'

'Would you say it's your favourite one-day race, or is it just a race where you thought, "It's on the calendar, I've got the form and the bike skills to do it"?' I enquired.

'It was definitely my favourite race on the calendar – there were two up there, actually. The one that captured my imagination, as a race, was the Tour of Flanders, but Paris–Roubaix seemed to suit me more, so it became my real focus and used up a lot of my mental energy in getting ready, preparing, as well as the stress of looking forward to it.'

'Why?' I asked.

'I think that comes from having that belief that you can actually win it, or have a chance of winning it. That is slightly different to the Tour of Flanders, where I knew that if the wind was in the right direction, and a couple of the favourites had some bad luck, then out of the thirteen or fourteen times I did it there was possibly one edition where I was sprinting for the actual win. But, realistically, the chances were really, really slim. Whereas Paris–Roubaix, out of nine attempts, there was a couple of occasions I really put myself in the right position. So I think you then mentally start looking forward to it, because there really is something to gain.

'And, to be honest with you, I just enjoyed racing it. I really did. Some races just take ages to do. You would be in a stage race, where it still suited my style, but it's two hundred kilometres and you look down at the bike computer after fifty K and you're half expecting to see one hundred and twenty kilometres, and it says only fifty! Whereas with Paris–Roubaix it was kind of, "Shit, this race is almost over. I've only just got going!" I will never forget the first time I rode it. It really did feel like the race was about ten minutes long. Yeah, it just went so fast. It was so much fun.'

I found this both refreshing and a positive boost for my own impending battle with the *pavé*. 'It's funny,' I said, 'that you say that. When I was reading Stuart O'Grady's book, he said that the first two times he did Paris–Roubaix he basically was shitting himself and he couldn't understand how people could go that fast when he was just barely keeping control of his bike. You didn't feel like that?'

'Not really,' replied Roger, 'but then I had a slightly different background. I developed through cyclo-cross. For me, sliding around in wet mud on roads and not really worrying was preparation, I suppose, for the cobbles. I do remember just enjoying it, but on the other side of the coin. Stu is just that little bit older than me. I raced the spring Classics from 2003, which was my first Paris–Roubaix, through to 2011, and I never had a wet race, so that's fundamental. I think Stu must have ridden in 1998 and I remember watching that race with Magnus Bäckstedt, because I was sharing a flat with him at the time. The conditions were just atrocious, so I can imagine: if that was your first attempt, and you're from Australia, and you've probably never seen a cyclo-cross race, let alone raced in one . . . well, I can guess it was a pretty big baptism of fire, to be honest.'

'What about the *pavé*, Roger? I sound like a broken record now, with the amount of people I've asked, but is it as lethal as everyone says it can be?'

'Well, the hardest bits for me were the three kilometres before the cobble sections begin. That last little surge before each sector of cobbles would be vital. In fact, most sectors of cobbles I would be trying to recover to get on to the cobbles first. You know, everybody wants to be in the first ten on the cobbles – it's one of the hardest parts of the race, and why I think Paris–Roubaix tends to suit faster riders, really. If you're used to being at the front of the peloton anyway, that bit of it is fairly easy, you'll have that sort of accelerant, that basic power, which means you can accelerate past people to get into the right place at the right time. Those were the kind of basic skills I had, and if you hit the cobbles in the first ten then you can see how many put the brakes on and how many go flat out, and then that's when you know the big guys really attack. That's only on a couple of sectors throughout the race, really. For the rest, the most important thing was hitting the faster sectors in the first ten and then taking a deep breath to start recovering, which is how I used to ride. When you do go fast on the cobbles you could really put yourself into all sorts of difficult places.'

'You must be proud,' I said, 'of coming third. You're the joint-top British finisher with Barry Hoban. And you then finished fourth in 2010. That must please you?'

'Yes, it's kind of funny. I think in any other race I would have been, but I'd set my targets on doing well in that race. But my dream as a kid was to win Paris–Roubaix . . . to come on to that velodrome – and that day [in 2010] I just remember feeling really strong and really competitive, and then I made a bit of a hash of it on the track. If I'd have just been hanging on and just sort of gone, "Thank goodness for that, I've made it and I made it in the front group, that was brilliant . . ." then fine. But I still feel that I lost that one.'

'The one that got away,' I commiserated with him, clearly recalling watching Eurosport on the sofa, shouting my head off, as I'm sure many others were.

'Yeah, rather than the third place that I got, that I snapped out of nowhere, kind of thing, which was a bit frustrating, to be honest. If you could rerun it you would do it differently, wouldn't you?'

'How do you feel about the likes of Wiggins hoping he can finish in the top three, or even win it? Do you think that's possible?'

'I think it's great. I think it would be a fantastic thing for the event. I think as a Classics rider – as a "Classics focus rider" – I always felt the Classics are an amazing story to be told. I don't think they're pushed or encouraged as much as they could be by the world of cycling, really, so to have a huge character, or name, that would introduce Paris–Roubaix to thousands of people that probably don't even know it exists would be amazing. So from that perspective, it's fantastic – you have someone who's won the Tour de France aiming to win Paris–Roubaix too – it says a lot about

Brad, in that he's a real traditionalist for cycling. It's really nice to have people that still have respect for the traditions of cycling. I know it's becoming a different sport, and a mainstream sport, and it's harder to be at the highest level, but how many riders have won the Tour de France and thought, "Right, I'm going to do Paris–Roubaix now"?'

'It's amazing,' I agreed.

Roger continued, 'It is amazing and it's so unheard of now that I just think, "Fair play to him." The one thing that Brad's always done is kept a focus on what he believes in. I think it's just nice that he respects and believes in the traditions of the sport, otherwise all we're going to have is one three-week race in the middle of July.'

'My final question is: what do you think about races that are held in such high esteem and tradition, like Paris–Roubaix, being open to amateurs like me? To be mass-participation events. I ask as I'm always aware of what Bernard Hinault thought of ordinary cyclists wearing Tour de France jerseys – that he just wanted to rip them off. I wondered if that kind of feeling translates to other riders when they see amateurs, complete amateurs, but with all the gear, all the bikes that people have nowadays, and they're riding the really tough courses – obviously a hell of a lot slower – but they're on this hallowed ground. How do you feel about that?'

'I completely sympathize with Bernard Hinault and his thoughts on people's jerseys,' Roger firmly stated. 'I was kind of brought up in that tradition, anyway. I was brought up in a cycling family, and it's back to the traditions of cycling again and, you know, if you'd earned the right to wear a national champion's jersey [then] that was who you were. You worked hard to earn the right to wear that; it was almost your badge of honour. So, I can appreciate it, but I can also understand why people want to wear them too. It is the same as fans wanting to be part of a team and wanting to be part of the whole experience, so I can see both sides of it. But, really, there is only one side of me riding on the Paris–Roubaix and Flanders races. But I just think participatory amateur events is the way cycling's going to go. It's a fantastic thing that can happen and the way I see it is that I hope that everybody that starts the Paris–Roubaix *Étape* looks at their average speed at the end of it and then watches the pro race in the afternoon and thinks, "Bloody hell!"'

'I will, believe me!' I laughed.

'Yes, people will have an affinity with it then, you know. It's really easy to sit at home and comment. The number of bike races where I've sat at home myself and watched and said, "I would have won that if I'd gone to that. How easy does that look . . ." I think [racing] brings a much greater appreciation and interest in the event and makes fans totally appreciative of what it feels like on the cobbles. Then, all of a sudden there's a little bit of awe, a little bit more respect and interest, and I don't think that can be a negative thing at all. I like the way that Ride London do their race – it's a platform that works really well. With a head start, you ride the same route, you've got the crowds on the roads already screaming. The crowds get more to watch, and if you haven't trained hard enough you won't finish, and that's the end of it. So there's all sorts of emotions: you'll feel like a superstar, you're riding on the same day as the race, you get cheered on, and there's a challenge to it, too. I'm sure you'll feel the same for Paris–Roubaix. Good luck, mate.'

Day of Days

'*Haaarrruuummmppphhh*, not already!' I mumbled.

I felt like I had dropped off to sleep only minutes ago. It was my own fault; whenever I'm nervous and dreading the coming day I always, without fail, stay up late, as though it is going to put off the inevitable. But the alarm on my mobile merrily chirped away in the darkness as I decided on five more minutes in a warm bed. Well, maybe ten minutes more . . .

I drifted off again to the tune of 'All You Need Is Love' by the Beatles, especially that opening fanfare of 'La Marseillaise'. Wait a minute, that is 'La Marseillaise'! I was suddenly wide awake and wondering what was going on. I dragged myself out of the still crisp white sheets of my queen-sized bed to switch off the digital fanfare. Starting to feel like I was going a little crazy, the abstract memory of Jo telling me she'd plug me into getting up on time swam back into the front of my mind. 'A nice little touch, darling.' I smiled as I located the mobile on my dresser table and switched it to snooze.

Yet again, I couldn't believe I was about to do this. Sitting on the edge of the bed, I looked over towards the window where the bike was parked, and studied its frame and forks. I really hoped they'd last the course today. I went over to it and ran my hands along the top tube and then squeezed the seat's padding – it had better do its job.

Showered and mulling over whether to try to eat something, I decided to have a shave. My paranoia of crashing meant I was determined to look professional and clean-cut, just in case any passers-by wanted a photo, you understand. In reality it just marked time until I knew I'd have to dress and take my bike to reception for the pick-up.

I looked into the mini-fridge and eyed up the succulent apple pastry I'd bought at the *boulangerie* the previous day for the express purpose of packing in some carbs. But with so much whirling around my head I couldn't stomach anything right now and decided on just a very strong coffee as I pondered what to wear. What kind of weather would we encounter today? My heart wanted rain, wind and lots of mud in order to fully endure and enhance this experience of a 'Day in Hell', but my head and legs were hoping it was benign and partially sunny. Dust in the eyes, mouth and lungs would be preferable to negotiating clinging mud and slippery *pavé*.

Hearing muffled laughter and a shout from outside, I walked back across the room to the window. From behind the net curtains, studying the dark clouds settling above, I looked down to the car park two floors below and noticed three bike riders in full kit setting off on their bikes into the gloom, obviously cycling to the pick-up point. They were in full, snazzy winter-weather gear, complete with gilets and even balaclavas, the type you see 'freedom fighters' wearing in Ukraine at the moment. This kick-started me into action. 'C'mon, son. It's show time.'

Just like my fellow riders, I decided to take no chances and the full set of winter gear was neatly placed on the duvet, set out in order from helmet to rain-shoe covers. I started to feel better and a little more confident as, garment by garment, I began to assemble a bike rider, even one with the legs of a skinny, hairy chicken. I ran through the vitals:

Pump? Check.

Four inner tubes and bike bag? Check.

Gels, bars and water bottles? Check.

Sunnys (sunglasses)? Check.

Route map and bus ticket? Yep.

Phone and money? OK.

Bike? Yes.

I delicately took out from my official starter pack my race number (1770) which was printed on to heavy-duty brown and black cardboard, with the 'Paris–Roubaix Challenge' livery around it, and attached it to the front of the handlebars. It was quite stylish compared to the usual sportive's black numbers on cheap, white plastic cards. It contained a computer strip at the back to record my progress across the various zones we would ride through – all very modern. I was equally impressed with the long fluorescent yellow strip containing all the twenty-eight sections of cobbles, how long they were, and what five-star difficulty rating each part of *pavé* was given, plus where the all-important feed stations would be. As far as I could see, this would be a vital piece of information and I thankfully took off the adhesive strip and placed it carefully along the top tube. I knew I'd be referring to it a lot during the day. I focused on section number 13, *Trouée d'Arenberg* . . .

There was one final ritual to perform. I carefully unzipped the top of my rucksack, and from a small freezer bag took out a nondescript piece of tattered sky-blue-and-white-striped ribbon from the medal my late father was awarded for serving in Korea in the 1950s. It had been issued by the United Nations, and this tiny fragment somehow connected me to him. I pinned the ribbon to the thermal vest beneath my race jersey – it meant the world to me.

'Bring me luck, Dad,' I whispered. And I headed out the door with my bike.

Coming out of the lift, I quietly ambled along the hotel's worn carpet towards the main reception and was met with what could

only be construed as a mini-MAMIL convention. Six guys dressed
just like me, and six pairs of tired, caffeine-fuelled, blinking
eyes mirroring my mindset of 'We who are about to die, salute
you . . .' A polite cough interrupted me and I turned to see the
nightwatchman, who was managing to look quite elegant and
grown-up compared to us lycra lovers. He smiled and enquired,
'Monsieur MacGregor? Room 211, yes? Your taxi is waiting for
you outside.'

I solemnly nodded, and then looked outside through the glass
doors to see a large, steel-grey Renault Espace gunning its engine.
'Well, this is it,' I thought with grim satisfaction, 'no point in hanging around with my fellows.'

'Are you British, mate?' A Yorkshire accent startled me for a
second, and I turned from the door to the nearest cyclist, who had
a full Garmin trade strip on, and a beautiful black Pinarello bike.
Nice, if you could afford it.

'Yes, just over for the race, thought I'd take a cab to the pick-up
to save on the stress of finding my way through the streets of Lille
at this time of the morning.' I gripped tightly on to the handlebars
wanting to be away and alone with my thoughts.

'On yer own, then?' He smiled, but his question simply reignited
that feeling of 'Johnny no mates'. The other riders sitting behind
him were either toying with the bikes, checking their food supplies,
texting on their mobile phones, or just staring at me.

'No, no, the two guys I came with headed out fifteen minutes
ago, as they fancied warming up with a ride, but I'm a lazy sod.'
Why? Why did I feel the need to say that?

'Ah, don't blame yer, we're following our tour guide in a few
minutes, when he gets up, the bugger. We did the Tour of Flanders
last week and it were great, good preparation for this one today,
eh?' Again, he smiled when he said this, but his nervousness shone
through and he was probably feeling the same as me. I gave him a
perfunctory smile and looked towards the door.

'Well, good luck. I hope it's as enjoyable as Flanders,' I said, and made to go. He nodded a good luck gesture, too, and I headed out to the waiting cab. I was usually upbeat and friendly towards fellow riders at domestic races, but this was a whole different league of stress and anxiety. With my shoe cleats loudly clickety-clacking on the polished reception floor, I made my way out into the very cold pre-dawn.

The driver, a Moroccan-looking guy, smiled, said hello in a heavy accent and helped me get the bike (minus its front wheel) into the boot of the vehicle. 'He can't have picked up a fare as sexy as me in ages,' I thought to myself sardonically. He already had the address for the pick-up outside the velodrome plugged into his satnav, and so without further ado we set off into the pre-dawn gloom with no fanfare, just total quiet, bar the hum of the engine and the car heater going full-tilt.

When you're sitting in the front of a cab, I think there is a tacit agreement that you're up for a conversation, and he asked me, without taking his eyes off the road, 'You do the big race today?'

For some reason, possibly because he wasn't connected to the race, wasn't a fellow rider, I felt uninhibited in talking with him. In fact, I felt like I needed to unburden my thoughts. 'Yes, the Paris–Roubaix, 170 kilometres and 52 of them on the cobbles – sorry, the *pavé*. You're taking me to where I get picked up by the coach to take me to the start at Busigny.'

I blurted all this out pretty quickly and was happily relieved he kept up with me and actually fired back a question. 'You enjoy something like that? You not getting tired, or . . .' he pointed to his bottom with a smile '. . . painful down there?'

And from there we began to swap stories – of why I cycle, why I wanted to take on this race, how he loved football and Real Madrid, why he wouldn't want to do what I was about to do, and, of course the obligatory, was I doing this on my own? But, joking aside, he managed to take my mind off my worries and I felt somewhat more relaxed, that is until we came to the velodrome and I saw the pick-up point. Mahmoud, as I found he was called, kindly and carefully got my bike out from his boot and watched as I fixed the front wheel back on. As I paid the fare, plus tip, I enquired whether he could pick me up at the finish later.

'It would be my pleasure, just call me on my mobile,' he said, handing me his card. With a big, warm smile he then patted me on the back, and I felt the better for having shared that cab ride with him.

The departure area resembled a scene from *Blade Runner*. Twenty or so coaches, with giant trailers on the back, were all lit up like oil rigs, looking pretty surreal in the fog, which made it seem as if they were floating on the road. Around them were hundreds of riders, all dressed in winter cycling gear of many colours and brands – some had helmets on, some sported those popular bandanas, and a few were even wearing their sunglasses! There was a palpable buzz of anticipation and impatience as everyone was keen to get their bikes loaded on to the trailers, get on the bus and get a good seat to chill out for the ninety-minute coach ride southwards to the start.

Slowly navigating my way through the throng, it hit me, for the first time, how international this event really was. Yes, I heard English and French being spoken, but also Norwegian, Swedish, Danish (let's just say Scandi), German, Spanish, Italian, Japanese, Portuguese, what sounded like Greek, heavily accented English– American, Canadian, Irish, South African, Australian and Kiwi. Here we all were, all with stories to tell of our reasons for wanting to ride this mad race, how we'd trained and how we'd managed to get to this point in time. This thought warmed me and I began to feel a strong connection to these strangers. It wasn't, however, always a two-way feeling, as quite a few of them either pushed or even barged past me with their bikes in their desire to get loaded up quickly. Indeed, I ended up getting hacked off with some of their antics at the queue I chose to join, so walked away to find a more sedate line of mainly Belgians, judging by their voices and the local club strips they were wearing.

Suddenly I was at the front of the line, with three guys behind me, but the coach driver then abruptly announced there was no more room in the trailer and we'd have to queue elsewhere. Clearly, he didn't appreciate the mindset of guys like us who were about to do untold damage to our posteriors on miles of *pavé*; we didn't move and instead gave him an icy stare. One of the Belgians shouted, 'Here, we go here!' and gestured to the rest of us to follow him. He quickly opened the luggage hatch, which slid up to reveal a giant empty space – lovely. We all detached our front wheels and carefully loaded each bike into the bowels of the coach, much to the driver's chagrin. We then handed him our green ticket stubs before boarding.

I made my way down towards the rear, where the toilet is situated (throwing up on many school trips had imbued me with this survival instinct), and found a double seat so that I could stretch out and make myself comfortable. Closing my eyes, I attempted to chill, listening to the hubbub from my fellow passengers as they quietly discussed what lay ahead. What will be, will be.

We headed off, the coach taking its place in a drawn-out convoy. Roubaix was asleep, dark, cold and foggy. I huddled up in my seat, trying to stay warm, and thought to myself, 'See you in seven hours, I hope.' The journey seemed like a dream, as the warm air of the bus's heater finally kicked in, and we all started to peel off our jackets and gilets in order to preserve their benefit once we were out on the road. The warmth, added to not having had much sleep, was a great combination for blankly staring out of the window as the bus rattled along a mixture of country and main roads.

The images that flew past were of a rural idyll, with the lights of sleepy villages occasionally breaking up the miles and miles of vast flat opaqueness that is the northern French countryside. Dawn started to break, with tiny shards of orange and yellow rays in the cement sky, but the further we drove, the more the fog enveloped the whole vista until you could hardly see much at all. I decided to go through my checklist again and to mentally prepare for the ride itself. Judging by how the chatter on the coach had died down, the others on the bus were doing the same. It wouldn't be long until we reached Busigny.

I was very aware of the historic poignancy of this area. Busigny, like many hamlets in the region, was on the perimeter of the Battle of Cambrai in October 1918, when the Germans were finally pushed back to their Hindenburg Line, and ultimately to their final defeat a month later. The village had served as a clearing station for the wounded coming out of the battle.

As we slowly made our way into the outskirts of Busigny, the mist gave way to reveal the iconic architecture one associates with Great War cemeteries, with one hundred or more immaculately maintained, pale sand-coloured headstones, in perfect formation, surrounded by lush, grassy green verges. In the middle of it, I could see a simple cenotaph with a cross. It was beautiful and tragic to see, especially when I thought about the role my own family played in the fighting. It certainly snapped me back into reality; no matter how hard our journey would be today, it was just a bike race. No one (hopefully) was going to die, or be seriously injured.

I could see others further down the front of the coach nudging one another and looking out at the view. Perhaps we were all think-ing the same thing, that almost a century ago, this really was 'the Hell of the North'. The sombre moment was broken as we came to a shuddering halt in the town square and, following the riders down the coach steps into the dawn, I dressed up in my jacket, gloves and hat again and waited my turn patiently to collect my bike and reattach the wheel.

In the square all around me were riders sorting out equipment, fixing tyres, testing brakes, piling supplies into jersey and jacket pockets, and all animatedly chattering. The buzz was building very quickly, and I looked over to where I could hear the noise of a tannoy at the other end of the square.

I wanted to get underway quickly, but suddenly the urge to eat finally kicked in. With all the nervous anticipation, plus the fact it wasn't even 7 a.m. yet, my stomach had finally spoken. I was relieved to see the usual sportive food and drink stalls next to the starting gate, parked the bike and gleefully took in what was on offer. Hunger does drive you to act, and so I must belatedly apologize to the lady running the stall who watched me rudely stuff a chocolate brioche, fig rolls, two bananas and a handful of dates into my mouth within minutes. All washed down with two cups of fresh coffee, which I gestured abruptly for her to give me. Not my finest moment, but she handled it with a grace and kindness these pages cannot possibly do justice to. *Merci, madame*, whoever you were.

The organizers had allowed for groups to start every five minutes, so, eager to get underway, I clipped one shoe into the pedal and coasted my way to the start gate, which was your typical, pro-race inflatable barrier. Its modern fabric and size looked weirdly at odds with the ancient surroundings. Taking my place amongst twenty or so riders, I listened to the instructions the race commissar was relaying over a loudspeaker.

Then it was, '*Un, deux, trois . . . bonne chance sur* 2014 Paris–Roubaix Challenge!'

The fifty or so locals who had turned up at this ridiculous hour to watch gave a loud cheer, some riders hugged one another, or high-fived and shouted encouragement. We were off!

Into the Unknown

Leaving the lights, noise and bustle of our *Grand Départ* in the distance, we seemed to enter the nether world of a spring dawn. The gloom was still clinging to the ground, and the fog refused to budge in the fields surrounding us, though thankfully we could see clearly ahead on the dank road, for a distance of about 250 metres. There was a chorus of bikes being tested as the riders around me clicked through their gears and we began to speed along in a long, classic train, two abreast. I was loving this already.

I seemed to be in a mini-peloton of approximately twenty-five or so riders, and as far as I could see they were all male. Several seemed familiar with one another as they rode along together, and I could pick up a few English accents towards the front of the group. I sat in, halfway back, as we increased our pace to a nice and steady 30 k.p.h. The roads were very smooth and wide, there was no traffic to worry about yet, but I still noticed an outrider on an official motorbike some way off in the distance, acting as our eyes and ears ahead, leaving us to concentrate on warming up sufficiently quickly after standing around for a while in the cold.

I was mindful not to blast off and waste energy – 'Leave that to others,' I thought, and indeed a couple of Italian riders, big stocky guys in very snazzy blue, white and green national jerseys and long bib tights, zipped off the group and disappeared down the road. If this were a sportive back home and I knew the route well and the type of roads I would be riding, I'd probably do the same thing. It's always good first thing to test the legs, but my nervousness kept me in check. I had to think about the goal: 'Just get to the velodrome in one piece, Iain.'

The pace increased again and the chatting stopped – we could hear the dawn chorus around us, the countryside waking up to the hum of well-oiled gears smoothly speeding along. For the next dozen kilometres or so, the main road undulated, but nothing like it would if I were riding in the hills of Kent and Sussex. This felt very much in my comfort zone, for now. We started to pass through small villages, and a few locals were out to watch the race, or simply going about their daily lives. Some waved, some didn't give us a second glance. I could feel the tension building amongst the group, as we knew we were coming up to the first section of cobbles – Section 28: Troisvilles to Inchy. As we barrelled along I recalled what William at Pavé Cycling had impressed upon me and prepared myself for battle. 'Ride on the crown.'

Troisvilles was seen as one of the 'Five Stations of the Cross' and the quasi-religious overtones do not overstate the significance of this section. Alongside the epic Wallers–Arenberg, the relentless Mons-en-Pévèle and the fearsome le Carrefour de l'Arbre, these were the great testing places for any would-be winner of Paris–Roubaix, and indeed any amateur just wishing to finish the race itself. All the books I had studied described all of these sections in colourful and dramatic language – these would be the key moments of make or break.

The one legendary section now missing from the modern race was the only real climb of the route, at Doullens. This was the first real obstacle that any rider had to overcome, and up to the 1950s it had actually been cobbled too. Before the invention of modern gearing and derailleurs, this was seen as the biggest challenge of the race, and where key selections were made. It has long since been dropped from the official route as more sections of *pavé* were uncovered and incorporated into the race, and I for one wasn't upset by this.

As it was the start of the first *pavé* section, Troisvilles was naturally labelled 'the Gate to Hell'. At only 2,200 metres, and given a three-star rating of difficulty on my race notes, I knew this would be a test, and one I could measure against what an actual four- and five-star *pavé* section would be like later on. Still, it was cobbles, it didn't matter what grade they were, they were still cobbles.

I snapped out of my thoughts as the race began to resemble the pell-mell rush to the first fence at the Grand National. Riders started to increase speed and position themselves apart from one another to ensure they wouldn't get taken down by fallers. Someone shouted out, 'Watch out for bottles on the floor, they'll be all over the place for this first section!' We were steaming along now on a main stretch of tarmac, with the fog still on our flanks in the fields, and I looked down at my Garmin to see we were hitting 40 k.p.h. as we moved as a single entity into a shallow left-hand turn.

Big mistake. We hit the section full on and the suddenness of it made me cry out in surprise, as though I'd just seen a rat in a Great War trench. The road started to turn to gravel and within seconds the bike and my body began manically to bounce and topple along the *pavé*. Finally, the moment had come. The horizon resembled rolling South Atlantic swells as I started to lose coherence and control . . .

'Fuck me!' I hear someone shout over the din of the rattling bikes. The violence of the juddering rocks my whole body as I fight to keep control of the bike and avoid the detritus lying all over the *pavé*. I focus on not hitting anyone, but all I can really see are dozens of different types and colours of water bottles all over the place. One rider stops and pulls over to the side and is laughing in shock or terror, I can't tell which, as I speed past him. I'm still turning a big gear, sticking to my race plan of maintaining focus, riding on the crown of the road and driving the legs as we descend quickly down a steady incline of cobbles for what feels like 1,000 metres.

The group I was with only moments ago has splintered completely and I feel like I'm completely on my own. The scenario reminds me of those old Great War pilots who were in the thick of a dogfight one moment and then suddenly can't see anyone for miles. As we reach the bottom of this gloomy descent, I feel in control but am slowing down. I start to climb up on to some sort of plateau and find it easier going and increase my speed accordingly. Feeling more confident as the *pavé* turns a dog-leg left, I just follow my instinct and try to navigate the turn as best I can.

Disaster strikes. I overshoot the left turn due to my nervousness (fearing that I'll overrun the bend and go into a hedge) and decide not to slam the brakes on but desperately try to unclip my right shoe to stop myself quickly and maybe be a little bit more in control. But, in an instant, it all goes Pete Tong. My cleat won't budge, my right leg's pulling and twisting action only jerks me further off-balance and my front wheel judders left at right angles to the ditch, which I then go into head first.

'Fuuuuucksaaaaaaaake, arrrrgh.'

As with any crash on a bike, it's over instantly, and though I can't see them yet, I hear other riders zipping by my prone body and bike. I manage to finally unclip my feet from the pedals, a little too late, and scramble up. The fear has gone, only to be replaced by abject embarrassment. The first section, and I bloody crash. Thankfully everyone seems to have passed, and I get the bike back on to the solid part of the road, rub my right shoulder, which took the brunt of the fall, and look around to see if I've dropped anything. In the gloom of this tight little lane I can't make out anything on the ground around me, other than my sunglasses, which have come out of my jersey front pocket. I pick them up quickly and clip back in.

It's an agonizing ride of 600 or 700 metres – my slow pace only increases the insane jolting as my tyres seem to hit every cobbled rut that is sticking out at an odd angle. My hands grip the top bars manically, as if I am suspended thousands of feet above a precipice and I daren't let go.

'Nearly . . . over . . . nearly . . . there . . . c'mon!'

As I reach the banner across the section of *pavé* that marks where the beautifully smooth road begins again I could get off my bike, kneel down and kiss it – but, equally, I am thrilled beyond words that I have finally ridden across a section of *pavé*. I have momentarily overcome the demons.

A local, middle-aged man, seemingly on a morning stroll with his white mongrel dog, is standing at the banner watching the action. He nods at me, smiles a knowing smile and, pulling on the dog's lead, heads back down towards the regular road where a few houses are situated. Only another 50 kilometres, across 27 sections of this to go . . .

I had a sip from one of my *bidons*; thankfully I had taken sound advice to ensure I wedged the bottles in firmly – judging by the plethora of bottles, gel packs, energy bars, and various other artefacts I rode through, there would be a lot of frustrated and thirsty riders out there later on. Clipping back in, I was thankful for the mental break to take stock. My bike and myself were still in one piece, I felt shook up slightly but not too shocked after my crash, and the weather was cool, though we were still fog-bound. The wind had died down slightly, but I was resigned to having to ride through it all the way to Roubaix; after all, that was part of the 'rites of passage' I had already signed up to.

I could hear a distant rumble of tyres on cobbles, and three riders whizzed by, not stopping after the end of the section, and I decided to get going and try to tag along on their wheel. It took

me a few kilometres to gain on them as they were ticking along at
a fair lick over some darkly undulating, empty roads, and I noticed
we were almost hitting 40 k.p.h. again.

Being on the end of the line is preferable, but it does have its
dangers, too. The main benefit is that one gets pulled along, expend-
ing less effort, as the riders in front punch a hole through the air
resistance for you. What I find levels out this advantage, especially
if you and none of your fellow riders speak the same language,
is that sudden bumps, holes and obstacles in the road very rarely
get flagged to you. The universal sign language of sweeping one's
left or right hand behind your back to indicate which way the rear
rider should avoid often gets forgotten. I am guilty of this at times,
so caught up in the moment you forget your obligations to the safe
riding of your group.

Hence my problem here.

I take stock again as we ride, quickly studying my bike, tyres,
and *bidons*, while also flexing my fingers to get the feeling back.
The stinging in my palms is only matched by the ringing in my
ears as I recover from the battering we've just taken. On the one
hand I'm chuffed and excited to have ridden *pavé* at last, but looking down at the route itinerary on the top tube I am daunted by
the remaining trials to come. The distance isn't a problem, more
the obstacles littered along the way. The guys in front of me are
chattering away in French and don't seem perturbed that I don't
follow through to take up my turn at the front – I doubt I could
keep up their pace if I did. For now I'm happy to take a pull and
get ready for Section 27: Viesly to Quiévy.

We keep up the tempo and I manage to view my surroundings
in detail. Even with the wintry conditions, the great expanse of
flat farmland stretches out in every direction around us. The trees
are still bare and lifeless, acting like signposts for our continued
odyssey north, the countryside, with its opaque agrarian vastness,
feeling very similar to the east of England, where I grew up. You

can really feel the history here, and the slower pace of life to match. A few locals are out and about, a mum and toddler wave hello as they amble down the street of a small village we speed through. I make a point of smiling and calling out, '*Bonjour!*' I want to enjoy the whole experience, the good and the bad.

The pace quickens and my compadres' gossip dies down as we see the banner ahead proclaiming 'Section 27: 1.8 kilometres'. I make sure to ever so slightly drop off the group, to allow room for mistakes but, yet again, I am taken aback by the ferocity of the *pavé*, and cling on to the top bars as my legs burn with the effort of turning a big gear. Surprisingly the guys in front of me opt for their smaller ring and their cadence comically explodes to over 100 r.p.m. as I sweep past them heading downhill and already I can see the finish some 600 metres away at the bottom of the lane. Feeling confident, I push on, staying on the crown as instructed by the professionals, and start to feel even more confident. A black-clad racer hurtles past me on the right-hand side, riding in the gutter, leaving me gasping in admiration, yet ever so slightly miffed, too, that he's broken my 'feel good' moment. At least I have those French guys in my wake.

However this 'feel good' factor lasts but seconds as we confront one of the longest sections in the race. Section 26: Quiévy to Saint-Python. My guide awards this baby four stars, and from the off it seems infinitely more difficult in terms of maintaining control and not falling off. I desperately start to weave back and forwards across the *pavé*, trying to find a line that won't unseat me, or wreck the front wheel, which is taking a battering. The vibrations are severe as we start riding up towards the plateau of the slope and I'm having to dig deep to maintain a decent speed, all the while thinking, 'This is bloody madness.'

Sweating like a farm animal, despite the wind chill from the stiff breeze cutting across our path, I try to mentally relax and let the bike go free to find its own way safely. I ease my grip on the bars.

A few more riders have crept up on me and by the time we come to a dog-leg to the right, we number ten or so and slow down accordingly so as not to cause a pile-up. On the apex of the corner, two kids are standing above us all on the grassy high bank, wrapped up in woollen hats and warm bomber jackets. This must be the highlight of their day, watching clowns from other countries try to survive their precious *pavé*. The spectacle seems to amuse them, judging by the smiles on their faces.

We plough on and looking up I see this section goes on towards the horizon and my heart sinks. Fearful I will blow up I reduce my cadence right down and tuck into the side of the track in order to let stronger or braver riders through. They pile in accordingly. Cycling is such a great leveller of the ego. An event like this quickly tells you where your talent lies in the great pecking order of the peloton. Right now I feel like the 'bottom feeder' I cycle like. I just want to survive.

The pace may slacken and heart rate quicken, but the drag of this hill seems never-ending. I clench my rattling teeth, grip the hoods (I was warned not to, but what the hell) and decide to treat this last kilometre as interval training. BANG, BANG, BANG goes my front wheel as I hit every single sett that seems to be protruding out of line. 'Keep it up, c'mon!' I shout at myself. The sweat is pouring from my brow as my head overheats with the winter hat sandwiched beneath my helmet. With stinging eyes and a very sore backside I am just about done in by the time we see the finish banner by a farmhouse.

I slow right down, coasting over the final ten metres or so of the *pavé* and come to a halt by an ancient-looking building. It's a very beautiful, eighteenth-century, classic French farmhouse, straight out of a Turner painting (or someone French who paints like Turner, perhaps). Ripping off my helmet, I wipe my eyes with the thermal hat, stretch my back and take a sip of water. Once you've stopped, the sounds of the countryside are equally as shocking as the vibrations. The silence is deafening. A stream of cyclists flows by and I realize the fitter guys who started off after me are now catching up. They all seem determined, focused, and very smooth in their style. I envy them as each one flies by. I take another sip and look off into the distance. It's so peaceful.

Two thoughts buzz around my brain: one, 'Can I do this?' And two, 'I don't want to finish last.'

Descent into Hell –
the Arenberg Forest

We flow along like salmon in a stream, seemingly unaware of our surroundings yet with a primeval urge to get to the end of the journey. The effects of my earlier crash are starting to now be felt: my right shoulder begins to throb, and the right knee develops a jagged pain every time I flex to push down on the pedals hard. It's bearable, of course, as my mind is focusing on the climax – well, to my mind anyway – of these past six months of training. Now is the time and the hour.

The mist has risen completely to reveal the opaque, bleak landscape I suspected I would see, broken up by the odd, lonely house dotting the fringes of the acres of fields. In the distance I can see a wood, and the famous colliery tower looming in the haze as my mini-peloton starts to crank up the cadence and I see for the first time Flemish, German and French flags, motor-homes, more gendarmes and lots of spectators. The Arenberg, at last, is in sight.

The hamlet of Arenberg brings to mind footage from 1980s news bulletins of striking miners. The pit village seems a provincial, small, ugly community; the housing is scattered around in clusters with one main road cutting through to the mine. It's clearly industrial, with no real thought of civic pride or well-being; it has been dropped there to house the workers, to do their job – period. There are soot-covered windows, doors and vehicles; roughly kept pathways and cement-grey roofing. You'd only come here for the work; there is no other reason you would want to live here unless you loved hunting mushrooms in the forest.

The long, straight road leads us up to the waiting spectacle. Having watched Paris–Roubaix over the years, I subconsciously know every house on this street, every dip in the road and all the features of the forest ahead – like the bridge cutting across the path soon after one enters it. The pro event regularly enjoys 30,000 spectators lining this forest track, and there are plenty out today, too – but, still, I don't really take in the dozens of people cheering us on as I am mentally tuning in for the battering about to hit me. I am torn between chanting, 'I am so up for this,' and the gut-wrenching fear of an impending knee-capping. I am a centurion of the Ninth Legion, entering the forbidden forest to witness destruction by hordes of Germanic tribesmen. Well, maybe not, but you get the picture. Roll the dice, and here we go. I tap my chest where my dad's war ribbon is pinned and quietly mutter a prayer.

We roll up to a white fence that is guarding the entrance to Arenberg, and the head of my group slows right down; gendarmes and race organizers are directing riders through the gap in the fence to begin their assault on the famous section. We can see the overhead rail bridge before us, and a chill goes down my spine as I look towards 'the Trench', the first 800 metres or so, sloping down to the bottom section, which looks dark, damp and danger-ous. I hear a Scouse accent hollering, 'Let's have it!' as he then comes to an abrupt halt behind our group, realizing he has to wait his turn like the rest of us to enter this bear pit. A sense of impatience permeates our group now.

From my memories of reading the race manual, this is where those riders taking on the shorter routes, who haven't as yet ridden any cobbled sections, go into the forest, too. We veterans of the *pavé*, on the other hand, obviously feel we've earned the right to be the vanguard for this fresh attack. We politely barge our way to the front of the waiting line and without further protest hop like sheep in a fold through the two-foot gap and start the race afresh. Welcome to hell, *mes amis*.

Now, over recent months, I have pretty much digested every book written about the race, and I am trying to stay focused before we hit the heavy stuff, but my mind wanders back to thinking about what Sean, Barry and William have all said to me:

'Ride on the crown.'

'Stay in the big ring, and keep up a good speed.'

'Don't fear it, embrace it and you'll be OK.'

'It's brutal!'

I click up on to the big ring and select a higher gear: I am going to take this bugger on, I am not going to be intimidated; I can see the rise to the finish and it'll be over before you know it – a few minutes' pain and it'll be done . . .

'*Fuuuuuuuuuuuuuuccccccck meeeeeeeeeeeeeeeeeeeeeeeeeee!*'

A portly German and his lanky pal, dressed in black and racing beautiful white Pinarellos, fly past me and generate enough noise with their tyres being pummelled to be heard over the general din and shouts of the fans who have come early to watch the amateurs suffer this spectacle. I can only describe the initial feeling of hitting these rocks (let's not bandy words about, that's what these bloody things resemble) as being akin to someone attaching you to a heavy-duty road drill, which itself is lashed to a team of wild horses. You switch on the earthquake-inducing machine and the horses then proceed to drag you at speed down a hill. Screaming all the way. This is *Ben Hur* for cyclists.

Keeping to the plan, I attempt to stay at the centre of the track, but realize pretty quickly that this *pavé* is very different to what I have traversed thus far. The setts are more irregular, and the terrain itself resembles a building site. Amidst the general hubbub of the surroundings, the noise is deafening, one's brain churning over like a washing machine. I feel like I have Metallica's latest offering blasting out at full volume in my skull. The crowd is bigger here than anywhere I have cycled through; people are setting up for tomorrow's elite race, parking camper vans, staking out pitches, erecting barbecues.

The evergreen forest rises around the track like in some scene from *The Shining* – despite all the preparation I had undertaken in terms of reading articles and watching old races on YouTube, it is still a pretty forebidding sight. On my left is a muddy verge, with the woods acting as a barrier; to my right a metal guard rail protects the fans who are standing, forming a beautiful man-made pathway. If you try to veer left you'll end up in a swamp, while steering into a metal fence is never popular. One simply has to try to get across.

The *pavé* gets worse as we progress through the Arenberg, and twice I luckily avoid huge, sharp setts sticking out of the path like ship-wrecking icebergs. Around me are riders either stopping due to tiredness, mechanicals, or wipe-outs. One rider in an Orica–GreenEDGE outfit powers past me with not much room to spare, only to pile into the back of my German friend, who is shouting and crying out as Orica–GreenEDGE narrowly avoids going over his handlebars, his front wheel hitting the side of the German, before fighting to regain control only to veer off right and into the gutter, where he lands with a deflating and juddering thud that must have hurt. A thought pops into my head from something I had read before: 'Is this where Team Cofidis's Philippe Gaumont suffered his horrific

crash in 2001, which almost cost him his life?'[27] But I'm too
preoccupied to see if the guy in the ditch is OK, I just make sure I
stick to the German and follow his line.

Several riders are walking slowly back towards us along the
pathway – they clearly have had enough, or their bikes have
suffered major mechanicals. More are doing the same further up
the section; this is attritional. I am taking it all in but my whole
body is badly vibrating as I frantically steer my ship through this
minefield. My vision is tumble-drying, my heart rate is hitting its
threshold and I'm actually starting to think I'm drunk.

We start to rise slowly towards what I can see must be the finish,
about 500 metres away, where there is a huge crowd with dozens of
riders milling around. My pace and cadence have slowed dramatically as I tire, and I decide to increase tempo in an effort to beat
this beast. By clicking up a gear and with a violent (instead of my
usual smooth) stamp on my pedals, I attempt to get moving. My
chain jumps and into the bottom ring it goes, thus my leg pushes
down quicker than expected and my groin hits the top tube pretty
hard. Waking me from my dream state, my testicles scream in
agony and I feel nausea coming. I slow right down again and blow
hard as half a dozen riders rumble past me, not willing to hinder
their own progress through this hell by seeing if I'm OK. Who can
blame them?

I squeeze every last ounce of myself into staying on the bike
and not vomiting. But going down accidentally on to the bottom
ring turns out to be a blessing in disguise, as I regain control, and
start to increase the cadence easily. My speed picks up and the

---

[27] Gaumont, later infamous for admitting a severe drug problem while a professional cyclist,
was leading the race when he powered towards the Arenberg only to crash heavily and suffer
a serious compound fracture of his femur. With his heart rate topping 190 b.p.m., it almost
cost him his life as he developed a huge haematoma, which was only treated at the local
A&E in Lille. He died of a heart attack, aged 40, in May 2013.

bike naturally steers itself. I begin to see how one can ride this ridiculous terrain, but it's a painful lesson. I loosen my manic grip on the top bar and allow the bike to jump beneath me as I push harder to drive it forward. I ride past a prone rider who's got a double flat by the looks of it, has lost his balance and gone over – he's swearing in Danish, I think (I've watched too much of *The Bridge*).

Gaining more control, and not fearing any impending disaster, I lift my head up from focusing on the wheel in front of me and start to take in my surroundings again. It is a beautiful place, certainly now that I'm nearing the end of it. Fleeting objects appear in the periphery of my vision, moving fast. Four or five guys are really motoring along the spectators' pathway towards the top of the sector, passing me quite easily as I struggle along. Now, I'm not one to gripe, but part of me feels this is taking the piss. Isn't the whole point of what we're doing to experience what getting through the Arenberg is like? Will it inflict Gaumont-type injuries upon us? I think not! If only I could ride that fast, for that long, even if it was on *pot belge*. I look over at them again as they disappear up the pathway, and it gives me new impetus.

Some light is forcing its way through the tall pines, and I feel like I'm emerging out of a dark tunnel, back to life; the *pavé* rises gently up to reveal the finish of the Arenberg, and I eagerly put in one last spurt of violent stamping on the pedals. Again, we're having to navigate a small gap through a white metal barrier, and on the other side are hundreds of happy cyclists.

I've made it! I have ridden the Arenberg. I am so shocked to have conquered my fears without a flat tyre or injury that I look down at my Garmin and laugh as I realize I was only in there for a few minutes, and I shakily ride over to a quiet corner twenty yards past the exit gate. Unclipping, I prise my backside off the saddle, stand astride my bike and look it over. It seems OK, though the bottom bracket looks a mess of mud, grit and scratches, and my tyres are covered in a film of mud. My hands are in agony and I strip off my mitts to reveal the makings of impressive blisters forming on both palms. I pour some water from a *bidon* on them and get myself ready to depart. I don't fancy hanging around – we still have another 15 sections of *pavé* to go. Despite this, and the ringing in my ears, I am joyous in completing what to me is the pinnacle of cycling. All the years I have read, watched and discussed this epic monument to professional cycling and here I am – at the end of a personal journey. I feel a little sad thinking this, but am snapped out of it by voices nearby.

A couple – for they seem naturally bonded to one another, wearing the same black and white Specialized kit, complete with matching silver helmets – roll up towards me with huge smiles on their faces. 'That was amazing!' shouts the tall young man, teeth gleaming through his stubble and wired-looking eyes. His petite, but muscular-legged girlfriend, blonde ponytail sticking out of the back of her helmet, stops beside him and they embrace one another, laughing.

'My whole body is on strike!' she happily moans.

I say nothing.

He gestures towards me with a nod of acknowledgement. 'Enjoy it?'

'Yes, it was tough going, but I loved it. Funny how you build it up in your mind—'

He cuts across me, 'Ah, we were dreading it, but it was worth it. That was our first section. How about you?'

Now there must be an amateur cyclist's code of not wanting to brag, but I feel compelled to do so. I raise myself subconsciously off my seat, puff the chest out, and look steely-eyed into the forest. I am back in Roman centurion mode. 'No, I've been riding for about two hours now, across eleven sections. It's been tough, but I'm OK so far.'

'Wow,' says the girl, 'we thought about the full route, but chickened out. You must be strong.'

'Yes, yes I am,' I think to myself, but say, 'Anyone can do it; it's all in the mind at the end of the day.' Could I have sounded any more like a wanker? 'Anyway, got to get going, don't want to stand around too long as I'll get cramp. Good luck with the rest of the race.' And with that Gary Cooper homily from any Western you care to name, I clip in and head out on to a well-maintained forest road, going towards the next section at Hornaing. 'Cheers, *bonne chance!*' I say.

I am so happy, I could cry. Needless to say, the *pavé* would now begin to fight back.

Punctures and Death by Tractor

I was sailing along, blissfully happy with the joy of beating the sacred forest, of taming the dreaded Arenberg. The monkey off my back, I started to relax into the ride at last. I was all alone, riding along the perimeter of the forest as it broke out into open countryside, the road skirting another hamlet and the sky revealing a brighter start to the mid-morning proceedings. I had to do something special. The euphoric urge of having to have someone know about what I had achieved forced me to pull over to the side of the road. A few stragglers shot past me, their whirring gears and tyres loudly humming on the steaming road; the riders excitedly chattering to one another in French. In a frenzy, I wrenched my winter mitt off my right hand with my teeth, and retrieved my mobile phone from the rear pocket of my gilet. Smiling to myself and buzzing with the effort of what had just gone before, I rapidly speed-dialled my home number. It rang out. My numb fingers then tried multiple times to locate my wife's mobile number and, finally succeeding, I waited impatiently for her to pick up.

'Hello?'

'Darling, hi, it's me. I did it!' My voice boomed over the stillness of the surrounding forest.

'Did what? Are you OK?' I could hear the TV, and my

son chuntering in the background as it dawned on me it might be 10 a.m.(ish) where I was, but it was early breakfast time on a chilled-out Saturday morning back home.

'Sorry, I forgot the time difference. I just wanted to tell you I did it!'

'It's OK, we're just sitting here on the sofa watching CBBC. What have you done? Not crashed, I hope? You can't have finished the race already?'

That raised a smile as I looked at the makings of a very large blister developing on the palm of my left hand.

'No, no. The Arenberg – I got across it in one piece. I can't believe it. It was bloody brilliant. The cobbles were *un-be-liev-able!*' The last elongated word echoed around the terrain as I watched yet more riders cruise past.

'That's great—' The phone line went dead. I saw that the signal was weak, and my guess was everyone was calling home to report the same news, or perhaps my phone was on the blink. The phone buzzed in my hand again with a text message, *Kids want their breakfast and I need mine, too. Love you, be careful. Xxx*

I studied the message for a few seconds, before I was startled by a thick Scottish voice right beside me: 'You OK, mate?'

Standing there was a middle-aged rider, very overweight – his girth bulging out of his very smart Rapha long-sleeve jersey, creating rolling folds – but with a very impressive set of muscular thighs and calves. 'Ah thought ye might be in a wee bit of trouble there, is it a mechanical?'

He looked genuinely concerned. His brown wavy hair was protruding out of the vents and the sides and back of his white Garneau helmet. With his Oakley racing shades on and a great big-bearded, toothy smile, I instantly warmed to him.

'No, thanks, but I'm OK, just phoning home to tell them I got through the last section.'

'Aye, that was something else, eh.' His Glaswegian accent was unmistakable. 'Fancy riding along for a wee while?'

'Sure, happy to.' I swung back on the bike, clipped in and looked up to see him speed off into the distance. He may have looked like Billy Bunter in lycra, but he definitely had a motor under that big bonnet. I set off in hasty pursuit.

Catching him up, we hit open road, a nice smooth tarmacked surface which felt, after the Arenberg, like a billiard table covered in velvet. The stinging in my hands, up my arms, and ending at the nape of my neck slowly dissolved as the pair of us ticked along next to one another. The sun was starting to break through the mist, the chill in the air was receding and all felt right with the world. As he chatted away I reached back for a chocolate bar, which I had kept specifically as a reward for getting over the Arenberg in one piece.

As I munched on the Cadbury's Whole Nut, the sweetness of the chocolate providing the instant sought-after pick-me-up, I noticed he'd stopped talking and was staring at me. Or, rather, staring at the half-eaten bar in my hand, with a look anyone who has a five-year-old child will recognize. Wanting to enjoy his conversation further it was a case of sacrificing something. 'Want some?'

'Don't mind if I do, thanks, mate,' and he grinned as I passed over a chunk, a bit bigger than I had intended, but he accepted it willingly. Over the next fifteen minutes or so, he told me about how he'd come to be here.

He had been a keen cyclist in the 1980s and somehow fallen out of love with it as adulthood, drinking and chasing girls took over. Reaching his fiftieth birthday the previous year, he realized, at a surprise party with his family, that everyone was amazed he'd reached the milestone. So, undergoing an epiphany of sorts, he decided to get his teenage son's bike out of the shed, cycle to work, and started to plan for a new goal. The spring Classics were always his favourite races, and even though the renowned climber Robert

Millar was a fellow Glaswegian, Sean Kelly was the rider he followed avidly. He'd bought the gear, a new ubiquitous Boardman bike, and hit the Campsie Fells to get fit enough for his all-time favourite race.

'This one.' He gestured with his head as he smiled again and clicked up a gear. 'I did the Tour of Flanders last week as training, and am hoping to get under six hours.'

Under six hours!? He clicked up another gear and the speed increased to the point where he was pulling away from me, despite my best efforts to maintain parity without making it obvious I was blowing hard.

I am sure we have all been there on a bike, in a sportive, or even just training with mates: you all try to test one another, *mano a mano*, to see who has the best legs that day, and who can suffer more pain, too. Well, this guy was starting to put the hammer down before we reached the next section of *pavé*. Now I was left with a dilemma. Do I take him on at his own game, reaching into precious energy stores and endure the burning in my legs, just for the macho hell of it? Or do I forego the fact that the bugger just ate some of my chocolate reward and is now speeding off into the blue, without even breaking sweat?

The right hand did twitch for a few seconds, hovering over the gear lever, but with numerous sections to traverse, the weather getting warmer, and not wanting to let pride come before a fall, I eased off the cadence. The effect of the disparity in our speeds was instantaneous. Like a bungee jumper, he suddenly sprang away from me as if I were stranded in melting tarmac on a sweltering day at the Tour de France.

'See you soon, buddy. Thanks for the chocolate, much appreciated!' he shouted over his shoulder as his large form quickly reduced in profile the faster he sped away from me.

That last line, for whatever reason, sparked something within me. 'Sod this, I'm having you, sunshine,' and the salmon rose to the lure.

Breathing hard, my thighs crying out in agony as I drove the cadence through several gears within seconds, I hit 45 k.p.h. and began to eat up the road between us. Like Captain Ahab after the white whale, my target loomed back into the cross hairs, though he didn't look like he was busting a gut to get away from me. He was now only 20 metres or so away and I was closing fast. We turned right off the main road, and hit the next section of *pavé* (Wallers to Hélesmes) just as I drew alongside him.

'Hello again, pal. Watch yourself here, this stuff looks pretty lethal, as well as bloody long.' The cobbles did indeed stretch out to the horizon.

Again, he seemed to ease away from me and, increasing his speed, he moved on to the crown of the cobbles in order to try to get the best lie of the road as we descended slightly, coming up to the iconic, huge stone pillars that guard the left-hand bend of Pont Gibus. This is the place that pays homage to the French cycling great Gilbert Duclos-Lassalle, who won back-to-back Paris–Roubaix races in 1992 and 1993, making his winning moves at this juncture in the race. As we passed through the brick sentinels, marked out in giant white lettering on the walls were the eponymous words 'Pont Gibus 92:93'. Your average rambler might walk past it in ignorance, but to a fan of this race, it's as iconic as one of the hairpins on the climb to Alpe d'Huez.

I smiled to myself as I realized he was slowing down and I was about to pass him on the right-hand side. The *pavé* there, although a little rougher in places, with some setts protruding, did allow more room for the rider to use the grassy verge if need be. I certainly needed it and began to dodge potholes, murky puddles containing God knows what, and humps which, coming at me at speed, involved bunny-hopping over. My luck couldn't last this long. Looking at my man gliding towards the bend ahead of me, I missed a pothole rearing up and the front wheel took the brunt of it.

The impact wasn't shattering, as I managed to maintain my balance and keep on riding. But I instantly knew it was a blow out as the bone-jarring rattling of the *pavé* increased tenfold and my teeth began to vibrate in my skull. Pulling over to the right side of the road where the verge expanded by a few extra feet, I dismounted and surveyed the damage. By this time a long line of riders were filing past me, and the helplessness of knowing you're getting left behind by the herd hit home. I felt very alone.

The voice erupted in my head again. 'Stop feeling sorry for yourself, man, get on with it, quickly!' Having gone through this procedure more times than I cared to remember, I went into auto pilot and quickly placed the bike upside down on the level grassy verge, and disconnected the front wheel, the now flaccid rubber tyre looking pathetic and done in. Sitting down cross-legged I placed the wheel on my lap and with my tyre levers began the laborious process of prising the tyre off the hub in order to get at the inner tube. Job done, pretty quickly. Pleased with my progress despite stinging hands and fingers, I took out the new, shiny rubber inner tube to replace the old, which I then shockingly threw away into the ditch (c'mon, we all do it), and kneaded it into the frame of the wheel hub. Within five minutes the tyre was back on and I was ready to pump it up and get on my way.

Wait a minute, where was the pump?!

I grasped around in the three pockets of my gilet and there was no familiar feel of said pump. Just gels, my race cape, and the few Pret bars I had left. I quickly stripped off my gilet and again, with panic setting in, manically grasped around. Still no pump and, what's more, two of the three spare inner tubes that were in my pockets were gone, too. With rising panic I studied the surrounding area, and again patted myself down to make sure it somehow wasn't tucked away somewhere else. Of course not, you idiot. The realization dawned on me: maybe it fell out when I crashed first thing this morning? What the hell was I going to do now?

I shook my head in disbelief as more and more riders, in a huge echelon, pounded down the *pavé*, the noise getting louder as more of them appeared. Dozens were flying by, leaving me here, stranded with this stupid, flat, bloody tyre, and nothing to fix it with. Fuck, fuck, fuck! I stared into the horizon thinking about all the training, the endless hours in the kitchen on the turbo, and the expense of getting out here. All for nothing.

Just as I was about to kick my bike in frustration, a nearby rider suffered a very loud explosion and his back wheel almost went from underneath him as the tyre instantly lost any traction it had enjoyed seconds before. Unclipping with lightning-quick reflexes, he managed to keep his balance and not bring anyone else down with him, as three or four riders skirted round his prone bike and pressed on.

Without any remonstrations of anxiety or anger, he simply dismounted properly and pushed his bike over towards where I was stranded.

'Well done in keeping your balance there. I thought that was going to be a nasty one,' I said, trying to smile and not look a bit weird, just standing around spectating a race I should be involved with.

'That's my third flat since we started, this stuff is murderous!' He had to shout over the rattling din as twenty or more riders came hurtling down the road, some shouting encouragement to us, others heads down, gripping their drops as they stamped on their pedals. It's a great spectacle, even if you're stranded.

His name was Sam, he was Irish, and looked a proper rider. Six feet tall, with a lithe frame, under 70 kilograms in weight, armed with T-Rex-like arms and powerful thighs, he was dressed all in black, save for a silver helmet and white shades. He smiled, upturned his bike and quickly set about the process I'd been happily undertaking only minutes ago. Except he had all his repair equipment. While getting out his new inner tube from his saddle pouch, he stared up at me with a questioning look. 'Giving up already, are we?'

I gestured with upturned hands. 'I've lost my pump, must have fallen out earlier on, can you believe it?' On the one hand I was thinking he was unlucky, too, but inside I was doing cartwheels, as I knew salvation had arrived!

'You should have said, here, take this while I get the tube in,' he said, throwing me his pump, and got down to squatting on his back wheel as he eased it out of the bracket in order to get at the tyre quickly. I could have kissed him. A complete stranger and he's saved my race.

'Are you sure?' A typical British response.

Without looking up, he grunted, 'Don't be stupid, how else are you going to get to Roubaix. Get on with it.'

I didn't need a second longer, quickly attaching the pump and letting rip with manic thrusts to get the tyre back up to the requisite 60 psi. I was back in business, baby. He was still fixing his wheel as I walked over to him and put my hand on his shoulder as I offered the pump back. Smiling gratefully he nodded and carried on with his own repair. I remounted and after allowing another group to steam past, rejoined the race, my brain, eyes and teeth soon beginning to rattle again.

The next few kilometres flew by. I was conscious I was down on my target of finishing in under 6 hours 30 minutes, plus the adrenaline kicked in as I tried to make up time on riders I had recognized throughout the race. I recalled from my teenage road-racing days that when you're riding at a certain speed you tend to encounter people with the same ability along the way. You may take diversions, be injured, have a breather, or suffer a mechanical. But, sooner or later, a familiar shape will hove into view and the battle recommences.

I was enjoying one such duel with a guy who was wearing Mark Cavendish's British road cycling outfit, and a pair of garish yellow socks with the black Flandrian lion rampart embroidered on to them. You couldn't miss him. I knew he'd clocked me a few times, too, and both of us seemed determined to match the other's efforts. We would find one another later on in a bizarre incident.

For now, the second feed station at Hornaing arrived, and I eagerly joined the mass of participants who needed replenishment. It was another beautiful, tightly packed little market square, adorned with a variety of stalls offering fruit, brioche and waffles – lots of waffles, though no coffee. I was gutted. I picked a spot away from the hubbub and took in the scene of a wall of lycra colours, glistening bikes and highly animated chatter in multiple languages. The buzz was brilliant – everyone was still coming down from the Arenberg, swapping tales of derring-do, pointing to scrapes, bangs and near-misses. I did spot a few riders coming into the market square who just kept on riding, as though keen to not be encumbered by this morass of humanity – time was ticking, after all. Scoffing my third waffle, I took a long slake of water from the *bidon* and got back on the saddle.

My legs were sore, my neck was starting to spasm, and my hands were purple from gripping the bars so tightly. 'Accept the situation, Iain, and it's easier to handle the pain,' I thought. I reminded myself of one of my favourite passages from Richard Askwith's magnificent tribute to British fell-running, *Feet in the Clouds*:

My legs flopped so limply I thought I would fall to the ground. But I knew – and had known, since about the fifth mile – that there was no question of my doing anything but continue. And this confidence created a layer of mental peace over the physical pain. Whatever I was feeling, whatever I might feel, I was stronger than those feelings, because I chose to be.

He might have added, 'Because I am 80 kilometres from the finish, in the middle of nowhere, and don't speak much French, either.'

Section 16, Hornaing to Wandignies-Hamage, was coming up, and briefly glancing at the yellow strip on my top bar I could see four stars next to it warning of the severity of the *pavé* to come. I found myself alone with my thoughts – the majority of people seemed to want to hang around at the feed station a while. The sun was now shining through the cloud cover, and warming my back. A headwind was picking up, though, and for the first time I started to feel an ache in my legs as I tried to maintain a bigger gear.

My plan to overcome the conditions was evolving, as all good plans must if they are to succeed. I had now decided to keep in the big ring for the tarmacked roads, and use my discretion for the *pavé*. If the cobbles were a little more benign, then I would stay in the gear I had approached them in, but where there were hazards and the jarring and shaking proved too much, then I'd click down and spin my way through. Equally, the early bravado of wishing to dominate and ride on the crown was fading to an acceptance that we can't all be Tom Boonen or Fabian Cancellara. No, I'd decided that whatever it took to get over those final stretches of cobbles, I would do it. Survival mode was kicking in and I was still only halfway to the velodrome.

This stretch of *pavé*, although one of the longest at 3.7 kilometres, proved a little more forgiving than the guidebook allowed. Before I knew it, I could see two large manor houses flanking the finishing straight and the white and red banner telling me it was coming to an end. Marvellous. Next, please; I was starting to enjoy it. Indeed, the subsequent two sections – Warlaing to Brillon and Tilloy to Sars-et-Rosières – were again straightforward: get your head down and get through it as best you can. The actual *pavé* was smoother here, and I found fellow riders feeling safe enough to ride as a group, rather than one after the other. As the route tacked back and forth, I periodically felt confident enough to look up and take the wind and dust in my face, and I could see riders criss-crossing the terrain ahead of me. It reminded me of a fairground shooting gallery, where the metal duck darts back and forth as you try to hit it with your air rifle. At least it was pointing me in the direction I needed to go, and spectators were now dotted around everywhere I looked. As the conditions were improving all the time, I stopped to switch my winter hat with my new race cap and shades.

We hit the main road once more and thoughts of actually finishing this thing started entering my head, despite not wanting to tempt fate. As we began a section that cut through cultivated fields, bordered by hedgerows, I could hear cheering and whooping – coming up a rise there stood twenty or so spectators, with a variety of VW vans, cars and caravans parked nearby. The urge to put on a show burnt within me and, head down, I made the effort to stay in the bigger gear. Within seconds a scream of, 'Look out!' perforated the din. Lifting my head up, I saw that the whole road was taken up by a tractor and I was about to enjoy a head-on collision with its giant bucket.

Years of cycling in London, and not a scratch. I come out here to the vast agricultural emptiness of northern France, and I pick out the only tractor for miles around. Violently clenching both brake levers for all I was worth, the wheels locked and the bike started violently pulling to the left as I fought to remain seated. I could see the farmer, mouth agog, just staring at me, as various riders coming up fast were now braking, trying desperately to not stack up behind me. I juddered to a halt inches from the giant metal bucket.

Much swearing now commenced in French, German, Dutch, Italian and, of course, good old Anglo-Saxon. The equally irate farmer refused to budge. I was shaking with the realization of how close that had been as we all got into single file and eased our way past the throbbing behemoth, its engine rumbling in neutral.

'I thought you were a goner there.' I got a pat on the back from a cheery Brit who owned up to being the one who'd shouted the warning in the first place.

'I'm glad you did. I just didn't see him at all; how can a bloody tractor come out of nowhere, in the middle of nowhere?!'

But he had, and he'd almost taken me out. A shiver went down my spine at the stupid confidence we have when doing these races – we want to ride like the pros, and just because an official outrider motors past we think the roads are closed, that we're protected and safe . . . Still shocked, I slowly carried on down the section, embarrassed and thankful that my brake cables were brand new.

As we came off the section and were hitting a left-hand bend, there was more carnage. A rider at the helm, in the black and blue Sky livery, was cranking up the speed to go for the next section, coming up fast to Orchies. I was third in a string of half a dozen riders with him when we proceeded to hit a dip on to more *pavé*. I could see the Sky rider might be over-cooking the turn, but he realized it too late; his bike went from under him and he hit the deck with a sickening thud, taking the worst of the battering on his left shoulder, kicking up a violent cloud of dry dirt.

We skirted around him, but by now it was an unwritten rule that we all stopped for one another, as others had for me. I slowed down to reassure myself that he was going to be OK – it had been a hell of a wipe-out. He lurched groggily to his feet, but was at least speaking and rubbing his bruised left side. Then he picked up his bike and rested against the side of the road, mumbling a few words to an old man who had also walked over to check on his well-being. He was possibly embarrassed, and probably in shock, but he abstractly waved us all to carry on. A calm came over me as I settled down again to the road ahead, hoping we'd all get home safely. Suddenly none of us were chatting to pass the time as before; it had all somehow become less fun and definitely more serious.[28]

---

[28] Later, back in England, I caught up with this rider on the Challenge Roubaix website. He thought he'd cracked a collarbone, and when he asked for advice from the old man who'd come to his aid, he was met with the legendary line, 'Well, what would a Flandrian do?' Was this Roger De Vlaeminck? Say no more. He cycled on, through ten more sections of *pavé*, in agony, and completed the course. Chapeau!

Drunken Aussies
and Eating the Velodrome

It felt like the hours were ticking over. Studying my Garmin I could see I'd covered over 100 kilometres and there were eleven sections of *pavé* to go. With most sportives back in the UK, especially in the south-east of England, having ridden past that milestone would almost certainly mean I was on a downward trajectory, fitness-wise. I would be down to my final gel, probably running low on liquids, and definitely tiring. But here, right now, I felt pretty good, surprisingly, and my legs still felt strong. The terrain here certainly helped. Yes, the *pavé* was hard, but I'd handled it OK so far and, with very little climbing to contend with (the steepest gradient had been a half-mile drag out of a large village ten miles back, and only five per cent), the mental strain was the toughest part.

I took the opportunity to pull over before the next section for a few minutes to study the pocket map the organizers had provided. I needed to get into my head what lay up the road; what I needed to prepare for. I had been told the Arenberg was tough, but that even tougher sections lay ahead. Now basking in benign weather, I studied the A4-sized map, adorned with a very large and garish Paris–Roubaix Challenge logo in the corner. Suddenly a whoosh as four riders flew past me, so close I could feel their slipstream.

Low and behold there were the tell-tale Flandrian socks belonging
to the rider on the end of the line. I could have sworn he turned his
head towards me and smiled!

The next section, Auchy-lez-Orchies to Bersée, seemed straightforward enough – still quite long at 2.6 kilometres, but flat and
cutting through barren farmland. That didn't worry me. More
riders passed by shouting encouragement as I mulled over the
section coming after it, the one I had been warned by William
at Pavé Cycling was tougher than the notes suggested. Mons-en-
Pévèle was a 3-kilometre undulating lung-buster, complete with a
tight right-hand turn roughly one-third of the way along, and some
serious, very rough setts. It was the stage where the favourites in
the pro race normally chose to make their final winning moves. In
the wet it was supposed to be a quagmire, so I was at least thankful
for the clement weather. Get past that in one piece and it would be
50 more kilometres to the finish. To the end. Thinking that gave
me optimism. This was doable, but I still had no pump, and only
one spare inner tube, so I needed patience, good judgement and
lots of luck.

We crossed over the main D549, and for once there was a stream
of traffic – by now the locals were out, busy with their weekend
affairs, plenty of them honking their horns in encouragement, and
a few were even pulling slowly over to the verge in order for us to
stream through without braking.

'Would never happen in Laaaandaaaan,' came a familiar
voice over my shoulder. I had met Stuart after my crash on the
first section. Once I'd got going again we rode together for a few
sections of *pavé*. He was a twenty-something, strongly built
redhead, with a real love of cycling – he'd even ridden over for
the race from his flat in Battersea. It had taken him a week but
he'd seen it as a colossal 'once in a lifetime' adventure, as well as
training for today. Indeed, he was far stronger than I was and
had taken off before the first post-crash feed station. He was all

smiles seeing me again and we swapped stories of the Arenberg, punctures and the weather.

'Serious stuff coming up now, Iain. I'm glad I have these beauties,' he said, pointing to his tractor-like 28-mm tyres. They made a very loud whirring noise, even on tarmac; on cobbles it was like being followed by a car. But they did the job, and I didn't have any issues with anyone customizing their ride to ensure they finished with their brains and backside still intact. I had seen quite a few guys riding custom-built mountain bikes, some even with suspensions, and their tyres were fat. You'd hear them coming up from a distance, and the looks of calm on their faces as they passed by betrayed how easier they were having it on the *pavé*.

'Do you mind if I crack on, I want to beat six hours if I can.' He looked like a gun dog eager to chase a shot duck.

'No problem, mate, don't wait for me. Good luck and watch yourself.'

'You, too, see you in Roubaix for a beer.' And with that he flicked the gear leaver, lowered his grip to the drops and bent into the headwind. Within seconds he was 50 metres ahead of me and by the time I turned off the D549 on to a local road he was some distance away, his dark form heading towards the familiar red and white banner strung across the entrance to the coming *pavé*, section 11. Although I had a few guys behind me, as I now led the string along, I felt incredibly alone.

I pretty much floated over the next section, though my bunny-hopping skills came to the fore a few times as, riding in the gutter for a lengthy kilometre or so, my luck ran out when I hit some rather ugly, muddy potholes where someone had basically taken out a few cobbles. If this had happened right at the very beginning I'd have crashed, for sure, but by now I still had strength and more confidence in navigating my way through this minefield. Hilariously, one rider a few yards in front of me, was a little over-zealous in the manoeuvre and took himself off into the adjacent ploughed field, where he vainly tried to maintain his balance for a few seconds before collapsing into a heap. That kind of thing would recur throughout the remainder of the race.

And so to Mons-en-Pévèle. Now, when you think of cycling, you might think of an archetypal summer's day, perfect for a picnic, for sipping gorgeous red wine and eating fresh cheese and baguettes picked up from a nearby picturesque market town. Sadly, this was April, the headwind had picked up, and I was about to experience the hardest ride I think I'll ever do.

The terrain was now billiard-table flat and I could see for miles. In the distance was Pévèle, with its enormous church spire dominating the skyline. The section was looking straight for a good distance and I knew we'd have two tight, right-hand bends to navigate through, so I was intent on keeping an eye on my speed. Despite this, as we entered the section I could see a decent-sized crowd sitting there on a distant hillock watching the spectacle as the next train of riders motored through.

My group, now eight in number, was coming up fast behind them. Ahead in the string that had just gone past the spectators, I noticed the familiar Cavendish jersey and yellow Flandrian socks. There he was, my nemesis, thundering down the corridor of humanity and noise! I don't know how this happened, but instantly the blood was up. Changing quickly to the big ring, and selecting an extra gear, I immediately stamped on the pedals and took off, leaving my guys behind me agog. The crowd of about thirty or more locals saw me coming and began whooping and hollering, which only increased the tempo and excitement; I was in the moment, I was on a mission. The shouts of the crowd and the incessant percussion of my wheels on the crown of the *pavé* were overwhelming me as I darted up a slight rise and turned into a slow right bend leading into a very long straight. For the first time, I actually got out of the saddle and started springing over this stuff. It felt insane, but addictive.

The pay-off arrived. Hurtling now along the centre of the track, with the group ahead – containing my prey – just metres away from me, and an urge building to simply fly past them, I felt an eruption at the back of the frame. The noise of the tyre on the *pavé* multiplied tenfold, as did the vibrations through the handlebars to my upper arms and neck, and with a sickening feeling in the pit of my stomach I knew I had suffered at least one flat, maybe two. God, I hoped not two.

Pulling over to the right-hand side of what was now a very long and dead-straight stretch of *pavé*, as my fellow riders powered along, not looking back, I knew I was stuffed. No pump, one spare inner tube and potentially two flat tyres to contend with. Bugger. Looking around at the flat landscape of ploughed fields and grassy verges, seeing how much further it was to even get to the end of this terrible section, my spirits started sinking slowly. I decided the best option was simply to walk. Get off this section, take stock and deal with it. 'Don't give up just yet,' I told myself.

It was now turning into a brighter afternoon and, as I trekked along the grass to the side of the *pavé*, I could see a large gallery of spectators in the distance. Perhaps one of them, anyone, might have a bike pump to help me out? But this wasn't the sort of crowd I thought it was. Far from politely, or enthusiastically cheering on the gallant riders, this seemed more like a mob of drunks at closing time. Approximately thirty or more, all in their twenties by the looks of them, they were definitely here to party, and it was only one thirty in the afternoon.

'*Wheeeeeeeyheeeeeeeeeeeey!*' they screamed in unison as a group of riders shot past them. This wasn't the sober exultation of glee one might hear from parents at a school race – rather a leering, lustily delivered roar, rising up from the pit of somewhere dark and musty; the type of noise you hear when a streaker hits the hallowed turf at Twickenham, or echoing down Blackpool promenade at midnight on a summer's weekend. Beer was seemingly the drink of choice, and they were all dressed to party – bikinis and cut-off denims for the girls, Hawaiian shirts, rugby jerseys and hoodies for the boys. How did I take in so much detail? Because I was trying to tiptoe past them without being noticed.

'Hey, here's a fella!' A blonde-haired partygoer, can of beer in hand and Aussie flag in the other, was staring straight at me, not ten metres away as I attempted to nonchalantly get past this debauched gallery without too much fuss. 'Just blend into the background, Iain.' No such luck. His mates, in that classic drunken process, took several seconds to cotton on to what he was saying, then refocused in my direction, and finally got what he was saying. A wave of smiles and what resembled leering, open-mouthed, astonished guffaws broke along their ranks. 'Keep walking . . . keep walking.'

'What's wrong with yer, mate, yer arse had enough, eh!?' Loud laughter erupted amidst more cheering for riders flying between us on the *pavé*, thus providing some respite from their attention. A sudden outbreak of silence was then followed by full-on cheering once again, deafening me as I was now directly opposite the whole gang. I mouthed 'puncture' at them, smiling and pointing to my back wheel.

'Are you French, mate, no speak English!?' shouted a very tall and long-haired surf dude, his arm strung around what I took to be his girlfriend. She didn't seem to mind anyway. More stood in front of him as he towered over everyone.

'Just nod, keep walking, don't engage, keep the bike between them and you.'

'Aw, I love these Frenchies, better than the bloody Poms. Let's give the man a cheer, c'mon.'

In one movement (which I have to say I was impressed with considering the condition they were all in), to a man they crouched low and started murmuring. The noise was building up quickly as they held out their arms straight and began to wiggle their hands. The murmur now turned to a guttural roar that was clearly building to a crescendo and the Mexican wave started at the end I had just walked along. The ripple of movement, the cheering, the alcohol, allied to the surroundings of desolate farmland, made for a very surreal scene.

They were all now standing to attention, arms raised straight into the air, beer spilling all over their heads, clothes and on to the *pavé* itself. There was laughter everywhere, but I decided not to speak, there was no sense in spoiling the party, so I simply stopped, put my hands together in mock thanks, blew them a kiss and quickly walked on. The need to ask them for help hadn't crossed my mind; I was thinking more about how the hell they were going to get home. Not my problem, of course. Onwards.

I kept ambling along the section, very aware that I was wasting time, and was in real trouble. I tried to wave some riders down a few times over the next five minutes, but no one seemed to want to lend a hand, which was dispiriting. Where was the unwritten bond of fellowship of the road? It seemed to have disappeared for Mons-en-Pévèle – this really was attritional, 'march or die' type stuff, and my confidence in thinking I'd get out of this calamity was fast disappearing.

Coming to the end of the straight, as it took a ninety-degree right-hand turn, pitching slightly downwards towards a further left-hander 400 metres on in the distance, I saw a middle-aged couple standing next to their classic Renault 4 white delivery van. They seemed to be locals on a day out, enthusiastically but soberly clapping each rider on as they passed on the tight turn. I stopped opposite their position, trapped on the far bank due to the flux of riders coming through. The guy cusped his hands to his mouth and shouted towards me, '*Bonjour, Ca va? Etes-vous en difficulté?*'

I vainly smiled and nodded to him as I rested my aching arms on the handlebars. This ten-minute break from cycling was one thing, but now my body was cooling down, the muscles were beginning to announce how sore they actually were. My neck, in particular, was throbbing right at the base of my skull. I shouted back about my flat tyre and the lack of a pump, and that I was walking to the finish. He raised his eyes to the heavens in mock indignation and then gestured for me to wait a moment while he rummaged in the back of his van. His wife smiled benignly at me as he emerged with a professional cyclist's pump, the type one plunges down with both hands and I quickly made my way over to their side of the *pavé* and started to take the tyre off the front wheel (thankfully the back tyre was OK). This wasn't a problem; what proved to be the handicap was my inability to focus on getting the sodding tyre back on once the new inner tube had been safely inserted. Like one of those trainee fighter pilots who have to complete simple hand–eye coordination tasks at high altitude without an oxygen supply, my brain said one thing, but my swollen, bruised hands did another. Try as I might, the blasted tyre would not fit around the rim, to the point where I believed I had the wrong size and, swearing loudly, threw it on the ground in disgust.

The couple, who had gone back to watching the race while I performed my simple task, turned around to catch my comic suffering. After one further failed attempt, the gentleman gestured that could he try for me and, accepting the offending apparatus, he put the tyre on in approximately fifteen seconds. '*Voila!*' he said, handing it back with no hint of arrogance, or trace of a smirk.

Holding the punctured inner tube, I told him in broken French how the replacement was my final one, and gestured a gun to my temple in mock execution. Making a comedic sign of the cross, he allowed me to mount the bike, and then getting behind my saddle, pushed me back out on to the *pavé*. This had all taken minutes, but the disconnect of the situation, due to fatigue, gave it a surreal time delay. It felt like an hour had passed by the time I reached the end of the sector. Before that, I suddenly came to a stop again, unclipped and, with riders flying past me like wildebeest, I looked towards the couple who were still watching me from a distance. '*Merci!*' I shouted, and we fondly waved to one another as I turned to crack on. Manners cost nothing, after all.

The next two sections – Mérignies to Avelin and Pont-Thibaut to Ennevelin – were short and I progressed through them in a blur of tired, bandy legs and sweat-soaked brow. The 'bonk' was kicking in as the sun finally burst out of the cool grey clouds. Toiling across another flat section as it wound its way across a ploughed field the size of an airport runway, the site of a mini-village of stalls, port-a-loos and parked cars told that I'd reached the final feed station, by the famous windmill at Templeuve. It was situated flush against a tight bend in the road, and thus was causing a slight jam as some riders stood waiting to enter the feed zone, while others queued waiting to get past and carry on. Refuelling my tired, zoned-out body and mind could not have come a moment sooner. Fatigue had crept up on me and was now taking control. Reasoning I was in calorific deficit after 125 kilometres of full-on effort, I haphazardly discarded the bike against a grassy knoll and without further ado made for the nearest stall of food. Half a banana, a huge handful of dates and four cheese Tuc biscuits later – all dispatched in seconds, washed down with a whole *bidon* of water – I let out a very large belch, much to the laughter of the guys nearest me, and the consternation of the lady serving.

Grabbing yet more waffles and refilling both my *bidons*, I lurched past the food area and made to sit down for a few minutes towards the back of the zone. Tiptoeing my way past the dozens of riders crashed out around the stalls and toilet area, I managed to stand right at the back, next to a wire fence. From this unique vantage point, in one direction lay a war zone of lycra-clad casualties scattered about the place, while if I turned 180 degrees all I could see for miles was farmland, nothing else, bar some hedge-rows and clumps of trees. If this were wintertime it would be totally barren. Taking a breather and lost in thoughts, I felt like Pip from Charles Dickens's *Great Expectations*, roaming around mist-shrouded swamps when he bumps into Magwitch. I bet his body wasn't aching as much as mine, though.

My legs were still very wobbly and I needed to sit down. Noticing a free spot in a row of seats, I darted between two guys lying on their backs, almost asleep, and grabbed it. The relief washed over me as I poured water over my head, steam erupting through the air vents of my helmet. I could see one guy sitting cross-legged opposite me on the grass, in tears, holding his arm as if it was sprained or broken. He looked in a lot of pain, perhaps contemplating whether he could carry on. I didn't want to intrude.

The rider sitting to my right – a blond, middle-aged man, in the retro jersey and shorts of the Molteni team made famous by Eddy Merckx in the 1970s – slapped his thigh. 'They're fucked,' he said, gesturing to his legs. 'I can't believe I'm feeling like this and we still have the worst section to go.' He had a thick accent that sounded Dutch, possibly Belgian. In any event, although he smiled when he said this to me, his eyes betrayed how 'fucked' he indeed was. His sodden jersey, opened to the navel, revealed red-raw skin, covered with sweat and grime. More significantly, I noticed an ugly cut on his left knee, and the blood had trickled down his shin, his sock now crimson-stained.

For the next few minutes we sat in the sun, swapped stories, weakly laughed at the stupid accidents and near misses, and generally looked for any excuse not to get back on our bikes. I told him about my hapless luck, lost equipment, and lack of precious inner tubes.

'I'd give you one of mine,' he said, 'but I have only one remaining spare left.' I was moved by how genuinely sorry he was not to help me out. 'Just take it easy going through Carrefour de l'Arbre,' he continued. 'Those cobbles are lethal. You're almost home after that section, it's easy riding. Take care, man.'

He groaned as he rose from his seat, offering it to the next rider who staggered over for a rest. I forced myself up too and with lead-like calves, stumbled my way back to the bike, now nestled underneath four other bikes. Extricating it took a few more minutes, which was no bad thing, and, remounting, I checked my map for succour. 'Yep, thought as much,' I grimaced at the remaining obstacles between me and the velodrome: two more relatively easy sections of *pavé*, and then the final sting in the tail of this race, two lethal sections of unadulterated rocks, debris, razor-sharp ruts, and potholes. Separated by a short burst of super-smooth asphalt. Take a fall on either section here and that's my race kaput. I really wished I'd had someone riding shotgun with me today, it was more stressful knowing I was out here on my own.

'Come on, you need to ride it as before; anything else and you will crash.' The little voice for once gave sound advice. I couldn't go slow on the dreaded stuff, it would make the bone-rattling intolerable, and my arms, shoulders and neck were in agony anyway. There was only one hope: go hell for leather and, if disaster strikes, hope to high heaven someone takes pity on me and I get assistance. Let's roll.

By the time I hit sector 5, Camphin-en-Pévèle, my confidence had returned and my speed and cadence was again pretty good and constant – for approximately 20 metres, before the *pavé* fought back. On a par with the terrain of Arenberg, the first part was tough: as my whole body was put through the wringer, I could barely register what was the best line to take, the condition of the road was ridiculously prehistoric. As the pro rider Chris Horner has joked, I think they actually did dump a load of rocks on this and mix it up with their rotor blades.

There was no constant pattern to give any relief. I was literally hanging on for survival, while pumping the legs as hard as I still could without going into the red. I couldn't see what my Garmin bleeped, but I could guess I was now beyond my threshold. It was lung-bursting, as the jolt of each hard, unforgiving rock inflicted more excruciating pain through my bruised joints. No wonder this is seen as the decisive section for the pro race, it's an assault course. Hitting this at 60 k.p.h. doesn't bear thinking about: you can keep the cobble trophy, I'll walk, thank you.

Others were passing me as I make a determined effort to defeat the beast, sticking to riding in a line as much as possible. Hitting a rock, though, I was momentarily unseated and wrenched my right cleat out, managing to stay upright as I slowed right down and frantically attempted to clip back in again. Like a sedated horse, the bike rolled slowly to the verge as I quickly upped the cadence and made good my escape from this hell. We hit the asphalt road and it felt like heaven on a seat. My backside was killing me, I felt I'd been at the bottom of a ruck of South Africans. Pain all over doesn't even come close to describing it. A blanket of agony tightly wrapped around you, maybe? Spinning slowly and weaving moderately from side to side bought me some time to recover as I tried to regulate my breathing – looking at the Garmin, my b.p.m. had hit 190, and was now trickling down beat by beat in single digits. I could feel my heart thumping away in my chest, up my neck and resounding in my overheated skull.

Ding, ding, the final round was to come. 'Beat this and you're home and dry, Iain. C'mon, let's have it.' The voice sounded confident, but my body was starting to shut down from the increased effort of once again picking up enough speed to get across the *pavé*.

The last five-star section, Carrefour de l'Arbre, proved to be as unforgiving as William and Alex had warned. A long straight opened up ahead of me, flanked by wide fields, steadily rising to a left-hand turn. Fighting my way through to this point, my heart sank as I looked up and saw the road disappear up a leg-sapping incline to the horizon. I envied, to the point of venom-induced hatred, those who I could see completing this task, stick figures in the bright glow, the crowd applauding their efforts as they crossed the final time-check marker. Meanwhile, I was crazily slaloming my way through the terrible *pavé*, great chunks of it rising up in front of me as I frantically swerved towards the gutters to avoid a potential knee-capping from one of the several potholes lying in wait.

'This is crazy, crazy, *crazeeeeeeee!*' I roared to myself, as I vainly kept pounding on the pedals, hearing laughter from others as they suffered the same fate. Metre by agonizing metre I made my way up this trench, the iconic Restaurant l'Arbre Gruson standing out on the horizon – until – freedom! The thwack of the tyres hit the time-check, followed by a tearful reunion with tarmac – and it was over. I crested the top of the rise, cycling past dozens of spectators, and turning a sharp right made my way past the parked cars on the side of the road. Looking back to the right I could see the long trail of riders still on 'Hell's Highway', grimly making their way to the finish, as I gulped great gasps of air trying to cycle and recover at the same time, my bike on autopilot heading downhill towards Gruson, the lactic acid burning in my calves and thighs.

'I really have had enough of this bloody stuff!' I cried as the *pavé* of Gruson came and went fairly quickly. The closer we were getting to Roubaix, the less I cared about a puncture. By now, the doctrine of keeping to the crown of the cobbles to have a smoother ride had been ditched for the simple urge to get over this thing any way, anyhow, riding on the grass verge or through the ploughed field if need be. My neck was numb with the vibrations and even my ears were throbbing. Again I grabbed a *bidon* and poured its contents through the helmet vents, the water running down my face and shorts. I felt a mess, like day three at Glastonbury. I was zoned out and willing the end to happen.

I noticed two older men, perhaps in their mid-fifties, spinning along ahead of me, both riding mountain bikes and dressed in

Italian national bibs and jerseys. The noise their tyres made, even on the tarmac, was like an angry swarm of bees and, for what-ever reason, it annoyed me. The little voice again chirped in: 'Flash bastards on their tractors, they haven't felt the pain I have. They're not getting further up the road than me.' To which I, Terminator-like, clicked up a gear, focused the cross-hairs on their backs and wasted my final battery life on hunting them down. Why? Simply to have a reason to get through the final section, I suppose.

So, head down, as my neck could now barely sustain the weight of my head, I focused on their legs and cycling shoes, whirring away in a high gear, not 20 metres ahead. They were merrily chat-ting away to one another, with not a care in the world. They didn't seem fatigued, nor beaten down by the day's events, which only bugged me more. Try as I might, I just couldn't summon up the reserves of strength required to actually pass them, even though the road ahead was quiet and empty. We threaded our way through wooded countryside and small rural hamlets, the terrain flat and unthreatening. Suddenly they turned right into a wood and I stuck with them, glued to their wheels. It was then that alarm bells rang out. They had no race numbers, they were on hired bikes, and we were all cycling into a campsite. They pulled over by a tent and for the first time noticed me behind them as I, too, pulled over to the other side and pretended to look at my Garmin, tapping the screen as if trying to locate some vital piece of information. Without further ado, and overcome with tired embarrassment, I turned around and pedalled away. Another time, *mes amis*.

Several riders sped by on the road as I rejoined the race, and with the quick pit stop having given me fresh impetus, I managed to get in their slipstream until the final sector loomed at the village of Hem. In truth, I can't remember much else than getting through it, the ancient *pavé* seeming incongruous next to modern-day housing. The village of Hem itself was quiet, even for a Saturday afternoon, and, checking my Garmin, I could see I was well past six hours for the race. But annoyance at not hitting my pre-race goal was tempered with a smile that was beginning to decorate my weather-beaten face. I was almost there – no more cobbles, I had managed to get over, intact, 58 kilometres of it. The world seemed beautiful, my fellow riders were now comrades-in-arms as we headed victorious towards the velodrome. But, never has a further 15-kilometre ride taken so long. My body and bike were battle fatigued.

Suddenly, the familiar industrial architecture and mixture of new town housing and nineteenth-century boulevards came into view: the outskirts of Roubaix. The intensity of local traffic increased, and it seemed surreal to be navigating my bike through a scrum of cars, lorries and motorbikes – didn't they realize a race was on? The main boulevard down towards the velodrome opened up before me and there were a dozen or so riders now in my slipstream. Flags and banners were draped along the whole route ready for the next day's race proper, but I enjoyed the sense of achievement as a final super-smooth stretch of *pavé* arrived, laid down the centre of the Avenue Alfred Motte in 1996. Much as it was comfortable to race across, to me, it was immense, known to aficionados as the *Chemin des Géants* ('the Road of Giants'), with every race winner immortalized on a plaque bearing his name embedded into the cobbles. I tried to read some of them, glistening in the afternoon sun as I sped past. I wanted to savour this moment for a great deal longer.

Alas, sooner than I actually wanted, the velodrome's entrance appeared on the right and, coming through the winding entrance, I was amazed to see so many hundreds of spectators crammed by the public barriers, cheering us all in. Whether they were waiting for loved ones, or simply locals there to watch the spectacle, the noise and atmosphere that rolled over me was a great 'natural' stimulant. And there they were: the ancient, beautiful wooden boards of the velodrome itself. Various riders were now roaring past me, bits between their teeth, as if knowing this was what it was *all* about. You have to finish in style. Plenty of them were enjoying their moment in the sun, duelling one another high up on the bank, before swooping down for the final 100 metres, eyes popping out, sprinting to the line.

As for me, I did speed up to get to the topmost section of the embankment, and noticed a few younger spectators banging on the advertising hoardings, thinking I was about to launch myself at suicidal speed to the finish. But, at that moment, I sat up. I thought of my long-dead father, and my mother who had passed away three months earlier, now at peace, hopefully together some-where, and of Jo and my kids. Would they be proud of me, would they understand why I had driven myself so hard to train and ride this crazy race? Was it worth all those hours of sweat, toil and tears on the turbo trainer, or battling wind and rain on the wintry hills of Surrey and Kent? I smiled at what Barry Hoban had said to me – 'It's brutal' – and of Sean Yates's assertion he would never ride it again. Now I knew what they meant, but I had come through it.

I took the final bend and, slowing, started heading down the bank and into the centre of the straight. Crossing the line, I was too tired to even break into a smile or raise my arms aloft in triumph. Though hats off to the guy who did indeed attempt the sprinter's pose as he crossed the line at speed after me – and went over his handlebars and ate the boards to spectacular effect, and much mirth. He was OK, he still smiled when he received his rather bling medal.

In a glow of weariness and happiness, I pedalled to the tented finish and, as is the custom, asked if I might have two medals, one for each of the kids. As ever, I was moved by the kind reply, and two medals were duly placed in my swollen and sweaty palms.

Finding a place in the centre of the field of the velodrome, surrounded by hundreds of heroes, I sat down with an ungainly thud on the grass, followed by a grunt of satisfaction. It did indeed feel a unique occasion. I had ridden through history. Painfully peeling off my mitts revealed ugly blisters the size of golf balls on each palm, and my backside was numb, but I was ecstatic. Lying back, propped up on one arm, I dangled the medals in front of me, their garishness hidden by the sun's reflection. 'Job done, kids,' I said triumphantly. I lay sprawled out on the grass, taking the warmth of the sun's rays, feeling the pain all over my body ebb away, and promptly dozed off.

Epilogue

The taxi ride back to the hotel was beautiful – I was finally travelling by other means than my own legs, and on blissfully smooth roads, though my backside was still aching. The taxi hummed along quietly in the glow of the evening sunset, its warmth and comfy rear seats battling my will to stay awake. The driver, Mahmoud, had laughed in genuine delight when I called him on my mobile to come and pick me up from the velodrome. 'Ahhhhhh!' he shouted in mock incredulity, 'you finish the race OK? No hurt yourself?'

We agreed to rendezvous at the entrance to the track, where a lot of like-minded riders were being greeted by relatives, loved ones and cab drivers, in a scene that resembled some kind of weird bike show at Heathrow Terminal 5. Feebly wheeling the bike to the exit I registered Mahmoud's huge smile instantly, and it felt I was greeting a long-lost friend. He knew my story, why I had come here, my reasons for this torturous journey and what it all signified to me. No one within 100 miles of where we stood smiling at each other at that moment did. It was a special pat on the back, well deserved and genuinely given. It meant a lot to me.

He took my bike, and gently took the wheel off and placed it all in the boot of his car. He opened the rear passenger door for me, and I felt like I was a newborn baby, being taken home by my father from the delivery room. I eased myself in and, for the first time that day, felt I was back amongst the living, that twenty-first-century comforts had been restored. Off we sped back to the hotel, and a superbly deep, hot bath that lasted well over an hour, a room-service meal of pasta, beer and cheesecake, and then bed. Had I really ridden the *pavé* today? It all felt like some film I'd just watched. It only took a sudden turn of my head, or raising of either leg or arm, to remind me that I had indeed put myself through hell. I kept myself busy for the next thirty minutes posting triumphant pictures of myself on Facebook for family and friends, and then calling Jo at home, retelling the near-death encounter with a tractor, and then answering her questions that all the parts that mattered were intact.

Rising late the next morning, I put on a display of gargantuan greed for the restaurant staff, scoffing an enormous cooked breakfast, followed by two *pains au chocolat*, and fruit salad, washed down with copious amounts of coffee. *Pavé* can do that to you, but the food never really washes away the memory of the pain. I rushed to pack as I was late for my date back at the velodrome – to watch Wiggo try to win the pro race.

Back in the stadium, I forewent the extortionate fee to sit with a crowd of well-heeled locals in the VIP area opposite the winner's rostrum, and took to the grassy knoll nearby, which had a perfect view of the giant TV screen showing the Eurosport coverage and was within a thirty-second walk of the pop-up beer stand.

The afternoon passed theatrically as I managed to befriend a group of Norwegians, most of whom had also ridden the full distance the day before. Swapping stories of derring-do is always more colourful when fuelled by a never-ending supply of Belgian beer; the guy who'd kicked his front wheel in frustration when upset at losing his *bidon* on the *pavé*, got his foot stuck in the spoke and then ended up going right over his handlebars, won the contest. We all raised a glass to his health when he revealed, underneath his race cap, a large bruise on his forehead, cut hands and a huge smile because he still finished the route, even with a few broken spokes.

As Wiggo and the elite final group battled through to the last sections of *pavé*, our Norwegian cousins stood up as one unit whenever their great compatriot Thor Hushovd came into focus on the big screen. A bellow of 'THOOOOOOOOOOOOOOOR!' rose up like some Viking blood oath; glasses clinked and beer was spilled. That would generally be followed by a very gentle, 'C'mon, G' squeaked out by a nearby guy from Devon who'd tagged on to our group and was desperate for Geraint Thomas to sneak a win. I knew whose camp I was in. More beer, thank you, Lars.

Alas, Wiggo, 'G' and even Tom Boonen were not at the races as a relatively unknown Dutchman, Niki Terpstra, snuck away for the glory. I say 'snuck away' but he put on a rather impressive time-trialling exhibition, haring along for dear life once he knew no one was going to follow him. Wiggo battled it out in style on the boards, and we roared him on. It had been a great race, and I still had my medal around my neck from the day before; I was the only one on the grassy knoll who did that day. Out and proud.

Saying farewell to my Scandi mates, I walked through the suburbs of Roubaix to catch a local train into the centre of Lille. The bricks and mortar of the old streets, boulevards and cafés would have been familiar to Paris–Roubaix's founders Théodore Vienne and Maurice Pérez back in 1896 – hardly anything had changed at all. The atmosphere, so close to the velodrome, was striking; this was still a semi-industrial, working-class community. The area looked rough around the edges now, but maybe it had always been this way, people scratching a living in the hinterland of Lille. A world famous legendary bike race was right on their doorstep, and I wondered whether it actually mattered to them?

It did to me. It was time to go home.

I had ridden various long rides across Britain, and suffered at times on some pretty tough sportives, but I have to say I felt completely at ease and satisfied on the train home to London. This race meant a lot to me, in many different ways. I had dreamt of riding these cobbles since I was a teenager, and it had certainly lived up to its reputation. Compared to the *Étape* the previous year, it was mentally tougher, certainly, but the history that surrounded it and the places I had traversed along the route had mesmerized me to the extent that I had blocked out a lot of the discomfort. It was like riding the Grand National course on a road drill, about a hundred times, with all the split-second terror and anxiety thrown in, too. But the memory of the fun, the comradeship and then finishing at that neglected, run-down stadium was something I would look back on with pride.

As the late winter sun showered the Lille terminus in golden twilight, the Eurostar train silently pulled away like a grand ocean liner, and finally – thankfully – I fell into my reserved seat for the trip home. Studying the compartment as I sipped my espresso, I noticed quite a few fellow cyclists making the same journey back to London; their tired eyes betraying either a struggle over the cobbles on the Saturday or a very hard drinking session on the Sunday lunchtime watching the professional race. We all seemed to generate the satisfied countenance of a job well done, and were now content to allow the general 'civilian' hubbub of the train to wash over us.

I decided one more look was in order, so, with a rueful smile, I stood up to grab my rucksack from the crowded overhead compartment, wrestled the bag free, sat back down, unzipped it, and pulled out a plastic tourist shopping bag that bulged at the bottom with a weighty object – my gift to myself.

The couple sitting opposite looked on with mild curiosity as I proceeded to take out an ugly piece of stone: nondescript, roughly hewn into a cube, grey in colour and shining brightly upon its wooden plinth. Like a shot-putter, I held it aloft in my palm, gazing up at its simplistic beauty, thinking it had been well worth the twenty euros at the velodrome café shop. I could see a few other travellers across the compartment looking at me, some perhaps recognizing what I was cradling. The rays of winter sunshine coming through the train window struck the cobble as I carefully placed it on the table. Maybe this was how Mr Ben had felt at the end of every trip through the tailor's shop? I wondered what the kids would make of it when I got home. I settled back into the seat and drifted into a semi-conscious doze, which was punctuated by the vibration of my mobile. It was a text message from my pal Kevin, who'd kindly loaned me his bike bag and had actually goaded me into riding the full distance in the first place. '*Chapeau*, Iain! Now, all you need to do is ride the Tour of Flanders next year!'

Now *that* would be a challenge . . .

Paris–Roubaix Winners

1896	Josef Fischer (GER) Diamant	
1897	Maurice Garin (FRA) La Française	
1898	Maurice Garin (FRA) La Française	
1899	Albert Champion (FRA)	
1900	Émile Boubours (FRA)	
1901	Lucien Lesna (FRA)	
1902	Lucien Lesna (FRA)	
1903	Hippolyte Aucouturier (FRA) Peugeot	
1904	Hippolyte Aucouturier (FRA) Peugeot	
1905	Louis Trousselier (FRA) Peugeot–Wolber	
1906	Henri Cornet (FRA)	
1907	George Passerieu (FRA) Peugeot–Wolber	
1908	Cyrille Van Hauwaert (BEL) Alcyon–Dunlop	
1909	Octave Lapize (FRA) Biguet–Dunlop	
1910	Octave Lapize (FRA) Alcyon	
1911	Octave Lapize (FRA) La Française–Diamant	
1912	Charles Crupelandt (FRA) La Française–Diamant	
1913	François Faber (LUX) Peugeot–Wolber	
1914	Charles Crupelandt (FRA) La Française–Diamant	

1915–18 No races

1919   Henri Pélissier (FRA) JB Louvet & La Sportive

1920   Paul Deman (BEL) La Sportive

1921   Henri Pélissier (FRA) JB Louvet & La Sportive

1922   Albert Dejonghe (BEL)

1923   Heiri Suter (SUI) Gurter–Hutchinson

1924   Jules Van Hevel (BEL) Alcyon–Dunlop

1925   Félix Sellier (BEL) Alcyon–Dunlop

1926   Julien Delbecque (BEL) Alcyon–Dunlop

1927   Georges Ronsse (BEL) Automoto

1928   André Leducq (FRA) Alcyon

1929   Charles Meunier (BEL) La Française–Diamant

1930   Julien Vervaeke (BEL) Alcyon

1931   Gaston Rebry (BEL) Alcyon

1932   Romain Gijssels (BEL) Dilecta–Wolber

1933   Sylvère Maes (BEL) Alcyon–Dunlop

1934   Gaston Rebry (BEL) Alcyon

1935   Gaston Rebry (BEL) Alcyon

1936   Georges Speicher (FRA) Alcyon

1937   Jules Rossi (ITA) Alcyon

1938   Lucien Storme (BEL) Leducq–Hutchinson

1939   Émile Masson Jnr (BEL) Alcyon

1940–42 No races

1943   Marcel Kint (BEL) Mercier–Hutchinson

1944   Maurice Desimpelaere (BEL) Alcyon

1945   Paul Maye (FRA) Alcyon

1946   Georges Claes (BEL) Rochet–Dunlop

1947   Georges Claes (BEL) Rochet–Dunlop

1948   Rik Van Steenbergen (BEL) Mercier–Hutchinson

1949   André Mahé (FRA)
  Victory shared with Serse Coppi Stella–Dunlop

1949   Serse Coppi (ITA)
  Victory shared with André Mahé Bianchi–Ursus

1950   Fausto Coppi (ITA) Bianchi–Ursus

1951   Antonio Bevilacqua (ITA) Benotto–Ursus

1952   Rik Van Steenbergen (BEL) Mercier–Hutchinson

1953   Germain Derycke (BEL) Alcyon–Dunlop

1954   Raymond Impanis (BEL) Mercier–Hutchinson

1955   Jean Forestier (FRA) Follis–Dunlop

1956   Louison Bobet (FRA) L. Bobet–BP–Hutchinson

1957   Fred De Bruyne (BEL) Carpano–Coppi

1958   Leon Vandaele (BEL) Faema

1959   Noël Foré (BEL) Groene Leeuw–SAS

1960   Pino Cerami (BEL) Peugeot–BP

1961   Rik Van Looy (BEL) Faema

1962   Rik Van Looy (BEL) Faema

1963   Emile Daems (BEL) Peugeot–BP

1964   Peter Post (NED) Flandria–Romeo

1965   Rik Van Looy (BEL) Solo–Superia

1966   Felice Gimondi (ITA) Salvarani

1967   Jan Janssen (NED) Pelforth–Sauvage–Le Jeune

1968   Eddy Merckx (BEL) Faema

1969   Walter Godefroot (BEL) Flandria–De Clerck

1970   Eddy Merckx (BEL) Faema

1971   Roger Rosiers (BEL) Ric

1972   Roger De Vlaeminck (BEL) Deher

1973   Eddy Merckx (BEL) Molteni

1974   Roger De Vlaeminck (BEL) Brooklyn

1975	Roger De Vlaeminck (BEL) Brooklyn
1976	Marc Demeyer (BEL) Flandria–Velda
1977	Roger De Vlaeminck (BEL) Brooklyn
1978	Francesco Moser (ITA) Sanson
1979	Francesco Moser (ITA) Sanson
1980	Francesco Moser (ITA) Sanson
1981	Bernard Hinault (FRA) Renault–Elf–Gitane
1982	Jan Raas (NED) TI–Raleigh
1983	Hennie Kuiper (NED) Aernoudt–Rossin
1984	Sean Kelly (IRL) Skil–Sem
1985	Marc Madiot (FRA) Renault–Elf–Gitane
1986	Sean Kelly (IRL) Kas
1987	Eric Vanderaerden (BEL) Panasonic–Isostar
1988	Dirk Demol (BEL) AD–Renting
1989	Jean-Marie Wampers (BEL) Panasonic–Isostar
1990	Eddy Planckaert (BEL) Panasonic–Sportlife
1991	Marc Madiot (FRA) R.M.O.
1992	Gilbert Duclos-Lassalle (FRA) Z
1993	Gilbert Duclos-Lassalle (FRA) GAN
1994	Andrei Tchmil (BEL) Lotto
1995	Franco Ballerini (ITA) Mapei–GB
1996	Johan Museeuw (BEL) Mapei–GB
1997	Frédéric Guesdon (FRA) Française des Jeux
1998	Franco Ballerini (ITA) Mapei–Bricobi
1999	Andrea Tafi (ITA) Mapei–Quick-Step
2000	Johan Museeuw (BEL) Mapei
2001	Servais Knaven (NED) Domo–Farm Frites
2002	Johan Museeuw (BEL) Domo–Farm Frites
2003	Peter Van Petegem (BEL) Lotto–Domo

2004	Magnus Båckstedt (SWE) Alessio–Bianchi
2005	Tom Boonen (BEL) Quick-Step–Innergetic
2006	Fabian Cancellara (SUI) Team CSC
2007	Stuart O'Grady (AUS) Team CSC
2008	Tom Boonen (BEL) Quick-Step
2009	Tom Boonen (BEL) Quick-Step
2010	Fabian Cancellara (SUI) Team Saxo Bank
2011	Johan Vansummeren (BEL) Garmin–Cervélo
2012	Tom Boonen (BEL) Omega Pharma–Quick-Step
2013	Fabian Cancellara (SUI) RadioShack–Leopard
2014	Niki Terpstra (NED) Omega Pharma–Quick-Step

Winners by Nationality

Belgium 55

France 28

Italy 11

Netherlands 6

Switzerland 4

Ireland 2

Germany 1

Luxembourg 1

Sweden 1

Australia 1

Bibliography

Askwith, Richard, *Feet in the Clouds: A Tale of Fell-Running and Obsession* (Aurum Press, 2003)

Bouvet, Phillipe, Callewaert, Pierre, Gatellier, Jean-Luc, Laget, Serge, and, Herlihy, David, *Paris–Roubaix: A Journey Through Hell* (VeloPress, 2007)

Cossins, Peter, *The Monuments: The Grit and the Glory of Cycling's One-Day Races* (Bloomsbury, 2013)

Fotheringham, William, *A Century of Cycling: The Classic Races and Legendary Champions* (Mitchell Beazley, 2003)

Fotheringham, William, *Fallen Angel, The Passion of Fausto Coppi* (Yellow Jersey, 2009)

Fotheringham, William, *Merckx: Half Man, Half Bike* (Yellow Jersey, 2012)

Friebe, Daniel, *Eddy Merckx: The Cannibal* (Ebury Press, 2012)

Hutchinson, Michael, *Faster: The Obsession, Science and Luck Behind the World's Fastest Cyclists* (Bloomsbury, 2014)

Kelly, Sean, *Hunger: The Autobiography* (Peloton Publishing, 2013)

Sidwells, Chris, *Cyclosportive: Preparing for and Taking Part in Long Distance Cycling Challenges* (A & C Black, 2011)

Sykes, Herbie, *Coppi: Inside the Legend of a Champion* (Rouleur, 2012)

Velominati, The, *The Rules: The Way of the Cycling Disciple* (W.W. Norton, 2014)

Woodland, Les, *Paris–Roubaix, The Inside Story: All the Bumps of a Cycling Cobbled Classic* (McGann Publishing, 2013)

Yates, Sean, *It's All About the Bike: My Autobiography* (Bantam Press, 2013)

Acknowledgements

I have read probably thousands of these acknowledgement pages across the span of my publishing career, and it is only now after completing the journey of my own book that I truly know why they are written. This book, as well as my actual journey to ride Paris–Roubaix, would never have been possible without the following people.

What began as a conversation in a pub, then led to a challenge to not only ride this race but then write about it, needs to be laid at the door of one man. A man of many faces, whether it be literary agent, publicist, eagle-eyed journalist, or opportunist publisher in his own right – Humfrey Hunter is your man. I am very grateful to my editor at Transworld, Giles Elliot, for allowing me the chance to tell this story, as well as remind me of the basic skills of editing a first draft. Huge thanks to Ian Preece for a magnificent job on shaping my ramblings into something close to a coherent narrative.

There are many people who work in and around professional cycling who have been exceptionally generous with their time in allowing some rank amateur, and indeed novice of cycling history, to question them at length regarding their own experiences of Paris–Roubaix. I am very grateful to William Fotheringham, Daniel Friebe, Richard Moore, Herbie Sykes, Peter Cossins,

Chris Sidwells and Tom Robbins for sharing their memories and opinions on the race. Also to David Luxton for connecting me with them. The chance to interview a few of my cycling heroes was probably the highlight of this whole process, and Sean Yates, Roger Hammond and Barry Hoban could not have been more accommodating. For my trip to France to unearth more facts about the race I would give special mention to François Doulcier, the boys at Pavé Cycling CC (William and Alex) and, of course, Eurostar for showing me it is possible to be stranded on a train platform for hours and not be bored. For looking after my physical well-being on a bike, I must give due credit to George and Vaidas at Vaidas Cycles, as well as Andy at Cadence Performance.

On a personal level, cycling is not just about pushing your physical limits, or riding a legendary race. It is more to do with riding out with friends and enjoying the scenery. I could not ask for better company than Arjen Jansen, Ben Worley, John Edmunds and Charles Colombo when out on the hills, even if I am trailing behind them. Equally, huge thanks goes to Kevin Morgan, who inspired me to ride the full route of Paris–Roubaix by calling me soft if I didn't, as well as loaning me his luxurious bike bag and recommending accommodation in Lille, pre-race. Also, a grateful bottle of bubbly to the brilliant Karen Farrington who offered crucial advice on the first draft. A hug of gratitude to my in-laws – Julie and Peter Bennett – whose love of cycling rubbed off on me whenever I visited their home. A true inspiration.

Finally, the three people who were in my thoughts hour after hour of training and actually riding this race, and to whom this book is dedicated with all my heart – Joanna, Cameron and Isla.

Index

Alcyon 50
Aldersley velodrome 85–6
amateurs
  and Paris–Roubaix race 109, 125,
    169, 176
  races opened to 176
  see also Étape du Tour
Amis de Paris–Roubaix, Les 118, 120–1,
  122–4, 129
Anquetil, Jacques 155, 158
Arenberg Forest 113, 115, 126, 160,
  162–3, 196–202
Armstrong, Lance 155, 166, 172
Askwith, Richard
  Feet in the Clouds 212
ASO 109, 121
Auchy-les-Orchies to Bersée section
  218
Auto, L' 44, 46–7
  promotion of Paris–Roubaix race
    44–5, 46–7
Automobile Club de France (ACF)
  12
Automoto 50

Bäckstedt, Magnus 174
Ballerini, Franco 72
Bartali, Gino 143, 155
Barthélémy, Honoré 51

Belgian riders 115
  domination of Paris–Roubaix race
    podium 65–75, 101, 115
  and Dutch riders 115
Belgium
  ethnic complexities 66
  German occupation of during Second
    World War 101
  popularity of cycling 67
Bennett, Peter 33
Bernard, Alain 121
Bevilacqua, Antonio 134
bike 54–63
  carbon frames 111–12
  evolution of 12
  perfect set up for Paris–Roubaix race
    109–13, 116–17, 159, 167–8
  tyres 110–11, 116, 158–9, 167–8
  wheels 110
bike fit 57–63
  Cadence Performance 58–63
  Vaidas Cycles 55–8
bike races
  evolvement of 13–15
Birnie, Lionel 54
Boonen, Tom 65, 69, 71, 74, 75, 114,
  127, 132, 167, 237
Bordeaux–Paris race 15, 17, 18, 19, 20
Brambilla, Gianluca 73

Breyer, Victor 21–2, 24, 47, 48
Brompton bike 2, 79, 83, 84
Brooks, Adam 87
Brunel, Philippe 70
Busigny 42, 182, 185
Buysse, Lucien 49

Cadence Performance 58–63
Cambrai, Battle of (1918) 185
Camphin-en-Pévèle section 227–8
Cancellara, Fabian 71, 94, 127, 132, 165, 170, 171
carbon frames 111–12
Carette, Henri 16–17
Carrefour de l'Arbre section 126, 170, 226–7, 228–9
Catchpole, Henry 103
Catford CC 28, 166
Cavendish, Mark 65, 147, 157
Challenge Desgrange–Colombo race 140
Christophe, Eugène 47, 49
Circuit Franco–Belge 160
Claes, George 65
Classics 66, 68, 69, 71, 74, 175
clothes 54
Clouston, Svein 27–8
cobbled roads *see pavé*
Coppi, Fausto 136, 137, 138, 139–40, 141–2, 143, 144
Coppi, Serse 135, 137, 139–40, 141–2, 144
Cossins, Peter 69, 74
  The Monuments 68
Courbertin, Baron Pierre de 11
Crupelandt, Charles 45
cycling
  evolution of 12–13
  popularity of in Belgium 67
  popularity of in France 14
cyclo-cross 73, 174
Cyfac 111

De Maeght, August 67
de Rooij, Theo 9–10

De Simpelaere, Maurice 102
De Vlaeminck, Roger 65, 70–1, 72–3, 74–5, 132, 161, 165
De Wetter, Albert 142
Dead Man's Penny 41–2
Defraye, Odile 67
Demeyer, Marc 65
Demol, Dirk 65
Desgrange, Henri 23–4, 44–5, 46–7, 48, 99
Dierickx, André 161
Dingley, Geoff 87
Ditchling Beacon 54, 76–7, 78
domestiques 137
Doulcier, François 119, 120, 121–30
Dreyfus affair 44
Duclos-Lassalle, Gilbert 127, 132, 167, 170, 208
Dutch riders
  and Belgian riders 115

Edinburgh 83–4
Edmunds, John 77–8, 80
Elliott, Malcolm 64
endurance racing 14–15
Étape du Tour 2–7, 9, 148, 169, 238

Faber, François 45–6
Fédération Cyclopédique du Nord 17
First World War 42–4, 46
Fischer, Josef 23, 24–5, 45
Flèche Wallonne, La 140, 141
Fotheringham, William 3, 64, 145, 163–5
  Fallen Angel 137
Français, La 50
France
  occupation of during Second World War 99–101
French riders 68
  winners of Paris–Roubaix race 45, 65
Friebe, Daniel 54, 70–4
Froome, Chris 65, 107, 157

Garin, Maurice 15, 23, 24, 25, 44

Gaudin, Damien 127
Gaumont, Philippe 127, 199–200
Giffard, Pierre 45
Gilbert, Philippe 74
Gimondi, Felice 161, 162
Gladiator 50
Goddet, Jacques 99, 100, 101
Granauskas, Vaidas 55–7
Grand Prix du Tour de France 100

Hammond, Roger 156, 165, 172–7
helmets 54
Hill Climb Classic 28
Hinault, Bernard 71, 72, 127–8, 155,
    158, 165, 176
Hincapie, George 134
Hitler, Adolf 101–2
Hoban, Barry 73, 113, 156, 156–63,
    164–5, 171, 175, 232
Hornaing to Wandignies-Hamage
    section 213–14
Horner, Chris 227
Hutchinson, Michael
    Faster 26

Italian riders 141
    winners of Paris–Roubaix race 65

John O'Groats to Land's End (1996)
    27, 53, 78
Joinard, Achille 144

Kelly, Sean 59, 64, 69, 126–7
Kint, Marcel 101

Lanigan, William 103–18
Lapize, Octave 45
Leblanc, Jean-Marie 163
Leenen, Frans 138
LeMond, Greg 80, 155
Liège–Bastogne–Liège 114
Liggett, Phil 163
Lille 43
Linton, Arthur 23, 25
Long Mynd (Much Wenlock) 86

Longworth, Francis 85–97

MacGregor, George 41, 42–3
McLoughlin, Joey 64
Mahé, André 135, 136, 138, 139, 142–4
Mahmoud (driver) 183, 235–6
Mann, Anthony 158
Mapei 6
Marmotte race 147, 148
Martin, Dan 114
Mayade, Emile 12
Maye, Paul 102
Merckx, Eddy 65, 70–1, 72, 73, 74–5,
    132, 155, 157, 161–2, 165
Messines Road 49
Meyan, Paul 21
Meyer, Charles 23
Milk Race 64
Millar, David 107
Millar, Robert 64
Minart, Louis 17
Mons-en-Pévèle section 126, 218,
    220–1
Moore, Richard 54–5, 63
Moore, Tim 54
Morgan, Kevin 146, 153
Moser, Francesco 127, 165
Moujica, Jacques 138
Museeuw, Johan 65, 74, 116–17, 118,
    125, 164

Nibali, Vincenzo 107
nutrition 54

O'Grady, Stuart 132, 134, 173–4
Olympic Games (1896) 11

Paris–Brest–Paris race 14
    (1891) 14–15
Paris–Marseille–Paris race (1896) 12
Paris–Roubaix: A Journey Through Hell
    126
Paris–Roubaix race
    (1897) 44
    (1943) 101

Paris–Roubaix race (*cont.*)
  (1944) 102
  (1949) 135, 137–44
  (1964) 160
  (1972) 160–1
  (1994) 164, 167, 170
  (1998) 174
  (2001) 199–200
  (2004) 172
  (2010) 175
  (2014) 170–1, 236–7
  and amateurs 109, 125, 169, 176
  and Belgian riders 65–75, 101, 115
  bike set up and tyres for riding
      109–13, 116–17, 159, 167–8
  crashes 127
  destruction of route during First
      World War 47–8, 49
  endorsement of by *Le Vélo* 20–2
  fan rowdiness 115–16
  halting of during First World War 45
  hardest sections 126
  holding of first race (1896) 22–5
  losing of prominence in turn of
      twentieth century 44
  origins and establishment 16–22
  pavé and tips for riding 9, 21–2, 31,
      44, 56, 68, 106, 112–14, 116–19,
      118, 122–3, 125, 128, 148–50,
      162–3, 167, 174–5
  prize money 19, 20
  promotion of by *L'Auto* 44–5, 46–7
  reasons why elite riders race in 69, 71
  records achieved by champions 132
  repair of *pavé* by *Les Amis de Paris–
      Roubaix* 123–4, 129
  rest zones 118
  resumption after First World War
      (1919) 48–52
  resurfacing of roads 98, 102, 118,
      120–1
  staging of during Second World War
      100–2
  toughness of 8–9, 158, 166
  and traffic 150
  and weather 127
  winners of 45–6, 239–43
  winning as a lottery issue 165–6
Paris–Roubaix race (2014) (for
    amateurs) 178–237
  Arenberg section 196–202, 204–5
  Auchy-les-Orchies to Bersée section
      218
  Camphin-en-Pévèle section 227–8
  Carrefour de l'Arbre section 226–7,
      228–9
  crash 190–1, 196
  fatigue experienced 225
  feed stations 212, 225
  finishing line 231–2
  flat tyre and lack of a pump 209–11,
      221–5
  Hornaing to Wandignies-Hamage
      section 213–14
  journey to start line 182–6
  landscape/scenery 192–3, 196, 199
  Mons-en-Pévèle section 218, 220–1
  pain experienced 212, 227, 228
  Pont Gibus bend 208
  preparation and rituals on day
      179–80
  Quiévy to Saint-Python section
      193–4
  riding the *pavé* 189–91, 193, 198–201,
      208–9, 213–14, 217, 219–21, 229
  tractor incident 214–15
  Troisvilles-Inchy section 188–9
  Viesly-Quiévy section 192, 193
Passchendaele, First Battle of (1917)
    42
pavé (cobbled roads) 21–2, 68
  bike set up and tyres for riding 19,
      109–13, 116–17, 167–8
  Paris–Roubaix race *see* Paris–Roubaix
  repairing of by *Amis de Paris–
      Roubaix* 122–4, 129
  tarmacking of 98, 102, 118, 120–1
  Tour de France 125
Pavé Cycling Classics 103, 108
Pélissier, Francis 49, 51

Pélissier, Henri 49, 51–2
Pérez, Maurice 17–20
Pétain, Marshal 100
Peugeot 50
Planckaert, Eddy 132
Post, Peter 132, 160
Poulidor, Raymond 156–7
Puncheur race 76–9, 80–2

Quiévy to Saint-Python section 193–4

Raas, Jan 134
Raleigh bikes 53
Raleigh Comp bike 2, 79
Rebry, Gaston 65
Ride London 177
Ridgeway 95, 96
Road of the Giants 119
Robbins, Tom 146, 146–51
Rockingham Forest Wheelers 64
Rockshox suspension 167, 170
Rossi, Jules 102
Roubaix Cycling Tourist Club 109
Roubaix (town) 16, 20
  occupation of by Germans during
    First World War 43
  occupation of by Germans during
    Second World War 99
Roubaix velodrome 17, 43, 48, 130–5
Rousseau, Paul 18, 20, 21, 24
Rovny, Ivan 73

'Safety Bicycle' 12
Second World War 98–101
Sidwells, Chris 28–30, 32, 83, 151, 156
Cyclosportive 30–1, 35
Simpson, Tom 29, 156
Six Day races 14
Sportive, La 50
sportives 31, 95, 145–6
Sportwereld 67
Stablinski, Jean 162–3
Strade Bianche 94, 95–6
Summerfield, Jeff 152–3
Sunday in Hell, A (film) 71, 72, 150

Sykes, Herbie 136
  Coppi 136

Tchmil, Andrei 164, 167, 170
Terpstra, Niki 237
Terront, Charles 'Charley' 15
Thiétard, Louis 102
Thomas, Geraint 157, 237
Thys, Philippe 9, 51
Tour of the Black Country 83–94, 97
Tour de France 44, 101, 108, 123–4,
    163, 169
  (2007) 147
  (2014) 107
  Étape du Tour 2–7, 9, 148, 169, 238
Tour of Flanders 67–8, 74, 94, 114,
    115, 151, 158, 169, 173
  (1967) 161–2
Tour of Lombardy 72
training 29–36
  intensity levels 31–2
  interval 34–5, 36–7, 54, 113
  Puncheur race 76–9, 80–2
  Tour of the Black Country route
    83–94, 97
  turbo sessions 29–30, 32–6, 79, 113
tribalism 74
Troisvilles–Inchy section 188–9
turbo trainer/training 29–30, 32–6, 62,
    79, 113
Turgot, Sébastien 127
Tyne Cot memorial (Flanders) 43
tyres
  and riding Paris–Roubaix race
    110–11, 116, 158–9, 167–8

UNC 143, 144

V-Sprint club 87
Vaidas Cycles 55–6
Vallaeys, Jean-Claude 120–1
Van Hauwaert, Cyrille 66, 67
Van Lerberghe, Henri 51
Van Looy, Rik 65
Van Petegem, Peter 65

Van Steenbergen, Rik 65, 140, 141–2
Vansummeren, Johan 114
Vel d'Hiv arena (Paris) 99
Vélo, Le 15–16, 17–18
  demise of 44–5
  endorsement of Paris–Roubaix race
    20–2
velodromes
  construction across France 13–14
Verbeeck, Frans 161
Vienne, Théodore 11, 17–20
Viesly–Quiévy section 192, 193
Voisine, Alex 105, 108, 109–10, 116,
  117

Waltonberg climb (Tour of the Black
  Country) 89, 90–1, 93–4
wheels 110 *see also* tyres
White Roads Classic (WRC) 94–7
Wiggins, Bradley 107, 127, 128, 155–6,
  165, 171, 175–6, 237
Woodland, Les 16
Worley, Ben 77–80

Yates, Sean 64, 156, 163–5, 166–71, 232
Yorks Hill 79, 94

Zandegu, Dino 162

Iain MacGregor has ridden a bike since the age of three and can fully recall every major accident he's suffered, even the one that knocked him out cold. He has worked in publishing for twenty years with some of the biggest names in sport and sports journalism.